PRAGMATISM AND THE PROGRESSIVE MOVEMENT IN THE UNITED STATES

The Origin of the New Social Sciences

John Lugton Safford

D1714063

UNIVERSITY
PRESS OF
AMERICA

LANHAM • NEW YORK • LONDON

Copyright © 1987 by

University Press of America,® Inc.

4720 Boston Way
Lanham, MD 20706

3 Henrietta Street
London WC2E 8LU England

British Cataloging in Publication Information Available

Library of Congress Cataloging-in-Publication Data

Safford, John Lugton, 1947-
   Pragmatism and the progressive movement in the United
States.

   Originally presented as the author's thesis (Ph.D.)—
University of California, Riverside, 1984.
   Bibliography: p.
   Includes index.
   1. Social sciences—United States—History—20th
century.   2. Social sciences—United States—Philosophy.
3. Pragmatism.   4. Progressivism (United States politics)
I. Title.
H53.U5S24   1987   300'.973   87-10524
ISBN 0-8191-6438-0 (alk. paper)
ISBN 0-8191-6439-9 (pbk. : alk. paper)

All University Press of America books are produced on acid-free
paper which exceeds the minimum standards set by the National
Historical Publication and Records Commission.

ACKNOWLEDGEMENTS

This work, in its present form, was written as a doctoral dissertation under the supervision of Professor John L. Stanley at the University of California, Riverside. Also reading the dissertation were Professors Francis M. Carney and Charles R. Adrian.

Four years earlier the author completed a Master's thesis titled <u>Pragmatism</u> <u>in</u> <u>American</u> <u>Culture</u> at California State College, San Bernardino, under the direction of the late Professor Robert R. Roberts. Significant portions of both the research and the writing were done at the time. It was Professor Roberts who suggested researching the connection between Pragmatism and the Progressive Movement, and it was that chapter from the thesis which was the basis for the present work. Also of help on the thesis were Professors Paul Johnson and Edward Erler.

Finally, the author is grateful to all those authors and publishing houses which allowed extensive quotation of their works.

TABLE OF CONTENTS

PREFACE

The primary thesis of this dissertation is quite simple. It is that "the new social sciences," the _sciences_ of man and society as they have come to be known at the end of the Twentieth Century, owe their origin and style to the academic philosophy of Pragmatism and the social movement called Progressivism.

The method used to establish the above thesis is also quite uncomplicated. First, the Pragmatism of William James is examined in order to show how radically the Pragmatic theory of truth differs from the traditional correspondence and coherence theories of truth. (In order to remind the reader that the word "Pragmatism" refers to a specific theory it and all schools of philosophy will appear capitalized by the author throughout the text.) Second, the writings of a number of the seminal thinkers of the Progressive period will be displayed in order to exemplify what they owe methodologically to Pragmatism. Here, because the space and scope of the work does not allow it to be exhaustive, the author has concentrated upon only some of the most relevant figures of the time. While the particular choices may have been idiosyncratic, the text as a whole will make it evident that they were sufficient for its purpose. Finally, some modern social scientists will be cited in order to exemplify the fact that the effects of Pragmatism are with us still.

One might argue that American history can be categorized in terms of its various reform movements: Abolitionism before the Civil War, Populism after the Civil War, Progressivism before and after the turn of the century, the New Deal between the World Wars, and the aspirations of the New Frontier and the Great Society after the Second World War. The now classic debate between John Hicks and his student, George Mowry, centered on whether or not Populism and Progressivism were distinct movements, with Mowry arguing that the Progressives were of an urban, educated class as opposed to the agrarian Populists. This work extends Mowry's thesis, holding that it was their education more than anything else that distinguished the Progressives. As reformers, they sought to improve -- indeed to _perfect_ -- the human condition on earth not by moral regeneration, but often by drastically altering the economic _system_ of production and distribution. On the whole, they were psychological epiphenomenalists: they believed that ideologies and psychological states were the effects of men's actions, not their causes. Like their predecessors, their concern was for the redistribution of wealth, prestige, and power in line with the nation's equalitarian traditions. Yet, as intellectuals and politicians themselves, their explanations for the causes of degeneracy were novel. Their methods became ends, and their legacy is a questionable faith in technique. Thus, although Progressivism took many forms, this work focuses on the Progressives as the new intellectuals of the turn of the century, the New Academia.

The secondary thesis is that the American philosophy of Pragmatism has worked to the detriment of a true science of society. A "scientist," as the term is used here, is someone who at least occasionally works at the theoretical edge of his discipline: he relates empirical conditions to laws, theories, and hypotheses about the nature of his subject. At the other end of the scale is the "taxonomist" who merely collects or documents "the facts," the ultimate positivist. In between is the "technician" who, using whatever rules and tools that pertain to his craft, arranges or manipulates "the facts" in order to achieve a predictable or desirable result. If his results were out of limits, were anomalous, it would constitute a problem for a scientist to investigate. A scientist, when working as such, is necessarily a philosopher in that he is searching for certitude. (A Ph.D. is a doctor of philosophy in his field.)

In order for there to be a science of society there must be people who are attempting to understand what the significances of the empirical conditions of society are by reference to laws, theories, and hypotheses. A high degree of such understanding about a living organism (and surely the individual parts of society are alive) would imply a teleology. Health -- the physical and psychological well-being of an organism -- is, for example, an objective good. Avoiding the fallacy of composition, one simply can assert that the quality of a society is measured by the collective health and well being of its individual members -- which, after all, are the only elements which are empirically real and, unlike a "team" a society has no purpose beyond the health and survival of its members. A social scientist, like a biologist, should be able to distinguish without bias a healthy from an unhealthy individual, and should be able to do the same for a society or a nation. At least this is what the Pragmatists tried to do.

x

One problem with the new social sciences is that its practitioners are bifurcated into "technicians" and "romantics." The technicians are quantifiers and the romantics are the new myth-givers such as John Rawls. Given the Pragmatic origin of the new social sciences, scientific progress can occur only when the two roles are combined in one, only when the technician and the man of vision are, at the least, in close communication. By and large, this has not been the case: for instance, when B. F. Skinner or Noam Chompsky advocate social change they are said to be acting "unprofessionally," or in only their personal capacities.

Yet, ironically, the hope and justification of Progressivism and the new social sciences is an element of Platonism that was explicitly rejected by his more nominalistic student, Aristotle -- namely, that to know the good is to do the good. Thomas Aquinas raised Plato's determinism here into the essence of human freedom when he held that freedom is one's ability to judge his judgment -- or, as John Dewey was to explain it, to consider the alternatives in the light of reason. For Plato, Aquinas, Dewey, and Karl Mannheim human "freedom" is merely the result of being stranded in an incomplete condition between the determinism of instinct at one extreme and the determinism of perfect knowledge at the other. The hope of the new social sciences was that they could compel men (at least educated men) to make all the right social and political decisions because they would "know themselves." C. Wright Mills's famous formula, "IBM plus reality plus humanism = sociology," fits perfectly into the Pragmatic tradition, where knowledge is seen as the means to earthly salvation. In this light it is not ironic that B. F. Skinner, author of Walden II and Beyond Freedom and Dignity, holds the same chair today at Harvard that William James held a century ago. Like Mills and Herbert Croly, Skinner speaks for both the romantic and the technician at once.

A deeper problem for the American social sciences is that their Pragmatic heritage is Nominalistic. Nominalism -- the theory that reality is located wholly in concrete individuals -- literally makes it difficult to see the (abstract) forest for the (concrete) individual trees. Epistemological Nominalism denies that things have or can be known by their essences. Here, definitions are mere names (terms) or conventions; universal terms (genus/species distinctions), collective terms, and abstractions in general, are but fictions for the purpose of manipulating a basically unknowable reality. Epistemological Nominalism is the basic assumption underlying the logic of quantification (as opposed to the older logics based upon qualitative distinctions). Thus much of the history of the Progressive Movement was one of great expectations followed by conceptual and factual disappointments. Lesser Pragmatists who were mere Positivists, were blinded and enfeebled by David Hume's is-ought dichotomy: description _alone_ did not render grounds for prescription.

More thoroughgoing Pragmatists, however, such as Thorstein Veblen, offered Sorelian socialist myths in order to make their research relevant; and, like Walter Lippmann and Sidney Hook, they were able to shift social myths radically in order to use the one that was most beneficially effective in practice. Still, because the myth of the "State," or the "Society," or the "People" is necessarily predicated upon epistemological Realism (where the locus of reality is in abstractions), the social myth could never be justified upon (Positivistic) scientific grounds. Epistemological realism is akin to metaphysical idealism. For the epistemological Realist a thing's essence is more basic than it is as a concrete, individual exemplar of that essence. This is what makes definitions meaningful -- especially those of universal terms, collective terms, and abstractions. Abstractions have a "higher reality" in that they are timeless; they do not generate or corrupt, come into being or pass away. Until only a few generations ago they were the subject matter of science and logic. Like the rules of plane geometry, they are always "there" to be discovered. As such, epistemological Realism is the underlying basis of traditional qualitative logic -- and a major target for attack by the Pragmatists. Again, for this reason when American social scientists go from description to myth based advocacy they are in danger of being labeled "ideologues" and "dogmatists." About the only "scientific" escape here has been American pluralism from James Madison to Robert Dahl, wherein whatever _emerges_ from the conflict of various and competing interests is _defined_ as the public good; and here the problem of objective advocacy disappears. A less scientific but more practical way out may be Theodore Lowie's advocacy of "juridical democracy," wherein the blackrobed priests of practical and natural law simply are given the power to settle the claims of competing interests in the name of the closest learned human approximation to the objective human good.

Yet, if there is to be political _science_, rather than merely an aesthetic interest in history and

comparative governments, political science must be the
architectonic science. It alone can combine and give
direction to all the other sciences. It is necessarily
a science of values.

Therefore, if the American social sciences are
going to continue in the Pragmatic tradition, it is
imperative that they make their humanistic value assumptions explicit, and test and revise their prescriptions
whenever possible. Because of the difficulty of carrying out laboratory experiments in order to isolate
causal variables, history and anthropology should regain
their high regard among the sciences for, as Dewey
remarked, history is the laboratory of the social
sciences. At least history should be seen as one of the
laboratories of political science, along with all the
other human sciences, because it is only over time that
most social prescriptions can be tried in practice. In
the end it may even be necessary to reevaluate our
Nominalistic methodology in the name of promoting the
objective human good -- or else admit that we are no
better than taxonomists and technicians. Perhaps, in
the end, this work may be looked on merely as a plea for
honesty and humility.

CHAPTER 1

THE ORIGINS OF PRAGMATISM: PEIRCE AND JAMES

Commentators often speak of Pragmatism as the only original American philosophy. This surely is debatable, and one would have to qualify such a statement in several respects before it would be credible. However, it is certain that Pragmatism was an original American philosophy and that it was highly influential. As Will Durant, who is perhaps the most popular commentator on the history of thought, has remarked:

> The reader needs no guide to the new and the old elements in this philosophy. It is part of the modern war between science and religion; another effort, like Kant's and Bergson's, to rescue faith from the universalized mechanics of materialism. Pragmatism has its roots in Kant's "practical reason"; in Schopenhauer's exaltation of the will; in Darwin's notion that the fittest (and therefore also the fittest and truest idea) is that which survives; in utilitarianism, which measured all goods in terms of use; in the empirical and inductive traditions of English philosophy; and finally in the suggestions of the American scene.[1]

What all forms of Pragmatism have in common is an emphasis on ends or results as opposed to either means or first principles. There is something particularly American about Pragmatism in William James's hands as he continually returns to the "cash value" of an idea. This chapter will attempt to clarify how Pragmatism originated as an obscure methodology of the physical sciences under C. S. Peirce and then changed into a general philisophy under James. This change was both crucial for its acceptance and indicative of popular American intellectual thought at that time. In the latter respect, Josiah Royce has given James the ultimate Hegelian compliment: ". . . James is an American philosopher of classic rank, because he stands for a stage in our national self-consciousness -- for a stage with which historians of our national mind must always reckon."[2]

Charles Sanders Peirce (1839-1914) normally is recognized as the founder of the Pragmatic method. A good deal is known about Peirce but, unfortunately, no one has as yet written his definitive biography. Unlike James, his fame is still in the process of emerging. Rather it has been the practice of most book-length works on his philosophy to begin with a short essay on Peirce, the man, as an introduction. There are almost no disagreements among them, only various omissions. The following biographical information will follow primarily the essay by Paul Weiss found in Richard Bernstein's Perspectives on Peirce (1965).[3] The Weiss biography is taken as authoritative because he is also the co-editor of Peirce's Collected Papers and has shown decades of interest in the man. All discrepancies or major additions will be footnoted.

Charles Peirce was born in Cambridge, Massachusetts, the second son of Benjamin Peirce, the foremost American mathematician of his time and a professor at Harvard. Many of both Charles Peirce's strengths and weaknesses are directly accountable to the fact that his father closely supervised his education, teaching him reading, writing, and (especially) mathematics, at home. According to Weiss, he also encouraged his son's eccentricities and failed to teach him how to get along in group situations.

Charles was precocious. He began the study of chemistry at the age of eight, had set up his own laboratory before he was a teenager, mastered the latest books on logic on his own, and invented code languages and mathematical games for his playmates.

Later his father sent him to several private schools as a preparation for Harvard. It may be significant to note that they were all local schools. Unlike James, Peirce did not have the benefit of study abroad in his youth. Judging from Peirce's later involvement in the classics of science, literature and logic it may be speculated that these schools stressed the "classical tradition," i.e. a proficiency in reading literature in Greek, Latin, French and German. He entered Harvard in 1855 and graduated in 1859 -- near the bottom of his class. This may be attributed to the fact that he was young and only motivated to work hard where his interest led him. It was as an undergraduate that he read Kant's Critique of Pure Reason three pages a night until he had it almost memorized.

2

In 1861 he joined the U.S. Coast and Geodetic
Survey. Among his greatest logistical achievements was
to maneuver his work stations so that he could continue
studying and lecturing at the same time. He hung on to
the job for thirty years. In 1862 he received an M.A.
from Harvard and in 1863 he received the first Sc.B.
that Harvard awarded. It was in chemistry and he got it
summa cum laude. He spent six months studying classi-
fication under Louis Agassiz at about the same time
that James also was studying under Agassiz. In 1864-
1865 he lectured at Harvard on the philosophy of
science. It is important to note that he came to
philosophy in a specialized way: he was looking for
answers to specific questions about the natural sciences, and about the way that logic can be used as a
tool of those sciences.

He was forced to give up his lectureship at
Harvard because of a personal dispute with the president. So, perhaps in order to stay close to the
academic life, he became an assistant at the Harvard
Observatory. Research work that he did there between
1872 and 1875 led to the only book he published in his
lifetime, Photometric Research (1878). He also did
pendulum and gravity research, for which he gained
international fame at the time he was the first American delegate to the international geodetic conference
in France. Partly because of the fame gained when his
assertions about the non-uniformity of gravity were
proven, he was put in charge of the U.S. weights and
measures in 1884 and sat as a member on international
commissions for the same purpose. He was the first to
propose the wave length of a particular light ray as a
standard unit of measure, a procedure accepted today by
all countries on the metric system.

The lack of a professorship was a large factor in
keeping his other works from being published. As A. J.
Ayer says, "He thought of himself primarily as a
logician in a sense in which logic comprehended the
analysis of all the processes of thought and inquiry
into the conditions of their truth, rather than just
the formal theory of valid deductive reasoning."[4] He
anticipated ". . . Wittgenstein in the idea that the
laws of logic had no formal content . . ."[5] He was
the only person until Schroder to advance Boolian
Algebra. Although he lectured for only a total of
eight years at Harvard and Johns Hopkins and had
relatively few students one of them was Mrs. Christine
Ladd-Franklin. He anticipated the Principia Mathemat-
ica (1910-1913) of Bertrand Russell and Alfred North

3

Whitehead (under whom Christine Ladd-Franklin did her doctorate). He also wrote on psychology, criminology, the history of science, early English and classical Greek pronunciation, Egyptology, did translations from Latin and German, prepared a thesaurus and an editor's manual, and much more.

However he was also handicapped by a number of difficulties which kept him from the fame he deserved. First, he was a poor lecturer. He had trouble making his thoughts and ideas clear to those who were not as well educated as himself. Second, his extensive background and penchant for precision best suited him for a very advanced class (a position to which he was never advanced in spite of his own and James's best efforts to get him a professorship). Third, his love life was scandalous; and this was something no university of his time could afford to have its professors known for. Fourth, he did not socialize well with others, especially his superiors. According to W. B. Gallie, "Peirce seems never to have been able to get on with anyone whom he did not greatly admire and who did not reciprocally admire him and treat him as an intellectual equal: in particular he found it hard to get along with university presidents and professors."[6] Finally (and ironically) he simply was not pragmatic in his dealings outside the laboratory. His finances were as badly managed as his love life. At one point he was forced to sell his private library, the best one on logic in the United States, to Johns Hopkins University in order to pay his debts. According to Gallie, Peirce in his old age was considered a "hopeless eccentric" who would try ". . . to escape his creditors by working in a loft the ladder to which he would pull up behind him."[7] During the last years of his life William James and his former students contributed to his maintenance. For this kindness he adopted the middle name "Santiago" which means "St. James" in Spanish. In summing up Peirce's idiosyncrasies one must conclude that he did not live "pragmatically" in the sense which the term has today; he either acted without regard to the consequences of his actions, or simply was unable to calculate probable consequences based upon past experience.

Concerning Peirce's Pragmatism his commentators unanimously credit the Cambridge "Metaphysical Club" as its origin or, at least, the earliest direct influence on its operation. This may be overrated.

The "Metaphysical Club" met fortnightly in the early 1870's for the purpose of intellectual discussion. Its usual format called for the reading of a paper by a member, followed by group discussion. Its most brilliant member was Chauncey Wright, referred to as either a radical Positivist or a naturalist, a man who intensely enjoyed debating as a sport. All the other members looked up to him and called him their "boxing master." Among those were Oliver Wendell Holmes, John Fiske, William James and the Benthamite lawyer Nicholas St. John Green. Green already had a leaning toward social jurisprudence and his effect upon the group is still an open question.

According to most commentators the entire group, with one exception, was "British-oriented".[8] Peirce, of course, was that exception. If they had been educated in the Great Tradition then Peirce felt that they had read it all with an English slant. He, on the other hand, was more at home with classical and Continental philosophers, especially Aristotle, Immanuel Kant, and John Duns Scotus. Before the "Metaphysical Club" first met he already considered himself to be a "Scotistic realist". In fact he claimed to be more of a Realist than Scotus himself.[9] Hence his unique education not only preceded his later group associations but also directed his responses. He was but an interloper in a group, a gathering of radical Nominalists, that was foreign to him. While William James was full of praise for contemporary French philosophers, Peirce thought that the last French philosopher had been Descartes. If anything, the effect of the club was not to shape his views, but rather to help him to articulate them.

When Peirce gave papers for the club they were usually on the topic of logic, a subject of little interest to the other members who were more interested in social philosophy, psychology, and jurisprudence. Peirce was unique in the group in that he was extremely well read in Medieval logic.[10] Since his logical background was so esoteric compared to theirs it is doubtful whether they could have been of much help to him in the discussions following his presentations. In fact most of the club members including James thought of him as exceptionally odd.

Finally when Peirce got around to framing the Pragmatic principle in 1877 (while on his way to a convention in France) it was long after the club was defunct, and it was done for a subject directly related

5

to his work as a physical scientist. The principle was translated from French into English a year later, but William James did not pick up the term for a full twenty years thereafter.

> Peirce's statement of the Pragmatic principle reads as follows: Consider the effects, which might have practical bearings, we conceive the object of our conception to have. Then, our conception of these effects is the whole of our conception of the object.[11]

Every word and comma of this was thought about and thoroughly intended just as it reads.

J. F. Boler contends that Peirce's Pragmatism makes sense best when it is used as a tool of a natural science. Understanding Peirce's Pragmatism is, thus, a matter of understanding its context. Boler says that, "In general a scientific hypothesis is not accepted because of where it comes from but because of where it leads."[12] Thus comes about Peirce's emphasis on "ends," "consequences," "effects" and "practical bearings." According to Gallie, "Pragmatism, in Peirce's hands was a logical tool . . ."[13] and a tool of the natural sciences. Pierce is a thorough philosophical Realist; for him the objects of scientific knowledge are objective, true, and repeatable. According to Ayer, Peirce, unlike James, did not equate a true proposition with one which is simply useful to believe.[14] Peirce's ". . . pragmatism," according to Boler, "warns that although we can dictate the questions, we cannot dictate the answers."[15] In his professional work Peirce was a member of the worldwide community of physical scientists. In his own study he was a member of the Scholastic-Continental-Realist tradition of thought.

Unfortunately for Peirce, his method was not something which would work only for fellow Realists. Instead he lived to see it changed to serve ends which he never intended or thought possible. Chief among those "kidnappers" who changed Peirce's intent was William James: in 1905 Peirce began calling his own method "Pragmaticism," a term ". . . ugly enough to be safe from kidnappers." However, since James repeatedly gives Peirce credit for originating "Pragmatism" Peirce's name has stuck to it.

6

Today the term "pragmatism" is applied to philosophical Nominalists, those who are the polar opposite to Peirce. For instance, Paul Boller describes Justice Holmes' position as "legal pragmatism."[16] To understand how this change came about one must look directly to James.

The biography of William James (1842-1910) presents the opposite problem from that of Peirce. First, there is far more material than can be used conveniently in a work of this size and scope. Two such sources are his letters collected and edited by his brother, Henry James,[17] and his authoritative biography by G. W. Allen.[18] There are several others; some such as R. B. Perry's The Thought and Character of William James (1936)[19] run two volumes in length. When James's own works are included the information becomes massive. Only a very small part of this whole is needed for the purpose of this work. The second drawback is that James's principal and best known biographers often appear to be "Jamesians". Either consciously or unconsciously they appear to present him as a sort of intellectual hero and standard to be admired. On the other hand his detractors, such as George Santayana and Mortimer Adler, are inclined to take the opposite extreme. When there is still so much passion aroused by a philosophy it may be indicative that the issues James treated are still alive today, that in a sense we are still a part of the same age. In order to emphasize the "kidnapping," only a relatively brief sketch of his biography is needed. Here R. B. Perry's general chronology[20] defers to G. W. Allen as the authority because Allen wrote one of the last biographies on James (1967). Thus, he was able to synthesize the earlier ones and to correct their errors.

As George Santayana puts it, "William James enjoyed in his youth what are called advantages: he lived among civilized people, traveled, had teachers of various nationalities."[21] The senior Henry James, according to Bernard Brennan, was a rich eccentric: "In his utterances he adopted the role of prophet and mystic, denouncing church and state."[22] His Swedenborgian mysticism allowed him to hold views which in other contexts would have been condemned as contradictory. He attended Princeton Theological Seminary for two years after graduating from Union College, but quit because he could not accept the doctrines of orthodox Calvinism. Still he remained concerned with religion throughout his life. This aspect of the father and its effect upon William cannot be over emphasized. As A. J. Ayer sees it, logic stood in the way of traditional religious arguments and it thus had to be shown that logic did not compass the whole of reality. Ayer says:

> This is of fundamental importance to the understanding of James's thought, since his desire to make room for religious beliefs, without relaxing his intellectual standards or manipulating the evidence, was also one of the principal motives for his pragmatism. In particular, it strongly colored his interpretation of the pragmatic theory of truth.[23]

The Senior Henry James, being independently wealthy, devoted his life to being a professional student and to educating his children. "This education," wrote Brennan, "was designed to minimize the influences of institutions and grim traditions."[24] The James children were continually moved from continent to continent and from school to school in order to broaden their backgrounds.

William James had been interested in art since childhood, and in 1860 he attempted to pursue it as a career. Upon finding that he was not cut out to become a painter he decided to attend Harvard. At that time two of his brothers enlisted on the Union side in the Civil War, but William held back for health reasons. He began, like Peirce, as a chemistry major but changed to physiology. This scientific training was the most rigorous he ever had and later helped hold in check his tendency to make broad generalizations. Also, like Peirce, one of his favorite professors at Harvard was Louis Agassiz, with whom he later went on an expedition to Brazil.

From his background in physiology James turned to medicine and received his M.D. from Harvard in 1869. He was in poor health all his life but managed to be productive in spite of the fact. He never practiced medicine but, instead, took up teaching anatomy and physiology at Harvard in 1873. Two years later he taught his first course in psychology. His primary interest in the field at that time was in how states of the body determine mental states -- a normal reaction for a person with his formal training. By 1876 he was promoted to the secure position of assistant professor of physiology at Harvard. Two years later he married and signed a contract to produce a book on psychology. His marriage was as nearly perfect as one could hope for and the Principles of Psychology (1890), which took him more than ten years to write, is a classic and monumental work in its field. Even his severe detractors admire it. His brilliant style of writing made even the dullest subjects come alive. He wrote like a public speaker and, in fact, most of his published works were originally delivered as speeches or lectures.

While logic had led Peirce to philosophy, James was finally led to it by physiology and psychology. Both logic and psychology at that time were still properly regarded as divisions of philosophy. It is worth noting that neither Peirce nor James had much early or formal training in philosophy. Rather, both were primarily concerned with solving problems presented to them from their own particular disciplines. The philosophers whom each chose to read were those who offered possible solutions to their respective problems.

Between the time James received his M.D. and started teaching he suffered a mental breakdown. Perhaps a reason for this can be found in the tension between his upbringing and his education; his emotion and his intellect. He could not bear the thought of a deterministic universe and, yet, that was the only sort of world that his studies had taught him to believe in. By reading Wordsworth and Charles Renouvier he managed to recover from his mental crisis.[25] Yet intellectually he still remained a determinist. When teaching psychology he reversed what is normally considered the mental cause-and-effect sequence, saying:

> . . . that the bodily changes follow directly the PERCEPTION of the exciting fact, and that our feeling of the same changes as they occur IS the emotion.
>
> . . . [W]e feel sorry because we cry, angry because we strike, afraid, because we tremble, and not that we cry, strike or tremble, because we are sorry, angry or fearful as the case may be. . . .
>
> The neural machinery is but a hyphen between determinate arrangements of matter outside the body and determinate impulses to inhibition or discharge

9

within its organs. When the hen sees a
white oval object on the ground she
cannot leave it; she must sit upon it
and return to it, until at last its
transformation into a little mass of
moving, chirping down elicits from
her machinery an entirely new set of
performances.[26]

He immediately goes on from there to describe and
account for human actions in the same biologically
compulsive manner. By 1890 he still said:

I now proceed to the most vital
point of my whole theory, which is this:
If we fancy some strong emotion, then
try to abstract from it all the feelings of its bodily symptoms, we find
nothing left behind, no "mind-stuff"
out of which the emotion can be constituted, and that a cold neural state of
intellectual perception is all that
remains.[27] (italics James)

This is from the Principles of Psychology. In the same
work he held that the seat of the human "self" is
located in the muscles of the face and throat.[28]

Perhaps the key to understanding James is to know
that he held contradictory beliefs. Again, he was
raised one way and then educated another. His Swedenborgian father taught freedom and humanism. Often
Ralph Waldo Emerson was a guest in their house. James
was basically religious and, yet, he had received the
latest scientific education. "Science" reduced literally everything to the laws of material cause and
effect, to nothing but matter in motion.

Santayana observes that, "There was a deep sense
of insecurity about him."[29] He wanted to embrace
both the world of "science" (as he knew it) and of
traditional human or religious values at the same time.
James was extremely sensitive to the predicaments of
the philosophy of his age, and had the gift of being
able to make them alive to others. James was utterly
appalled by the idea of a mechanistic universe and most
of all by the automaton theory of mind. He thought
that while the deterministic scientific theories were
basically true man still must be a free moral agent.

As W. B. Gallie says:

> But though he felt this to be so,
> he lacked the logical power to see and
> say clearly why it was so: and the main
> thread of his philosophical development
> consists in his persistent efforts to
> find philosophical justifications for
> his initial feeling or hunch against
> current materialistic doctrines. To
> this end he welcomed aid from the most
> diverse quarters.[30] (emphasis Gallie)

In A. J. Ayer's words, William James

> . . . sought the advantage of being
> tough-minded with regard to any ques-
> tions of natural fact; and tender-minded
> with respect to morals and theology.
> What attracted him to Pragmatism was
> that it seemed to him to make both
> possible.[31]

It permitted him to have the best of both worlds, to
hold contradictory beliefs at once, to reconcile what
for James was equivalent to the problem of theodicy.
This is a use for the Pragmatic method which made
Peirce, the logician, so unhappy. In truth when James
listened to Peirce lecture he confessed that he did
not understand him and later made his famous description of Peirce as, "flashes of brilliant light revealed
against Cimmerian darkness!"[32] According to Gallie,
James's

> . . . openly anti-intellectualistic
> teachings stand in definite opposition
> to the intellectual temper of Peirce.

> But, unlike Peirce, James was never
> greatly influenced by the spirit of the
> laboratory and never drawn to reflect
> closely on its methods. ... Moreover
> -- and here again he stands in marked
> contrast to Peirce -- James confessed
> himself "mathematically imbecile" and
> "a-logical if not illogical," and in one
> of his last books he publically and
> solemnly "renounced logic".[33]

Peirce's great weakness lay in moral and aesthetic
philosophy. He was primarily a physical scientist and
a logician, and probably could never have achieved popular fame. James, on the other hand, had a life-long

11

interest in all types of value theory -- especially religion -- and it was religion that was in a time of crisis in the United States. Thus he shone brilliantly in a sphere which held the public interest, one which did so in the strongest of ways. Any breakthrough in this area which supported tradition, security, or "common sense" was bound to gain immediate recognition.

James's unique contribution was to combine epiphenomenalism with religion. In his Pragmatism: A New Name for Some Old Ways of Thinking (1907) he declared: "'The True,' to put it very briefly, is only the expedient in our way of thinking, just as 'the right' is only the expedient in our way of behaving."[34] (emphasis James) In the same work he said that, "On pragmatic principles, if the hypothesis of God works satisfactorily enough, it is true."[35] Although he goes on to claim that he believes in higher forms of consciousness,[36] such gods still would have a material basis, standing to us as we do to our cats and dogs.

James, as a psychologist, thought that emotion or "temperament" was primary in directing the human power of reason.[37] If all thought is but epiphenomena, then so too is reason. Human needs become drives that dictate what is looked for or thought about. He was sensitive to too many varieties of philosophical experience to believe, or put his faith in, any of them as reflections of Truth or Reality. He was fond of the Hegelian, Josiah Royce, as a friend and as a disputant, but he certainly never believed in the Absolute or in any such systematic philosophy. Rather, for James the "true" was equated with the useful, not with either a correspondence or a coherence theory of reality. In a truly pluralistic universe there are infinite possibilities. Ayer claims that he was reacting against the logic of the neo-Hegelians.[38] However Ayer also recognizes that James's "radical empiricism" stressed the importance of even the subjective sensations and needs, such as religion. Religion is useful. He was a subjectivist and a thoroughgoing Nominalist. Needs and sensations certainly are real at one level, even though they are epiphenomenal and not objective. "Thus, for James," says Ayer, "it is an essential characteristic of religion and moral theories that their role is to satisfy our emotional and practical demands."[39]

This is the use to which James put his Pragmatism in "The Will to Believe," a use which Peirce called "suicidal". This remark is quoted by numerous scholars such as Ayer and W. B. Gallie who agrees that it is a completely unwarranted extension of Peirce's Pragmatism.[40] Gallie comments further that, "Quite apart from the quality of their respective philosophical equipments, Peirce and James were antithetical intellects."[41]

"The Will to Believe"[42] (1896), originally delivered as an address before the Philosophical Clubs of Yale and Brown Universities, probably did more to make James's fame than anything else. This is the most concrete instance of his advocating a position rather than just making an analysis or a description. His main adversary is William Kingdom Clifford who, in "The Ethics of Belief" (1879),[43] had defended the point that men ought only to hold those beliefs which they have examined and of which they are reasonably sure. This was a moral imperative because one's beliefs represent tendencies or predispositions to actions -- and actions affect others. Darwin and the whole age of natural science had made the traditional beliefs in God untenable to a rational person such as Clifford. Men life Clifford, such as Thomas Huxley and Herbert Spencer, were extending the scope of Darwinian science so as to supersede religion altogether, to unmask it as but the opposite of science -- as superstition.

James fearlessly -- and perhaps foolishly -- went into battle with both Thomas Huxley and William Clifford. He called the latter an enfant terrible,[44] accused him of not recognizing his own passional nature,[45] and opted for Pascal's phrase, "Le coeur a ses raisons que la raison ne connait pas."[46] True beliefs are those which are useful or profitable ones, even if contradictory and regardless of their correspondence to ultimate reality. More still, for James, in the case of future events faith can actually create its own desired end or object. This is the Pragmatic value of faith. He explains:

> The desire for a certain kind of truth here brings about that special truth's existence; and so it is in innumerable cases of other sorts. Who gains promotions, boons, appointments, but the man in whose life they are seen to play the part of live hypotheses, who discounts them, sacrifices other things for their sake before they have come, and takes risks for them in advance: His faith acts on the powers above him

13

as a claim, and creates its own verification. ... There are, then, cases
where a fact cannot come at all unless a
preliminary faith exists in its coming.
And where faith in a fact can help
create the fact, that would be an insane
logic which should say that faith
running ahead of scientific evidence is
the "lowest kind of immorality" into
which a thinking being can fall. Yet
such is the logic by which our scientific absolutists pretend to regulate
our lives![47] (emphasis James)

There is something powerful and inspiring about this on
a religious level. It should make one think back to
James's Swedenborgian father. Yet it is easy to see
how Peirce, the logician and philosophical Realist,
called it "suicidal". Will faith in the existence of
God "create the fact"?

No; but allowing people to believe in virtually
anyting will encourage experimentation and "progress".
It may be speculated that what James really wanted to
do was to free human action from the bonds of either
scientific or religious restraint.

James accepted the inverse of the traditional
relationship between logic and reality: for Peirce a
true theory would work in practice, its prior truth
ensuring its subsequent workability; whereas for James
whatever "worked" was the highest evidence of a true
theory. For this James has been criticized by every
major logician of our time including Russell, Whitehead
and Ayer. However, Royce appears ultimately to have
been right: James seemed to embody the intellectual
spirit of his age and the public loved him for it. He
was widely accepted in spite of his faults and in spite
of the shouts of those who pointed out his logical
absurdities. He appeared as a wise old man who offered
salvation from a mechanistic and deterministic science.

On the other hand contemporary materialists, such
as George Santayana were revolted. Santayana lamented:

. . . when his book on Pragmatism
appeared, about the same time as my
Life of Reason, it gave me a rude shock.
I could not stomach that way of speaking
about truth; and the continual substitution of human psychology -- normal

14

madness, in my view -- for the universe, in which man is but one distracted and befuddled animal, seemed to me a confused remnant of idealism, not serious.

The William James who had been my master was not William James of the later years, whose pragmatism and pure empiricism and romantic metaphysics have made such a stir in the world.[48]

Later, Herbert Schneider explained,

William James, the most religiously empirical of them all, was catholic in his sympathies precisely because he was protestant in his interests. Having achieved for himself an irreligious "healthy-mindedness" after years of struggle, he was free to extend the broadest sympathy to "sick souls". His Varieties of Religious Experience (1902) is therefore not an objective account of religion, but a clinical diagnosis of religious diseases. The sicker the soul the better it suited him, for such cases admirably illustrated his philosophy of consciousness.[49]

It was not merely the variety of religious experiences, but the abnormality or "subliminal" quality of religious consciousness that seemed to James the essential fact of religion. And he presented his clinical cases of "sick souls" not in order to raise problems of mental health, but rather in order to show that "healthy mindedness" is an abnormality for religion.[50]

Perhaps Schneider understood James better than did Santayana. James appears to agree with Karl Marx, and even more so with his personal friend Sigmund Freud. Dogmas are connected with restrictions; restrictions create an unnatural condition, or sickness, in an acting being; and the conscious manifestations of such a condition is religion.

In his last work, The Meaning of Truth: A Sequel to 'Pragmatism' (1909), James tried to defend himself from the attacks of the professional intellectuals, those who accused him of simply trying to make people feel good. In the preface he argued,

> I had supposed it to be a matter of common observation that, of two competing views of the universe which in all other respects are equal, but of which the first denies some vital human need while the second satisfies it, the second will be favored by sane men for the simple reason that it makes the world seem more rational. To choose the first view under such circumstances would be an ascetic act, an act of philosophic self-denial of which no normal human being would be guilty. Using the pragmatic test of the meaning of concepts, I had shown the concept of the absolute to mean nothing but the holiday giver, the banisher of cosmic fear. One's objective deliverance, when one says 'the absolute exists' amounted, on my showing, just to this, that 'some justification of a feeling of security in the presence of the universe' exists, and that systematically to refuse to cultivate a feeling of security would be to do violence to a tendency in one's emotional life which might well be respected as prophetic.[51] (emphasis James)

> My treatment of 'God,' 'freedom,' and 'design' was similar. Reducing, by the pragmatic test, the meaning of each of these concepts to its positive experiencable operation, I showed them all to be the same thing, vis., the presence of 'promise' in the world. 'God or no God?' means 'promise or no promise?' It seems to me that the alternative is objective enough, being a question of whether the cosmos has one character or another, even though our own personal answer may be made on subjective grounds.[52]

What is significant is that he virtually accepted his critics' charges, but without allowing that they proved him wrong. Unlike his older contemporary, Karl Marx, James was perfectly happy that the people should have

16

an opiate in religion. Religion provided (or justified) ideals which most men could not arrive at through
their intellects. If men were unlimited potentials in
a process of evolution, then religious ideals might
provide the blueprints for them to evolve into gods.

Henry Steele Commager says of pragmatism, "Because
it taught that men hold the future in their own hands,
it was drenched with optimism."[53] However he also
states that, "Of all the philosophies to which Americans
have subscribed, pragmatism lent itself most unavoidably
to vulgarization."[54] Such ". . . a philosophy
sponsored by democracy suffered the consequences of
that sponsorship."[55] Yet what even Commager fails
to see is how it would be used by the intellectuals
and, after a generation, how even they would suffer
the consequences.

FOOTNOTES FOR CHAPTER 1

[1] Durant, Will. The Story of Philosophy: The
Lives and Opinions of the Great Philosophers. New
York: Washington Square Press, Inc., 1962, p. 518.

[2] Royce, Josiah. The Basic Writings of Josiah
Royce, Vol. I. ed. J. J. McDermott. Chicago, Illinois: University of Chicago Press, 1969, p. 208.

[3] Bernstein, Richard J., ed. Perspectives on
Peirce; Critical Essays on Charles Sanders Peirce.
New Haven, Connecticut: Yale University Press, 1965,
pp. 1-12.

[4] Ayer, A. J. The Origins of Pragmatism;
Studies in the Philosophy of Charles Sanders Peirce
and William James. San Francisco, California: Freeman, Cooper and Company, 1968, pp. 4-5.

[5] Ibid., p. 5.

[6] Gallie, W. B. Peirce and Pragmatism. New
York: Dover Publications, Inc., 1966, p. 35.

[7] Ibid., p. 36.

[8] Wells, Rulon. "Charles S. Peirce as an
American." Bernstein ed. Perspectives on Peirce;

17

Critical Essays on Charles Sanders Peirce. op. cit.,
p. 18 n9. This is taken as but one example.

[9] Boler, John F. Charles Peirce and Scholas-
tic Realism; A Study of Peirce's Relation to John Duns
Scotus. Seattle, Washington: University of Washington
Press, 1963, p. 7.

[10] Ibid., p. 4.

[11] Peirce, Charles Sanders. The Collected
Papers of Charles Sanders Peirce. eds. Paul Weiss
et al. Cambridge, Massachusetts: The Harvard University Press, 1960, p. 258.

[12] Boler, op. cit., p. 15.

[13] Gallie, op. cit., p. 21.

[14] Ayer, op. cit., p. 8.

[15] Boler, op. cit., p. 14.

[16] Boller, Paul F. American Thought in Transition: The Impact of Evolutionary Naturalism, 1865-
1900. Rand McNally and Company, 1973, p. 16 164.

[17] James, Henry. The Letters of William James.
Boston, Massachusetts: Little, Brown, and Company,
1926.

[18] Allen, Gay Wilson, William James: A Biography. New York: The Viking Press, 1967.

[19] Perry, Ralph Barton. The Thought and Character of William James, 2 Vols. Boston, Massachusetts:
Little, Brown and Company, 1936.

[20] Ibid., pp. XIV-XX.

[21] Santayana, George. The Works of George
Santayana, Vol. VII. New York: Charles Scribner's
Sons, 1936, p. 39.

[22] Brennan, Bernard P. Williams James. New
York: Twayne Publishers, Inc., 1968, p. 16.

[23] Ayer, op. cit., p. 180.

[24] Brennan, op. cit., p. 24.

[25] Ibid., p. 34.

[26] James, William. "What is an Emotion?" Collected Essays and Reviews by William James. ed. R. B. Perry. London, England: Longmans, Green and Company, 1920, pp. 247-249.

[27] James, William. The Principles of Psychology, Vol. II. New York: Henry Holt and Company, 1890. p. 451.

[28] Ibid., Vol. I. pp. 300-302.

[29] Santayana, op. cit., p. 40.

[30] Gallie, op. cit., p. 24.

[31] Ayer, op. cit., p. 182.

[32] James, William. "What Pragmatism Means." Pragmatism and American Culture. ed. Gail Kennedy. Boston Massachusetts: D. C. Heath and Company, 1950. p. 1.

[33] Gallie, op. cit., p. 22.

[34] James, William. Pragmatism; A New Name for Some Old Ways of Thinking. New York: Longmans, Green and Company, 1943, p. 222.

[35] Ibid., p. 299.

[36] Ibid., p. 299.

[37] James, "What Pragmatism Means," op. cit., p. 2.

[38] Ayer, op. cit., p. 176.

[39] Ibid., p. 186.

[40] Gallie, op. cit., pp. 25-26.

[41] Ibid., p. 29.

[42] James, William. "The Will to Believe" (complete). Religion from Tolstoy to Camus. ed. Walter Kaufmann. New York: Harper Torchbooks, 1964, pp. 221-238.

[43] Clifford, William Kingdom. "The Ethics of Belief" (complete). Religion from Tolstoy to Camus. ed. Walter Kaufmann. New York: Harper Torchbooks, 1964, pp. 201-220.

[44] James, "The Will to Believe," op. cit., p. 225.

[45] Ibid., pp. 226-227, 228, 231.

[46] Ibid., p. 233.

[47] Ibid., pp. 234-235.

[48] Santayana, George. "A General Confession." The Golden Age of American Philosophy. ed. Charles Frankel. New York: George Braziller, Inc., 1960, pp. 272-273.

[49] Schneider, Herbert. "Radical Empiricism and Religion." Essays in Honor of John Dewey; On the Occasion of His Seventieth Birthday October 20, 1929. New York: Henry Holt and Company, 1929, pp. 336-337.

[50] Schneider, Herbert. A History of American Philosophy. New York: Columbia University Press, 1947 (third printing), p. 559.

[51] James, William. The Meaning of Truth; A Sequel to 'Pragmatism'. New York: Longmans, Green and Company, 1909, pp. ix-x.

[52] Ibid., p. x.

[53] Commager, Henry Steel. The American Mind; An Interpretation of American Thought and Character Since the 1880's. New Haven, Connecticut: Yale University Press, 1950, p. 96.

[54] Ibid., p. 100.

[55] Ibid., p. 101.

CHAPTER 2

THE REACTION OF JAMES'S CONTEMPORARY PHILOSOPHERS
TO HIS THEORY OF SELF AND CONSCIOUSNESS

The purpose of this chapter is to show the relationship of James's Pragmatism to the other dominant philosophies of his time, especially Idealism and Materialism. Josiah Royce is used as the representative Hegelian Idealist, and George Santayana the spokesman for classical Materialism. These philosophers were chosen because they were James's popular American contempories, knew him personally, and often made reference to him in their writings. Although James's best known European critics were G. E. Moore and Bertrand Russell, they will be passed over because theirs was simply a more concise (and less revealing) restatement of Santayana's position. Instead, Georges Sorel and V. I. Lenin will be used to illustrate the European reaction. James's theory of the self and of consciousness is stressed because it is central to both his own Pragmatism and the methodology of the new social sciences.

The approach continues to be historical because the point is not to discover what James "really" had in mind, but to exhibit how others made use of what he said.

In 1880 Josiah Royce wrote to James saying:

> In each moment we construct such a world because we are interested in doing so. The final basis of our thought is ethical, practical. These things are so because a given moment of activity must have them so. "Give me a world" is the cry of consciousness; and behold, a world is made even in the act of crying. ... Some of this you will, I think, agree with; some of it at all events I have learned from or through you.[1]

In an essay written two years later Royce says:

> Change the book you are reading, and your whole notion of the universe suffers some momentary change also. ...

Your change of attention qualitatively
alters your apprehension of truth.[2]

At every moment we are not merely
receiving, attending, and recognizing,
but we are constructing. Out of what
from moment to moment comes to us, we
are building up our ideas of past and
future, and of the world of reality.
Mere dead impressions are given. We
turn them by our own act into symbols
of a real universe. We thus constantly
react upon what is given, and not only
modify it, but give it whatever significance it comes to possess.[3]

Definite belief in external reality
is possible only through this active
addition of something of our own to the
impressions that are actually given to
us. No external reality is given to us
in the mere sense-impressions. What is
outside of us cannot be at the same
time within us. But out of what is in
us, we construct an idea of an external
world; and we ourselves give to this
idea all the validity that for us it
can ever have.[4]

Interestingly, Royce puts even more stress upon
the consequential aspect of reality than James does.
The fact that we actively choose which aspects of given
experience to make significant makes us ultimately
responsible for our beliefs and, thus, for the world
which we create. In this respect Royce sides much more
closely with Clifford than with James. Even though
Royce, in a letter to C. S. Peirce, described James
as ". . . my most intimate friend outside my own
family,"[5] he was quite willing to criticize James for
his lack of responsibility. From James's position the
will to believe is primary for an acting being, it is
an extension of the will to live; but, since it is so
primary or biologically based, it precedes consciousness. The activities of a conscious individual are the
results of his prior beliefs. In order to create his
beliefs, to create himself, an individual would have to
exist before he existed, would have to create himself
before he was created. Rather, for James it is the
body which creates consciousness.

22

In 1882, fourteen years before James first delivered "The Will to Believe" as a lecture, Royce wrote of him:

> A person for whose opinions I have much respect once said to me, that he disclaimed all responsibility for the beliefs that he held on certain very important matters.

> "I try," said he, "to conquer prejudice; but having done this, I can do no more. My belief, whatever it is, forms itself in me. I look on. My will has nothing to do with the matter. I can will to walk or to eat; but I cannot will to believe. I might as well will that my blood should circulate."

> Despite his disclaimer, I thought, and yet think, that he has made his beliefs very much for himself, and that these beliefs do him honor, as the statue does honor to the artist that chisled it. [6]

Royce could not bring himself to believe that James's beliefs had been fashioned from "wholly passive matter." He reflected that the powers of material circumstance were great, but continued:

> But my friend was a man of energy, and controlled the current of his thought. He fought hard . . . and he was so far conquered as to be the master of a very manly and many-sided system of doctrine. I think him responsible for this system . . . As a man is, so he thinks. [7]

Royce finds his solution to James's problem through a sort of Kantian approach to what is good in itself -- a good will. There is an ambiguity in the term "will": at one time it can mean a drive and at another a choice, often both together. James uses it as a drive, a force, or a motive power. Royce uses it as a selective force. He says:

> . . . attention, in its most elementary forms, is the same activity that, in a more developed shape, we call will. We

23

attend to one thing rather than another, because we will to do so, and our will is here the elementary impulse to know. Our attention leads us at times into error. But this error is merely an accompaniment, the result of our will activity. We want to intensify an impression, to bring it within the sphere of knowledge. But in carrying out our impulse, we do more than we meant. We not only bring something into clearer consciousness that was before out of clear consciousness, but we qualitatively modify this thing by attending to it. ... Attention seems to defeat, in part, its own object. Bringing something into the field of knowledge seems to be a modifying, if not transforming, process.[8]

For Royce the ultimate basis of the self is the will: It exists from birth, is itself a force with choice and, thus, is responsible, both morally and causally, for creating or manifesting itself.

Plainly, since active inner processes are forever modifying and building our ideas; since our interest in what we wish to find does so much to determine what we find; since we could not if we would reduce ourselves to mere registering machines, but remain always builders of our own little worlds -- it becomes us to consider well, and to choose the spirit in which we shall examine our experience. Every one is certain to be prejudiced, simply because he does not merely receive experience, but himself acts, himself makes experience. The great question for every truthseeker is, In what sense, to what degree, with what motive, for what end, may I and should I be prejudiced?[9]

Royce can avoid the problem that James poses because of the difference between potential and actual existence. The will is an actualizing force, in a sense a potential for actualizing since it does not act with mechanical necessity. It is a potential force for creating itself in actuality, and, as such, is responsible for the <u>attitude</u> that it adopts in the process.

24

Unlike James's self, which is the epiphenomena of the movements of his mouth and throat, Royce's conscious self might be described as the creation of his will. Even though speech is important for the development of a distinctively human mind, Royce finds that "Thought has other modes of expression than through the forms of speech," such as creative actions.[10]

Royce may be credited with anticipating the Pragmatists, Thomas Cooley and G. H. Mead, with the concept of "the significant other" in the emergence of the self. This is not surprising in view of the fact that significant perceptions and interpretations were the data by which Royce's will created its (actual) existence. It creates itself in its relationship to other selves and, secondly, as over against the brute facts which function as matter. Royce says:

> A man is conscious of himself, as a finite being, only in so far as he contrasts himself, in a more or less definite social way, with what he takes to be the life, and, in fact, the conscious life, of some other finite being. ... Our conception of physical reality is secondary to our conception of our social fellow-beings, and is actually derived therefrom.[11]

Thus not only does the self learn to define itself in its interaction with other selves, but it is also the case that most of what is taken for physical reality is, in fact, a matter of convention. "Matter" is understood socially or conventionally.

According to J. G. Cotton, "Without our neighbors we simply would not be aware of ourselves as selves at all. Such is the thesis of Royce."[12] Why, then, did not Royce get the credit for a theory that went to Cooley and Mead? Unknowingly, Cotton provides the answer when he says: "Royce has a way of saying that our estimate of ourselves depends upon what others think of us, or upon what we believe others ought to think. But these are by no means identical. For in our belief about what our neighbors 'ought' to think of us, we retain our own measure of independent judgment."[13] For Mead, the Pragmatist and "social behaviorist," there is no independent existence (socially speaking) and certainly no independent judgment.

25

Another area in which Royce took James to task was over the knowledge of <u>other</u> selves, the conscious states of others. Royce says, "There can be no direct perception of other minds. For this general reason, 'working hypotheses' about the interior reality which belongs to the mind of my neighbor can never be 'converted into the cash of existence'."[14] James was forced to resort to analogy, and Royce says that this is ". . . fatal to the whole pragmatic theory of knowledge. Surely an argument from analogy is not its own verification."[15] Royce missed the chance to attack the argument from analogy as wholly improper under these circumstances: it is suitable for judging an unknown individual case by reference to the well known general case; but in the case of the conscious states of others it is applied from the basis of only one known case (the individual who is directly conscious of only himself) to over a billion unknown cases. Still, Royce's point is well taken.

Royce's solution is to use the criterion of coherent new information as the sure sign of another mind.[16] There is a dialogue; new ideas are communicated by means of symbols; and it all depends upon a continuous series of mutual interpretations -- virtually the same structure as the now classic argument made by H. H. Price some twenty-two years later.[17]

As early as 1881 Royce expressed agreement with James that there was no "mind-stuff." For James there was nothing independent of matter, and for Royce there was nothing, no "stuff," independent of consciousness. In an interesting way, their radical positions were rather compatible on this issue. It was James's treatment of the objectivity of the given of consciousness which bothered Royce. Royce wrote a letter to him that year, saying:

> There is just one doubt in much that you say about the general definition of reality: Do you or do you not recognize this reality to which you speak as in its known or unknown forms independent of the knowing consciousness? Sometimes you speak as if "Sentiment" were all, sometimes as if there were something above the "Sentiment" to which the latter conformed. ... For me the sentiment of reality, the determination to act thus and so, the expectation of certain results, all these facts

26

of the active consciousness are together the whole truth. There is needed or known or conceivable above these facts of consciousness absolutely no transcendent reality.[18]

For Royce the data of consciousness is objective, upheld by the Absolute (or God). Still, in practice Pragmatism was compatible with metaphysical Idealism: their differences lay beyond the concern of all those but professional philosophers.

Whereas James and Royce were best friends and their philosophies were compatible in practice (with Royce from time to time calling himself an "Absolute pragmatist", there was little or no good feeling between James and Santayana. In fact Santayana was one of the only two students in his entire career that James actively disliked. (The other was Theodore Roosevelt.) For his part, Santayana began his professional studies with the rigors of "Catholic philosophy" (presumably Thomism) and detested James's lack of system, precision and certitude.

Santayana had a difficult time saying anyting about James that was not in some way demeaning. He says that James had an ". . . irregular education; he never acquired that reposeful mastery of particular authors and the safe ways of feeling and judging which are fostered in great schools and universities."[19] He could not stand James's apparent lack of consistency. However he knew it to be a part of his method. He conceded that, "In reality, James was consistent enough, as even Emerson (more extreme in this sort of irresponsibility) was too."[20] Continuing, Santayana claims that "His excursions into philosophy were accordingly in the nature of raids."[21] Santayana believed that James's popularity rested upon his poorer works -- The Will to Believe, Pragmatism, and The Varieties of Religious Experience -- rather than on his best work, The Principles of Psychology.

Although James's psychology was his most scholarly and well researched work, Santayana saw that it gave a clue to his later direction. According to Santayana, James did not dare to accept the conclusions of his own research because they would have pointed to a mechanistic universe.

He preferred to believe that mind and matter had independent energies and

27

could lend one another a hand, matter operating by motion and mind by intention. This dramatic, amphibious way of picturing causation is natural to common sense, and might be defended if it were clearly defined; but James was insensibly carried away from it by a subtle implication of his method. This implication was that experience or mental discourse not only constituted a set of substantive facts, but the only substantive facts; all else, even the material world which his psychology had postulated, could be nothing but a verbal or fantastic symbol for sensations in their experienced order. So that while nominally the door was kept open to any hypotheses, regarding the conditions of the psychological flux, in truth the question was prejudged. The hypotheses, which were parts of this psychological flux, could have no object save other parts of it. That flux itself, therefore, which he could picture so vividly, was the fundamental existence. The sense of bounding over the waves, the sense of being on an adventurous voyage, was the living fact; the rest was dead reckoning. Where one's gift is, there will one's faith be also; and to this poet appearance was the only reality.[22] (emphasis Santayana)

Santayana says that, "I think it important to remember, if we are not to misunderstand William James, that his radical empiricism and his pragmatism were in his mind only methods; his doctrine, if he may be said to have had one, was agnosticism."[23] Santayana defines James's agnosticism as ". . . feeling instinctively that beliefs and opinions, if they had any objective beyond themselves, could never be sure they had attained it."[24] Thus Santayana felt that James was philosophically shallow and a subtle form of religious hypocrite:

All faiths were what they were experienced as being, in their capacity of faiths; these faiths, not their objects, were the hard facts we must respect. We cannot pass, except under

28

the illusion of the moment, to anything
firmer or on a deeper level. There was
accordingly no sense of security, no
joy, in James's apology for personal
religion. He did not really believe; he
merely believed in the right of believing that you might be right if you
believed.

It is this underlying agnosticism
that explains an incoherence which we
might find in his popular works. ...
Professedly they are works of psychological observation; but the tendency
and suasion in them seems to run to
disintegrating the idea of truth,
recommending belief without reason, and
encouraging superstition.[25]

Santayana finds that James had no ultimate basis --
no ground at all -- for claiming that his fine psychological observations were not "instances of delusion."
Thus Santayana deplored the lack of basis for a "judicial attitude:"

In The Varieties of Religious
Experience we find the same apologetic
intention running through a vivid
account of what seems for the most part
(as James acknowledged) religious
disease. Normal religious experience is
hardly described in it. Religious
experience, for the great mass of
mankind, consists in simple faith in the
truth and benefit of their religious
traditions. But to James something so
conventional and rationalistic seemed
hardly religious; he was thinking only
of irruptive visions and feelings as
interpreted by the mystics who had
them.[26]

Santayana compared James's study of religion in The
Varieties to a surgeon who could guarantee the success
of his operation, but not the life of the patient. He
compared James's "Will to Believe" to Pascal's Wager,
and shows it to be fallacious for the same reasons:
first; there are a multitude of choices, not just two
alternatives. Second; the motive is base:

29

. . . such a wager -- betting on the
improbable because you are offered big
odds -- is an unworthy parody of the
real choice between wisdom and folly.
There is no heaven to be won in such a
spirit, and if there was, a philosopher
would despise it.[27]

To be boosted by an illusion is not
to live better than to live in harmony
with the truth; it is not nearly so
safe, not nearly so sweet, and not
nearly so fruitful. These refusals to
part with a decayed illusion are really
an infection of the mind. Believe
certainly; we cannot help believing; but
believe rationally . . .[28]

Note, however, the phrase, "we cannot help believing." In this much Santayana agrees with James. The
difference is that Santayana is a species of philosophical Realist: there is but one objective reality, and
only it is worthy of human belief -- the universe is
not plural. Santayana does not believe that James could
live with truth or certitude if he found it.

Philosophy for him had a Polish
constitution; so long as a single vote
was cast against the majority, nothing
could pass. The suspense of judgment
which he had imposed upon himself as a
duty, became almost a necessity. I
think it would have depressed him if he
had had to confess that any important
question was finally settled. ...
Experience seems to most of us to lead
to conclusions, but empiricism has sworn
never to draw them.[29]

Rather, Santayana thinks that James drew his false
conclusions from a true psychological fact; the fact
that will and belief do influence one's actions.

We do not need a will to believe;
we need only a will to study the objects
in which we are inevitably believing.
But James was thinking less of belief in
what we find than of belief in what we
hope for: a belief which is not at all
clear and not at all necessary in the
life of mortals.[30]

30

Santayana not only agrees that beliefs, will, and desire do influence actions; he takes Clifford's position in the extreme, saying: ". . . indeed, I think we can go farther and say that in its essence belief is an expression of impulse, of readiness to act."[31] Like the Pragmatists, he finds that human beliefs and impulses become adjusted to the facts of reality through actions. Again the difference between James and Santayana lies in Santayana's commitment to the brute knowable objectivity of the physical world. For this reason Santayana claims that James is at his worst when he claims that faith in success can be what is needed to bring about a successful conclusion.

> Here again psychological observation is used with the best intentions to hearten oneself and other people; but the fact observed is not at all understood, and a moral twist is given to it which (besides being morally questionable) almost amounts to falsifying the fact itself. Why does belief that you can jump a ditch help you to jump it? Because it is a symptom of the fact that you <u>could</u> jump it . . . ... Assurance is contemptible and fatal unless it is self-knowledge.[32] (emphasis Santayana)

He invoked Socrates to say that courage without wisdom is folly. Yet he is closer to James's position than Clifford's in holding that "Scepticism is . . . a form of belief. Dogma cannot be abandoned . . ."[33] However he qualifies this by saying, "The brute necessity of believing something so long as life lasts does not justify any belief in particular . . ."[34]

When writing about Bertrand Russell in <u>Winds of Doctrine</u>, Santayana devotes twelve pages to Russell's criticism of Pragmatism. Santayana both paraphrases Russell and quotes him at length on this subject, with Russell as a vehicle of criticism so as not to cast doubt on his own motives. Russell is excellent for this purpose because he took the same sort of delight as Santayana did in attempting to make Pragmatism look absurd. Sometimes Santayana would step in to help him; for instance when Russell was explaining how the Pragmatists paid inadequate attention to the facts, Santayana added:

> For we should presently learn that those facts can be made by thinking,

31

that our faith in them may contribute to their reality, and may modify their nature; in other words, these facts are our immediate apprehensions of facts . . . Thus the pragmatist's reliance on facts does not carry him beyond the psychic sphere; his facts are only his personal experiences. Personal experiences may well be the basis for no less personal myths; but the effort of intelligence and of science is to find the basis of the personal experiences themselves; and this non-psychic basis of experience is what common sense calls the facts, and what practice is concerned with. ... [T]he bedrock of facts that the pragmatist builds upon is avowedly drifting sand.[35]

Through the selective use of Russell's criticisms and his own remarks Santayana paves the way to suggest that the "psychological point of view" of Pragmatism, "might be the equivalent to the idealistic doctrine."[36] Thus accusing James of being a secret Idealist was the ultimate that Santayana could do in discrediting him. He also uses an historical approach to achieve the same result as he achieved through quoting Russell's analysis:

Such economical faith, enabling one to dissolve the hard materialistic world into a work of mind, which mind might outflank, was traditional in the radical Emersonian circles in which pragmatism sprang up.[37]

. . . [T]hey have declared that consciousness does not exist, and that objects of sensation (which at first were called feelings, experiences, or "truths") know or mean one another when they lead to one another, when they are poles, so to so to speak, in the same vital circuit. The spiritual act act which was supposed to take things for its object is to be turned into "objective spirit," that is, into dynamic relations between things.[38]

It certainly was not James's early materialism
that bothered Santayana but, rather, his pervasive
Nominalism.

> In William James . . . psychology
> was the high court of appeal. Ulti-
> mately he wrote his <u>Varieties of
> Religious Experience</u> -- by far his most
> influential book -- in which he showed
> his strong inclination to credit super-
> normal influences and the immortality
> of the soul.

> All this, however, was a somewhat
> troubled hope which he tested by all
> available evidence; and his most trusted
> authorities were often French, Renouvier
> and later Bergson . . . It was only
> later that he produced the sensational
> theories by which he is known, at least
> by hearsay, all the world over: his
> <u>Pragmatism</u>, in which the reality of
> truth seemed to be denied, and his
> article entitled "Does Consciousness
> Exist?" where he answered this question
> in the negative.[39]

He considered James to be a philosophical coward, one
who could not bear the consequences of his underlying
materialism. Santayana says, "I cannot understand what
satisfaction a philosopher can find in artifices, or in
deceiving himself and others. I therefore like to call
myself a materialist . . ."[40]

Indeed Santayana claims to be a thorough-going
materialist. Matter is primary, the only "stuff" which
is real in the nature of being. He says:

> I am not tempted seriously to
> regard consciousness as the very essence
> of life or even of being. On the
> contrary, . . . consciousness is the
> most highly conditioned of existences,
> . . . nor does its origin seem more
> mysterious to me than that of everything
> else.[41]

Santayana, at the opposite extreme from Idealism, very
clearly reduces mind to an epiphenomenon of matter.

. . . [W]hile the designation of substance as mind-stuff is correct, it is
by no means exclusively or even pre-
eminently proper. ... In so far as
mind has stuff at all under it and is
not purely spiritual, the stuff of it is
purely matter. ... Moreover, organization requires a medium as well as a
stuff; and that medium in which the
mind-stuff moves is avowedly space and
time. But what can exist in space
except matter . . .? Mind-stuff is
therefore simply an indirect name for
matter . . . and nothing but a confusing
attachment to a psychological vocabulary
could counsul for its frequent use.

I find, then, that in the psychological sphere, apart from pure feeling
or intuition, everything is physical.
There is no such thing as mental substance, mental force, mental machinery,
or mental causation. [42]

Santayana considered James to be at his best in the
passage in his Psychology where he declares that one is
sorry because he cries, angry because he strikes and
afraid because he trembles. After giving a vivid
account of the human passions run wild in love and
anxiety, he explains it in a manner reminiscent of the
way James explained the same phenomena by reference
to the "machinery" of a chicken:

All this is the psyche's work:
. . . and our superficial mind is
carried by it like a child, cooing and
fretting, in his mother's arms. Much of
it we feel going on unmistakably within
our bodies, and the whole of it in fact
goes on there. ... The psyche is an
object of experience to herself, since
what she does at one moment or in one
organ she can observe, perhaps, a moment
later, or with another organ; yet of her
life as a whole she is aware only as
we are aware of the engines and the
furnaces in a ship in which we are
traveling, half-asleep, or chattering on
deck; or as we are aware of a foreign
language for the first time . . . without distinguishing the words, or the

reasons for these precise passionate
outbursts. In this way we all endure,
without understanding, the existence and
the movement of our own psyche: for it
is the body that speaks, and the spirit
that listens.[43]

Unlike James, Santayana saw the necessity of positing
an unconscious psyche, a natural program for maintaining the life of the body. Of the psyche he says, ". . .
to keep us alive is her first and essential function.
It follows naturally from this biological office that
in each of us she is one, vigilant, and predetermined
. . ."[44] It has that same essential function in both
plants and animals.

He says:

The whole life of the psyche, even
if hidden by chance from human observa-
tion, is essentially observable: it is
the object of biology. Such is the only
scientific psychology, as conveived by
the ancients, including Aristotle, and
now renewed in behaviorism and psychoanalysis.[45]

One might speculate that if James had been a
philosophical Realist like Peirce, then Santayana might
have called himself a Pragmatist -- albeit grudgingly
and with many qualifications. This is because of
Santayana's insistence upon the practical knowability
of an object world, and of the efficacy of reason
which, as a tool, allows men to live in harmony with
nature.

Reminiscent of Pragmatic learning theory,
Santayana says that, "The guide in early sensuous
education is the same that conducts the whole Life of
Reason, namely, impulse checked by experiment, and
experiment judged again by impulse."[46] He says that,

. . . perception and knowledge are . . .
normally and virtually true: not true
literally, as the fond spirit imagines
when it takes some given picture . . .
for the essence of the world; but pragmatically, and for the range of human
experience . . .[47]

35

Thus also, there is nothing to prevent consciousness -- spirit --from having knowledge of its source.
Santayana says,

> In other words, consciousness is
> naturally cognitive. Its spiritual
> essence renders it an imponderable
> sublimation of organic life, and invis-
> ible there; yet it is attached histor-
> ically, morally, and indirectly to its
> source, by being knowledge of it.[48]

It may be said that James's two major contemporary
American critics held complimentary notions of the
nature of consciousness. For Royce, the act of defining one's separate conscious self as over against the
rest of consciousness creates something which functions
as "matter." Santayana, on the other hand, is acutely
aware of the fact that "all matter is alive",[49] ready
to actualize its potentials under the right conditions
of motion and complexity.

Royce and Santayana both agree that the self can
know itself and, thus, live in an objective harmony
with its surroundings; whereas for James the epistemological Nominalist, there is no such universal objectivity, and it might profit the organism simply to
experiment with its life-style. It is this lack of
assurance which made Pragmatism radically different.

The Marxist materialists also are disturbed by
Pragmatism's lack of assurance. V. I. Lenin criticized
James and Dewey as "subjective idealists."[50]

Actually Lenin admired one part of James's philosophy, his radical empiricism. Earlier philosophers,
such as David Hume, had started with sensations and
ended up reducing mind to what they started with.
"But," according to Lenin,

> experience is not merely the immediate
> experience of the given; it includes
> also -- and this in our view is James's
> great philosophical innovation -- the
> relations implied by the given, and
> which form the rigid fabric between all
> immediate experience and past or future
> experience. If experience consisted
> only of immediate experience, we would
> have only sensations and not science; we

would not even have perception in the full sense of the word.[51]

Lenin finds that James's theory of the mind allows the spectator to perceive relationships, instead of mere isolated phenomena. "Thus, it seems that the new orientation which has appeared in philosophy and which has been given the name of pragmatism marks an indisputable advance in the scientific and philosophical conceptions of mind."[52] Pragmatism is progressive and almost scientific in that it gives up all claim to a priori explanations, and relies on experience as its guiding principle.[53]

Where James went wrong was when he wrote The Will to Believe. Lenin faults James for ascribing "teleological laws" to mere thought.[54] In Lenin's view,

> The teleological concept of psychological law is in essence nothing but scientific facing for metaphysical conceptions, which made tendency, the will to live, instinct, the will, and action, the basis of everything that exists. Moreover, it has been accepted, elucidated and developed by the pragmatists, the adherents of the primacy of action. For them functional psychology and teleological psychology are synonymous terms.[55] (emphasis Lenin)

For the Marxists objective economics, not psychology, determines beliefs and actions.

Lenin defines the moral doctrines of Pragmatism as: "a mysticism of action. This attitude is not new. It was the attitude adopted by the sophists, for whom there was also neither truth nor error, but only success."[56] (emphasis Lenin) "Moreover, in regard to the problem of truth, pragmatism has become synonymous with skepticism, just as, in regard to morality or faith, it has become synonymous with irrational traditionalism.[57] (emphasis Lenin)

Lenin maintains that, "Reason in the final analysis is nothing but free examination."[58] Apparently one meaning of freedom for Lenin is freedom from the interference of the will. Whereas the pragmatists and the philosophers of the past had sought to impose (will) inter-connectedness or systemization upon experience, only Marxists allow experience to reveal how it really is systematised. Others have distorted reality, but not the Marxists because, as Lenin says, ". . . our knowledge becomes systematised in exactly the same way as it is given to us, and the relations of the given have the same value as the given itself."[59] (emphasis Lenin)

Just as Marxism is a form of Continental Rationalism, it is obvious that Lenin is a philosophical Realist. Truth must fit the theory or system which he holds. There is only one set of truths, those which he perceives. Again according to Lenin,

> Only those concepts that succeed are true. But one has yet to discover whether they are true because they succeed or whether they succeed because they are true. Pragmatism is always inclined to choose between these alternatives in favour of the first. Common sense apparently, can only choose the second.[60] (emphasis Lenin)

What is shocking for a materialistic Realist like Lenin is that under James's Nominalistic system truth itself might change from day to day. In this Lenin explicitly agrees with C. S. Peirce in the latter's criticism of James.[61] There is little wonder that the Marxists, or any other people who hold their positions with near absolute certainty, would be threatened by James's radical Nominalism.

On the other hand there was at least one influential European philosopher, Georges Sorel, who was indebted to James's emphasis upon the will. H. S. Thayer, who is one of the best known recent defenders of Pragmatism credits Sorel as being a variety of Pragmatist.[62] Sorel reflects the Bergsonian anti-intellectual sort of Pragmatism that stems directly from The Will to Believe. Believing in certain myths (e.g. the myth of the general strike) will not only justify violent actions but bring them about. For Sorel, like James, there is a sense in which believing makes it so.

Thayer says, "There are clearly certain broad similarities between Sorel's view of the function of the myth for social groups and James' argument in The Will to Believe concerning the benefits of belief to certain individuals."[63] The difference in application was that whereas James saw that beliefs might

38

comfort and motivate individuals, Sorel saw that they might solidify and motivate whole masses. Since his time it has been recognized that almost all mass movements require an ideology, no matter how strange or absurd it might be. It is "pragmatic" when one makes use of the principle that the Chicago sociologist, W. I. Thomas, discovered while researching The Polish Peasant in Europe and America: "That which is believed to be real is real in its consequences." What James had done, and what he was criticized bitterly for, was to overlook the important distinction between ontologic reality and consequential reality.

According to Thayer, "It was in 1921, in De l'utilie du Pragmatisme, that Sorel stated his partial acceptance of James's pragmatism and argued for its 'usefulness' as a means of settling controversies."[64] James had written The Will in the context of the battle between established religion and evolutionary naturalism. What Sorel did not like about James was his Protestantism, but, like others, it was something that he could dispense with without changing the methodology that was the core of Pragmatism.

Sorel was a disillusioned Catholic, and yet still too much of a romantic to accept the rationalism of Karl Marx. Instead he used a Jamesian approach to consolidate Christianity, Marxism and the a-rational vitality of Henri Bergson into his brand of "socialism." In a letter prefacing his Reflections on Violence Sorel justified his instrumental use of myth:

> In employing the term myth I believed that I had made a happy choice, because I thus put myself in a position to refuse any discussion whatever with the people who wish to submit the idea of a general strike to a detailed criticism, and who accumulate objections against its practical possibility.[65]

Unlike Plato, who adored stability, for Sorel the movement, the flux and creativity is everything. For this reason he is actually hesitant to see the class conflict resolved.[66]

Sorel saw Marx as a romantic, and this is the one quality about Marx which he admired. Of course Marx would not have appreciated this because he did not believe that his effectiveness depended upon myth. Sorel explains,

39

Like all romantics, Marx supposed
that the _Weltgeist_ operated in the heads
of his friends. There is a certain
amount of truth to this doctrine. ...
But we must be careful not to mistake
such scholastic schemes for laws oper-
ative in the future.

The pretension displayed by Marx in
speaking scientifically of the march
toward socialism is very defensible if,
like him, we admit that we are on the
eve of a catastrophe . . .[67]

Whereas Marx believed steadfastly in his "iron
laws," Sorel put his emphasis on psychology. According
to Irving Louis Horowitz,

Like Le Bon, he envisions the
moment of revolution as a phenomenon
made possible by the coalescence of
psychological factors. Revolution is
the point at which individual psychology
connects itself to universal history.
Because of this the study of objective
factors alone can never yield a knowledge of when or how revolutionary
transformations take place.[68]

Horowitz says that "Sorel was anti-rationalist in
much the way Rousseau was. Both feared the consequences of a society which, in its hyprocrisy and
artificiality had the effect of changing men from doers
into knowers . . ."[69] Yet he adds that a strange
kind of "Platonic elitism rather than Marxian egali-
tarianism was the chief instrument urging Sorel to seek
salvation in the producers."[70] Rather he sees Sorel
combining socialist Christian myths in an attack on
traditional Platonism:

. . . socialism shares with Christianity
an inability to detail the precise
changes in the world, and cares even
less whether the qualities of the
apocalyptic vision will be fulfilled in
empirical history. Socialism is neither
utopian vision nor scientific discipline. It contains elements of both
but its core is the practice of the
heroic life. ... Political action

emanates from the shadow world of the unconscious.

Traditional Platonic elitism, because of its intense rationalism, found no overt support in Sorel's philosophy. Sorel rejected Plato's view that the leaders of society know absolute truth while the masses lack such scientific insight. The distinction is rather between those people who can discover the psychological tone of the masses and are able to translate these feelings into actions by means of the myth... Leaders are not made by either the quantity or quality of knowledge they possess; but in virtue of how many men they can captivate and galvanize by the projection of a novel myth. The leader is the charismatic myth-manipulator, the mass are myth-believers. The useful lie serves to direct men into action and at the same time creates the basis for leadership. The reversal of rationalism is completed by Sorel to the last detail.[71]

For Horowitz it is clear that "The myth of the general strike leads inevitable to socialism as a myth."[72] "Sorel was saying that the mystery is not in the concrete parts of socialist society, but in socialism qua socialism. Socialism has a motivational and manipulative value only because of its ideals . . . "[73] while the rest is necessarily left undetermined.

Horowitz traces Sorel's development as a radical:

Long before Sorel discovered the utility of the Communist Manifesto in educating the labouring class circles, he considered the New Testament as the most valuable, commonly understood, guide to mass action. Yet apocalyptic myth, the suddenness with which sweeping social changes are brought about, was the common ground of Christ and Marx. The apocalypse, with its sublime faith in inevitable success, stands over science, the way action towers above discourse. Just as it is the centre of

41

Christian radicalism the apocalypse is
the basis of socialist radicalism. The
myth need not contain a single fact
which could come to pass. Its importance inheres in its ability to give
organization to the vague projections
which each person has to make about
life. The myth is stronger than a
fact; it is a belief. The will to
believe makes possible great social
upheavals.[74]

The last sentence is, of course, a reference to the
religious outcome of the psychology and philosophy of
William James. Horowitz says that, "The religious zeal
of Sorel was never really destroyed."[75]

Perhaps one more way to understand Sorel's position is to compare it to the "Freudian Marxism" of
Herbert Marcuse. Turning Marx inside out, Sorel fears
capitalism because it may make the lives of men too
easy, making them all soft and decadent. In Sorel's
case it is more of a "Jungian Marxism," a perpetual
fight against an archetype called "capitalism;" but a
fight which must never become successful because that
would end it. As Horowitz states,

To assume that men fight to preserve the strength of what they are
resisting is a logic that surpasses even
sublime wisdom. Underlying Sorel's view
is an instinctual psychology which
declares the battle to be the thing.
It is James' "fighting instincts,"
Nietzsche's "warrior spirit" and Bergson's "intuitive urge to battle" given a
class conscious coat of armour. The
position rests on a theory of human
nature as aggressive, and a theory of
society as regressive.[76]

It is easy to see how violence can be a cleansing force
for Sorel. Perhaps he was an influence on Frantz
Fanon. Horowitz adds:

The development of psychoanalysis
has tended to support Sorel's belief in
mythology as both the initial condition
of fresh scientific speculation and, no
less, the limiting condition of science.
When Freud wrote that "it may perhaps

42

seem to you as though our theories are a kind of mythology... But does not every science come in the end to a kind of mythology," he merely confessed what Sorel had been asserting all along.[77]

What he did achieve was to take the first step in framing a theory of politics which insisted on the central-ity of _irrational_ human impulses and false ideologies in the determination of the social relations of men. In this sense, he was a forerunner of the sociology of knowledge.[78] (emphasis original)

Today one may argue that the social sciences are themselves substituting for mythologies. It is to be expected that the need for them as such will continue, and also that the study of the role of myth in social action will increase. This is, perhaps, the most human way to understand human motivation because only man is the myth following animal. (Certainly it is doubtful that he is a "rational animal.") Horowitz concludes on the side of James and Sorel:

The need for mythology is a neces-sary adjunct of any theory of history which at one and the same time demands a clear-cut command to effective human action. Sorel seems to be saying that men will not act if such action involves violations of their real or imagined interests, or if such action is pre-sented to the mass as a scientific or intellectual necessity. ... Sorel assumes that men who doubt the universal significance of a proposed act will justify passivity. ...

Myth is needed to overcome the probabilistic world of scientific fact. ... Their ability to stimulate activity is the supreme measure of the worth of ideologies.[79]

Other scholars are of similar thought about the role of myth and social action. For instance Raphael Patai says,

One strongly feels that the pattern of group violence that is prevalent in our day to a degree Sorel would never have dreamed of, can be satisfactorily explained only along these lines. The epidemic spread of protest, violence, and other group action, not only in the United States ...but also in many other parts of our embattled planet, cannot be explained in any other way. It is not any actual sudden worsening of the global situation that has created the present wave of violent protest by today's youth: it is, rather, the mystical presentiment that by engaging in a quasi-Sorelian "general strike" they can hasten the advent of Utopia . . .[80]

Here it is not the intellect -- not the logos, the reason, impartial judgment -- that actually causes motivation. The intellect is calculative. It is analogous to a computer; it only manipulates the "facts" which have been put into it beforehand. Value originates outside of logic and is prior to it. Values are elements, not products, of the reasoning process.

Both James and Sorel had a great influence in Italy. Thayer quotes a revealing passage from an interview with Mussolini in the London Sunday Times of April 11, 1926:

The pragmatism of William James was of great use to me in my political career. James taught me that action should be judged rather by its results than by its doctrinary basis. I learnt of James that faith in action, that ardent will to live and fight, to which Fascism owes a great part of its success . . .[81]

Benito Mussolini had even been a member of a group that called itself "The Pragmatic Club."[82]

Pragmatismo can be traced directly to James. Its foremost native spokesman was Giovanni Papini (1881-1956), who met James in Rome in 1905. He already had a high regard for James and after the meeting came almost to idolize him. They continued to exchange letters, with James forming an equally high opinion of

44

Papini, almost to the point of seeing his own reflection in him. According to Thayer, "James had . . . begun to think of pragmatism as a philosophy, a program, a world-wide intellectual movement of which he was the founder; and after meeting the Italians, he was suddenly conscious of being the leader."[83] He even wrote articles on Papini and Pragmatismo.

It was not long until the Italian Pragmatists came under attack from two directions. The first was the Catholic Church which saw Pragmatismo as a form of Modernism -- a way of thinking which it pronounced heretical. The second came from the Italian academic philosophers, such as Benedetto Croce. After James died the second and third major Italian Pragmatists, Giovanni Vailati and Mario Calderoni, died in 1909 and 1914, respectively, and Papini converted to Christian mysticism. Italian Pragmatism flourished for only ten years and died in the disillusionment of the Great War. However, that high point coincided with the formative years of Il Duce. Papini decreed, "From induction by Will to Believe, there is given a single aim: aspiration to be able to act (Wille zur Macht)."[84] With the help of other European influences the "will to believe" became the transition to the "will to power."

The most pronounced and continuing effect of Pragmatism outside the United States was in England. James's Pragmatism reached England before the Pragmatisms of his epigoni and, according to Thayer,

> The most famous pragmatist outside the United States was Ferdinand Canning Scott Schiller (1864-1937). At the height of his influence early in the present century, Schiller was regarded the equal of James as leading spokesman for pragmatism. On the continent, far more attention was directed to the works of James and Schiller than to any of the other pragmatists.[85]

However, unlike James, by mid-century his name had vanished so completely that people mistook his name for that of the German poet.

Schiller was quite influenced by James and, according to Thayer, "He attempted to persuade James to drop the name pragmatism in favor of humanism. For humanism, Schiller contended, represented the broader movement into which pragmatism fitted as a part."[86]

(emphasis Thayer) That may have been the best insight of his career, except that he failed to notice that Fascism was also a part of that movement. Still, one might argue that the popularity of Fascism was, in part, due to the fact that it posed as a brand of humanism.

Often it is speculated that Pragmatism never died; it just changed names variously in order to avoid being associated with all the criticism directed at William James. James's Pragmatism, especially his epistemological Nominalism, his "cash value" notion of truth and "believing makes it so" view of reality, became a focal point for innumerable critics and defenders. The following chapters will document some of the effects of Pragmatism in its country of origin.

FOOTNOTES FOR CHAPTER 2

[1] Royce, Josiah. The Letters of Josiah Royce. ed. J. Clendenning. Chicago, Illinois: The University of Chicago Press, 1970, p. 89.

[2] Royce, Josiah. Fugitive Essays. Cambridge Massachusetts: Harvard University Press, 1920, p. 355.

[3] Ibid., p. 360.

[4] Ibid., p. 361.

[5] Royce, The Letters of Josiah Royce, op. cit., p. 280.

[6] Royce, Fugitive Essays, op. cit., p. 345.

[7] Ibid., p. 345.

[8] Ibid., p. 354.

[9] Ibid., p. 362.

[10] Royce, Josiah. Royce's Logical Essays; Collected Logical Essays of Josiah Royce. ed. D. S. Robinson. Dubuque, Iowa: William C. Brown Company, 1951, p. 16.

[11] Royce, Josiah. The Basic Writings of Josiah Royce, Vol. I. ed. I. K. Skruspskelis. Chicago,

Illinois: The University of Chicago Press, 1969, pp. 248-249.

[12] Cotton, James G. Royce on the Human Self. Cambridge, Massachusetts: Harvard University Press, 1954, p. 44.

[13] Ibid., p. 50.

[14] Royce, The Basic Writings of Josiah Royce, op. cit., Vol. II, pp. 478-479.

[15] Ibid., p. 750.

[16] Ibid., p. 751.

[17] Royce devised this method in 1916. Twenty-two years later, in 1938, H. H. Price used virtually the same argument in one of the most famous articles ever written on the subject of other minds. Why Royce did not receive any credit in it is anybody's guess. See: Price, Henry Habberly. "Our Evidence for the Existence of Other Minds," Philosophy, XII, No. 52 (1938).

[18] Royce, The Letters of Josiah Royce, op. cit., pp. 107-108.

[19] Santayana, George. Character and Opinion in the United States; With Reminiscences of William James and Josiah Royce and Academic Life in America. New York: Charles Scribner's Sons, 1921, p. 64.

[20] Ibid., p. 67.

[21] Ibid., p. 67.

[22] Ibid., pp. 70-71.

[23] Ibid., pp. 74-75.

[24] Ibid., p. 75.

[25] Ibid., pp. 76-77.

[26] Ibid., p. 80.

[27] Ibid., p. 86.

[28] Ibid., p. 87.

[29] Ibid., p. 82.

[30] Ibid., pp. 87-88.

[31] Ibid., p. 87.

[32] Ibid., p. 89.

[33] Santayana, George. "Scepticism and Animal Faith." The Works of George Santayana, Vol. XII. New York: Charles Scribner's Sons, 1937, p. 14.

[34] Ibid., p. 15.

[35] Santayana, George. "Winds of Doctrine." The Works of George Santayana, Vol. VII. New York: Charles Scribner's Sons, 1937, p. 104.

[36] Ibid., p. 105.

[37] Ibid., p. 107.

[38] Ibid., pp. 107-108.

[39] Santayana, George. The Birth of Reason and Other Essays. ed. D. Cory. New York: Columbia University Press, 1968, pp. 132-133.

[40] Ibid., p. 134.

[42] Santayana, George. "Realms of Being." The Works of George Santayana, Vol. XIV. New York: Charles Scribner's Sons, 1937, p. 340.

[42] Ibid., p. 374.

[43] Ibid., p. 331.

[44] Ibid., p. 329.

[45] Ibid., p. 326.

[46] Santayana, George. The Life of Reason: Or the Phases of Human Progress. New York: Charles Scribner's Sons, 1953, p. 6.

[47] Santayana. "Realms of Being" (1937), op. cit., p. 344.

[48] Ibid., p. 343.

[49]   Ibid., p. 327.

[50   Lenin, V. I.   Collected Works, Vol. 38:
Philosophical Notebooks. Moscow: Foreign Languages
Publishing House, 1963, pp. 609, 614.

[51]   Ibid., p. 469.

[52]   Ibid., p. 448.

[53]   Ibid., p. 470.

[54]   Ibid., p. 452.

[55]   Ibid., p. 452.

[56]   Ibid., p. 454.

[57]   Ibid., p. 458.

[58]   Ibid., p. 455.

[59]   Ibid., p. 459.

[60]   Ibid., p. 458.

[61]   Ibid., p. 457.

[62]   Thayer, H. S. Meaning and Action; A Critical
History of Pragmatism. New York: The Bobbs-Merrill
Company, 1968, pp. 320-323.

[63]   Ibid., p. 321.

[64]   Ibid., p. 322.

[65]   Sorel, Georges. Reflections on Violence.
trans. T. E. Hulme. New York: MacMillan Publishing
Company, 1974, p. 43.

[66]   Sorel, Georges. From George Sorel: Essays
in Socialism and Philosophy. ed. J. L. Stanley.
New York: Oxford University Press, 1976, p. 40.

[67]   Sorel, Georges. The Illusion of Progress.
Berkeley, California: University of California Press,
1969, pp. 207-208.

[68]   Horowitz, Irving Louis. Radicalism and the
Revolt Against Reason. London, England: Routledge and
Kegan Paul, 1961, p. 121.

[69]   Ibid., p. 129.

[70]   Ibid., p. 120.

[71]   Ibid., p. 136.

[72]   Ibid., p. 137.

[73]   Ibid., p. 137.

[74]   Ibid., pp. 134-135.

[75]   Ibid., p. 135.

[76]   Ibid., p. 119.

[77]   Ibid., p. 134.

[78]   Ibid., p. 126.

[79]   Ibid., p. 133.

[80]   Patai, Raphael. Myth and Modern Man. Englewood Cliffs, New Jersey: Prentice-Hall, Inc., 1972,
p. 92.

[81]   Thayer, op. cit., p. 322.

[82]   Ibid., p. 323.

[83]   Ibid., p. 327.

[84]   Ibid., p. 331.

[85]   Ibid., p. 273.

[86]   Ibid., p. 274.

CHAPTER 3

JOURNALISM FOR THE NEW INTELLECTUALS:
HERBERT CROLY AND WALTER LIPPMANN

It is unlikely that Pragmatism would have flourished as it did without popular journalistic support.
Chief among these popularizers was Herbert Croly (1869-
1930), the first editor-in-chief of the New Republic
from its inception in 1914 until 1928.

Croly was a first generation American at a time
when it was normal to be what currently goes by the
expression "a hyphenated American": his father came
from Ireland and his mother from England. According to
Charles Forcey, "Born of a newspaper-and-magazine-
editing family, he was a member of the upper middle
class."[1] Herbert's father was "managing editor of
the New York World and ultimately editor-in-chief of
the New York Daily Graphic."[2] His mother was the
editor of Demorest's Monthly and Godey's Ladies Book --
and, on Forcey's word, an ardent feminist.[3]

Even though Croly married into a wealthy family[4]
he did not fit in comfortably with the station in life
to which he was entitled. Surely one explanation for
his marginal character is to be found in the reform
minded zeal of his parents. His father eventually lost
his job at the Daily Graphic because he was too much a
reformer for the owners[5] -- and so directed much of
his energy toward preparing the boy to carry on the
family mission. Both of the elder Crolys, in Forcey's
account, were ardent advocates of Auguste Comte's Positivism and his new religion of science and humanity:

> Positivism, as its name implies,
> would end the ancient negative struggle
> between faith and reason; instead,
> religion cleansed of superstition would
> be fused with science to bring reason to
> a new beauty and a new strength. So
> rational a religion appealed strongly to
> Herbert Croly's parents. ... Beginning
> in 1868 frequent meetings were held in
> the Croly home, where initiates went
> through Positivism's peculiar ritual.
> When Herbert was born the the next year,
> he became, with symbolic propriety,
> the first child in the United States
> to be christened in the new "Religion

of Humanity." The christening was appropriate because the religion of humanity was something Herbert Croly never entirely abandoned . . .[6]

Given Herbert's Positivist background, it is little wonder that the behaviorist and determinist elements of Pragmatism appealed to him. Yet, given the example of his parents, one can understand how, in Forcey's apt description, ". . . Croly's search for the great leader became a neurotic obsession . . ."[7] In 1886 Herbert was packed off to Harvard where he majored in philosophy -- on and off for eleven years until 1897 without obtaining a degree. (In 1910 Harvard gave him his baccalaureate in recognition of his best known work, The Promise of American Life, published the previous year.) Forcey credits George Santayana as being influential on Croly's politics, especially with regard to his vision of socialism as being run by a natural but nonhereditary elite.[9] "Yet," he continues, "neither Royce's idealism nor Santayana's naturalism was the real solvent of Croly's baptismal creed. Indeed, Croly took the pragmatism of William James as his creed."[10]

Croly's great achievement was to perceive the unity of James's system. Free will and determinism are brought together through science: after all, any sane person does in fact will to ameliorate life and to make progress in whatever is the most efficient manner of doing so. Moreover, the people who demonstrate the path which everyone so wills will go down in history.

Similarly to Thomas Aquinas, Croly anticipated Karl Mannheim on the relationship between freedom and knowledge. The goal was a perfect state wherein all consequences are taken into account, and what he intends by "democracy" is but the most efficient means to that end. According to Croly, "Democracy must stand or fall on the platform of possible human perfectibility."[11] "For better or worse, democracy cannot be disentangled from an inspiration toward human perfectibility . . ."[12]

What sentient beings desire is, at the least, a materially comfortable life. Thus, for Croly, ". . . the Promise of American life has consisted largely in the opportunity which it offered of economic independence and prosperity."[13] "The Promise . . . is a promise of comfort and prosperity for an ever increasing number of good Americans."[14] "The substance of

52

our national promise has consisted . . . of an improving economic condition, guaranteed by domestic political institutions, and resulting in moral and social amelioration."[15]

In order to promote comfort and prosperity in the most efficient manner Croly saw it necessary to destroy the myths which reinforced the old individualism. Specifically, this took the form of an attack on the theory of natural rights which inhered in individuals, the Constitution which generated them, and the laws which the capitalist system generated. Methodologically, it was an attack on epistemological Realism.

For Croly, "An individual has no meaning apart from the society in which his individuality has been formed."[16] "Association is the condition of individuality."[17] This principle became more evident when one looks at nations, and it underlay Croly's distaste for international socialism. Domestically the American system is an "experiment": ". . . our system is at bottom a thorough test of the ability of human nature to respond admirably to a fair chance . . ."[18] As such, it can be improved.

Croly dismissed as tried and proven false the notion that a minimum of government automatically will guarantee the American Promise.[19] "The experience of the last generation plainly shows that the American economic and social system cannot be allowed to take care of itself, and that the automatic harmony of the individual and the public interest, which is the essence of the Jeffersonian democratic creed has proven to be an illusion."[20] Like the Populists he believed that ". . . the prevailing abuses and sins, which have made reform necessary, are all of them associated with the prodigious concentration of wealth, and of power exercised by wealth, in the hands of a few men."[21] Even though he agreed further that all true reform has a moral element, Croly added that moral reform alone is insufficient.[22] "The plain fact is that the traditional American political system . . . is just as much responsible for the existing political and economic abuses as the Constitution was responsible for slavery."[23] Thus he called singularly moral reform "a species of higher conservatism."[24] The inequalities that developed simply followed the internal logic of the system: "No amount of moral energy, directed merely towards the enforcement of the laws, can possibly avail to accomplish any genuine or lasting

reform."[25] "Reform exclusively as a moral protest
and awakening is condemned to sterility."[26]

Croly cites Charles Beard to show that the U.S.
Constitution was a class document:

> It is estimated that the friends of
> the new Constitution did not amount to
> more than about one-sixth of the pos-
> sible voters. This small minority was
> able to impose its will upon the mass of
> its fellow-countrymen, because its
> members were energetic, intelligent,
> resourceful and united.[27]

Without naming the Populists, Croly describes them as
the sort of people who originally opposed the new
Constitution, but whose interests were primarily "local
and agrarian." The implication was that the Populists
of his own generation had and would continue to fail
for the same reasons. Croly cites Beard's evidence
that the ". . . Constitution was, if you please, 'put
over' by a small minority of able, vigorous and unscru-
pulous property owners."[28] Yet Croly was more subtle
than Beard, seeing that the Constitution had outlasted
the Federalists.

The ultimate failing was that the populace ". . .
failed to understand the proper relation between
popular political power and popular economic social
policy."[29] Like Justice Holmes, Croly took the
Nominalistic position that laws should be ". . .
subordinated to the government instead of the government to the Law."[30] Croly's criticism of legal
formalism runs as follows:

> The serious criticism which can be
> directed against the [American] tradi-
> tional system is that it did not provide
> a sound and candid method of making
> popular political responsibility real
> and effective. The people are to be
> made responsible, not by acquiescence to
> a benevolent monarchy of the Word, but
> by their own disposition and power to
> prefer the public good. If democracy is
> to endure, its own essential goodwill is
> the function which must be fortified,
> and its good-will can be fortified, not
> by the abdication but by the exercise of
> its own activity.[31]

54

The future of democratic progressivism depends upon the truth of its
claim that the emancipation of the
democracy from the continued allegiance
to any specific formulation of the Law,
and its increasing ability to act upon
its collective purposes, is far more
likely to contribute to the moral
stamina and the collective enlightenment of the people.[32]

Focusing on the Constitution, he says,

Its essential defect is that of
treating the spiritual property of the
nation as a fund to be protected instead
of a fund to be increased by the manner
in which it is employed. It is not a
money treasure which is held in trust by
the Constitution. It is the life of the
American nation. Its rules and its
organization can derive their force
only from their congruity with the
national will and from the vitality of
the national will itself.[33]

In this last quote one might detect a similarity with
Woodrow Wilson's doctoral thesis: i.e., that parliamentary government is superior to the U.S. system of
checks and balances, and that freedom to experiment
is more valuable than limiting the possible abuses of
power. Croly concludes:

Does not the most effective protection which any man and any nation can
enjoy consist in faith in the purpose of
their own life and freedom to employ
every method and every instrument
required for the realization of their
ends? In short, does not the exagger-
ated value which has been attached to
constitutional limitations . . . tend
to undermine the foundations of human
nature and human will upon which the
whole superstructure of a progressive
democratic society must admittedly be
built?[34]

There can be no doubt that Croly was a moral
reformer, yet the casual reader must be warned not to
see him as a Populist who trusted all his energy to the

55

Spirit of Righteousness. Croly did believe, like Montesquieu, that "The principle of democracy is excellence . . ."[35] (emphasis Croly) "The foundation on which our government has come to be builded is unquestionably the character of the American people . . ."[36] Yet Croly reveals himself when he makes an indirect reference to James: "Perhaps the most fruitful lesson taught by modern psychology is that men do not act well because they are enlightened, but that they are in large measure enlightened because they act well."[37] Possibly without knowing it, Croly is in agreement with Aristotle's dictum that men become virtuous by doing virtuous things. Thus what he seeks is not so much to reform men as to get them to act well.

The foregoing explains why Jamesian myths are only instruments, expedients which can be superseded when necessary. Only now can one understand the enigmatic passage of Croly's about "the redemption of the national Promise" which reads, "Like all sacred causes, it must be propagated by the Word, and by the right hand of the Word, which is the sword."[38] For Pragmatists the Word is always at bottom only Nominal -- although it usually comes in philosophical Realist or Hegelian garb. The instrumental myth might even be a "scientific" law. On the other hand whenever direct action works better, then perhaps the sword is called for. It should come as no surprise that the German Count, Otto von Bismarck was Croly's contemporary European hero.

Once Croly had dispelled the myth of the Law he was forced to create a new myth which would promote social action. This was the notion of the American People.

Here the reader becomes acutely aware of Croly's chagrin. After all, in his time Civil War veterans still were plentiful, imigration was at its high tide, and the frontier only recently had come to an end. The only truly native Americans still contested the Arizona Territories with the cavalry. A philosophical Nominalist should see only different groups of people united temporarily for specific purposes. On the political level he should see something akin to Madisonian pluralism.

Croly says that "A nation . . . is a people in so far as they are united by traditions and purposes . . ."[39] This definition suffers because the United

56

States had so many regional traditions. He flirts with Bismarck's Hegelian definition -- "an invisible multitude of spirits" -- but finds it difficult to swallow. He rejects "the majority" while keeping majority rule as a necessary condition of the rule of the people -- even though,

> . . . the actions or decisions of a majority need not have any binding moral and national authority. Majority rule is merely one means to an extremely difficult, remote, and complicated end; and it is a piece of machinery which is peculiarly liable to get out of order.[40]

These "arbitrary and dangerous tendencies" of the majority are mitigated by "the cherishing of a tradition, partly expressed in some body of fundamental law" and by the notion "that the true people are, as Bismarck declared, in some measure an invisible multitude of spirits -- the nation of yesterday and tomorrow, organized for its national and historical mission."[41] The preceding was from a poorly written sentence which required the running explanation that went with it. What Croly might have said outright, but didn't dare, is that "the true people" is a Pragmatic myth. For Croly "the true people" is what he wills to be the "historical mission," "the collective purpose," or "the democratic consumation" of national fraternity. He insists,

> The people are not Sovereign as individuals. They are not Sovereign in reason and morals even when united into a majority. They are sovereign only in so far as they succeed in reaching and expressing a collective purpose. ... They are Sovereign in so far as they are united in spirit and in purpose; and they are united in so far as they are loyal one to another, to their joint past, and to the Promise of their future.[42]

Summarizing what Croly has said up until now: the American Promise or telos is the materially bountiful life which, itself, is the foundation for all higher values. The first step is "The emancipation of popular political power and responsibility from the overruling authority of the Law and the courts . . .,"[43] i.e.,

57

from Realism. "A prudential democracy would be a democracy without power, without character, and without ascendancy."[44] There is a place in Croly's scheme for "individual and social reason," and the laws derived therefrom:

> They have their use for a while and under certain conditions. They constitute the tools which the social will must use in order to accomplish certain specific results or to reach a useful temporary understanding of certain social processes. In this sense democracy is necessarily opposed to intellectualism and allied to pragmatism.[45]

A descendant of Plato's Noble Lie is necessary because "Individuals and societies are not natural facts. They are wilful [sic.] processes -- moral creations."[46] "The people are made whole by virtue of the consecration of their collective effort to the realization of an ideal of social justice."[47] The ideal itself may vary from nation to nation. In the particular case of the United States, "The national experience of the American people has prepared them to live by faith."[48] That is to say, Americans are the least in need of "the right arm of the Word."

For Croly, "Democracy does not mean merely government by the people, or majority rule, or universal suffrage."[49] At one point he admits the Nominalistic truth that, "The whole people will always consist of individuals, constituting small classes, who demand special opportunities, and the mass of the population who demand for their improvement more generalized opportunities."[50] So, as if setting the stage for John Rawls, Croly uses the fraternity principle to square the other democratic principles of liberty and equality: "The two subordinate principles, that is, one representing the individual and the other the social interest, can by their subordination to the principle of human brotherhood, be made in the long run mutually helpful."[51] The faith in fraternity in fact becomes the democratic telos and its defining characteristic. Thus, "The foregoing definition of the democratic purpose is the only one which can entitle democracy to an essential superiority to other forms of political organization."[52] In the past the formal impartiality of the system has created discrimination and inequality. Now,

Under the proposed definition, on
the other hand, popular government is to
make itself expressly and permanently
responsible for the amelioration of the
individual and society; and the necessary consequence of this responsibility
is an adequate organization and a
reconstructive policy. . . . [I]f any
critic likes to fasten the stigma of
socialism upon the foregoing conception
of democracy, I am not concerned with
dodging the word. The proposed definition is socialistic . . .[53]

Croly goes on to argue against international
socialism on what is the best of Pragmatic principles,
evolution. "The great weakness of the most popular
form of socialism, however, consists in its mixture
of a revolutionary purpose with an international
scope."[54] It emphasized <u>universal</u> laws, independent
of time, place, and circumstance. Pragmatism on the
other hand, was an offspring of Darwinism. Evolution
comes about through struggle and competition: without
other nations to compete with at best there would be
only stagnation. To be nice to Croly he should be
called a social nationalist.

In socialist nationalism the myth of the People
and the myth of Democracy are mutually reinforcing.
Also, the goal of both is a state that can never be
either fully developed or even fully comprehended.

Progressive democracy is bound to
keep its immediate and specific program
disengaged from its ideal of social
righteousness. The immediate program is
only the temporary instrument, which
must be continually reformed and read-
justed as a result of the experience
gained by its experimental application.
. . . The goal is sacred. The program
is fluid.[55]

For instance, the U.S. Bill of Rights was mistaken for
a goal and solidified -- instead of being seen as but a
tool. Rather American politics should be ". . . an
expedition sustained by faith in the ultimate value of
a clearly discerned goal, but ignorant of any authentic
itinerary save that which can be worked out by means of
a resolute and alert persistence on the road."[56]
Shortly after quoting John Dewey, "the wisest of modern

educators,"[57] on the necessity of direct participation in social life, Croly notes that the people must rise to their challenge and see it through:

> Thus we must fall back once again upon the creative creative power of the will, which insists, even though its brother, the reason, cannot ascertain. ... What the situation calls for is faith. Faith is the primary virtue demanded by the social education of a democracy -- the virtue which will prove to be salutary -- in case human nature is capable of salvation. Only by faith can be established the invincible interdependence between individual and social fulfillment, upon the increasing realization of which the future of democracy depends.[58]

> Thus the progressive democratic faith, like the faith of St. Paul, finds its consumation in a love which is partly expressed in sympathetic feeling, but which is at bottom a spiritual expression of the mystical unity of human nature.[59]

Croly's socialism is a tool based on its assumed efficiency. He justified it as follows:

> When a people are being nationalized, their political, economic, and social organization or policy is being coordinated with their actual needs and their moral and political ideals. Governmental centralization is to be regarded as one of the many means which may or may not be taken in order to effect this purpose. Like every other special aspect of the national organization, it must be justified by its fruits.[60]

Thus government control is but "a matter of expediency."[61] "All rights under the law are functions in a democratic political organism and must be justified by their actual or presumable functional adequacy."[62] Again, rights are interpreted Nominally.

Accepting James's behaviorism leads Croly to look at the national experience as a school, and to see the necessity of a schoolmaster. "The national school is, of course, the national life."[63] "The nation, like the individual, must go to school; and the national school is not a lecture hall or a library. Its schooling consists chiefly in experimental collective action aimed at the realization of the national purpose."[64] Unfortunately, men everywhere are "unregenerate." So,

> The policeman and the soldier will continue for an indefinite period to be guardians of the national schools, and the nations have no reason to be ashamed of this fact. ... Everyone in the schoolhouse . . . must feel one to another an indestructible loyalty. ... The existence of an invisible loyalty is the condition of the perpetuity of the school.[65]

In Croly's eyes even the most successful businessmen in the capitalist system are not free -- they are just better at the same general act of moneymaking. Moneymaking is "interested" behavior, and for Croly "The truth is that individuality cannot be dissociated from the pursuit of a disinterested object."[66] "In so far as the economic motive prevails, individuality cannot develop; it is stifled."[67] Of course he never takes up the question of how unfree people would be if they all were compelled to strive for an alternate, but equally uniform, national ideal.

Yet Croly's device to "create harmony between private and public interests"[68] is just that, to convince all men to work energetically for "disinterested" motives, the most effective one being "the national ideal." Because they are creatures of social conditioning, ". . . men will always continue chiefly to pursue . . . those ends recognized by the official national ideal as worthy of perpetuation and encouragement."[69] "What a democratic nation must do is not to accept human nature as it is, but to move in the direction of its improvement."[70] Notice how men must be improved; this is the law of evolution. Again this leads to socialism:

> The ultimate end is the complete emancipation of the individual, and that result depends upon his complete disinterestedness. He must become

61

interested exclusively in the excellence of his work; and he can never become disinterested in his work so long as heavy responsibilities and high achievements are supposed to be rewarded by increased pay. ... The only way in which work can be made entirely disinterested is to adjust compensation to the needs of a normal and wholesome life.[71]

Croly claims that the Populist reformers could not make the transition to Progressivism because the Populists were but reformers of the system, whereas the Progressives understood the necessity of changing the system itself.[72]

The Progressives found themselves obliged to carry their inquisition to its logical conclusion -- to challenge the old system, root and branch, and to derive their own medium and power of united action from a new conception of the purpose and methods of democracy.[73]

"The great object of progressivism must always be to create a vital relationship between progressivism and popular political education."[74] Knowledge necessitates the actions of those who have it, and that is a higher form of freedom.

Croly posits a leadership principle, claiming that given the leader's "Disinterestedness" he "can hardly go astray."[75] Perhaps the leadership supposition is necessary if one sees that political enlightenment does not reach everyone equally. After all,

There is only one way in which popular standards and preferences can be improved. The men whose standards are higher must learn to express their better message in a popularly interesting manner. The people will never be converted . . . by argumentation, reproaches, lectures, associations, or persuasion. They will rally to the good thing, only because the good thing has been made to look good to them . . .[76]

Croly, who was an architect by training, compares the great statesman to "the exceptional architect":

> He will be molding and informing the architectual taste and preference of his admirers. ... In so far as he succeeded in popularizing a better quality of architectural work, he would be by way of strengthening the hands of all of his associates who were standing for similar ideals and methods.[77]

Moreover, leadership for the exceptional man is an obligation:

> The peculiarly competent individual is obliged to accept the responsibilities of leadership with its privileges and its fruits. There can be no escape from the circle by which he finds himself surrounded. He cannot obtain the opportunities, the authority, and the independence which he needs for his own individual fulfillment, unless he builds up a following; and he cannot build up a secure personal following without making his peculiar performances appeal to some general human interest.[78]

> The common citizen can become something of a saint and something of a hero, not by growing to heroic proportions on his own, but by the sincere and enthusiastic imitation of heroes and saints, and whether or not he will come to such imitation will depend upon the ability of his exceptional fellow-countrymen to offer him acceptable examples of heroism and saintliness.[79]

Looking first to Europe for democratic exemplars Croly says, "The most luminous and the most soaring expression which the progressive democratic faith has ever received was uttered by the Italian Mazzini; but the Italians of his generation were not prepared to live by it."[80] Prophets before their time are at best only tragic.

On the other hand, Germany had become an overwhelming success. Everything worked. Bismarck had

63

made obvious to all the advantages of the paternal
state.[81]

> Germany alone among the modern
> European nations is . . . carrying the
> cost of modern military preparations
> easily, and looks forward confidently to
> greater success in the future. She is
> at the present time a very striking
> example of what can be accomplished for
> the popular welfare by a fearless
> acceptance on the part of the official
> leaders of economic as well as political
> responsibility, and by the efficient and
> intelligent use of all available means
> to that end.[82]

According to Croly, "The test of German domestic
statesmanship hereafter will consist in its ability to
win the support of the industrial democracy, created
by the advance of the country, without impairing the
traditional and existing practice of expert and
responsible leadership."[83] The existence of this
expert and responsible leadership proves that "The
democrats who disparage efficient national organization
are at bottom merely seeking to exorcise the power of
physical force in human affairs by the use of pious
incantations and heavenly words. That will never
do."[84] Words should never have such power. For
Croly it was obvious that "The German national
organization means increased security, happiness,
and opportunity of development for the whole German
people."[85] The German example proved that "A
nationalized democracy is not based on abstract
individual rights . . ."[86]

Considering carefully Bismarck's wars, Croly found
that ". . . the partial abuse of victory does not
diminish the legitimacy of German aggression. A war
waged for an excellent purpose contributes more to
human amelioration than a merely artificial peace, --
such as that established by the Holy Alliance."[87]
(Notice his example as a refutation of Realism).
Bearing the preceding in mind Croly predicts, "The
federation of Europe, like the unification of Germany,
will never be brought about by congress and amicable
resolutions. It can be effected only by the same old
means of blood and iron."[88]

Croly justified colonialism on the same basis
as did John Stuart Mill; it benefits the colonies.

Moreover, he added that it makes war less likely among the advanced countries because of their extended economic vulnerabilities and drained off energies. Colonialism is a form of "tutelage": ". . . at least for a while the Asiatic population may well be benefited by more orderly and progressive government. Submission to such a government is a necessary condition of subsequent political development."[89] Second, "The truth is that colonial expansion by modern national states is to be regarded, not as a cause of war, but as a safety-valve against war."[90]

Looking to his America, Croly dismissed the Populists as not understanding what they were about. William Jennings Bryan could never accomplish lasting reform because he distrusted the means necessary to the end: a strong national government, the guidance of various experts, and trust in "the exceptional man"[91] as political leader. Instead, Croly's designated "hero"[92] of the reform movement was Theodore Roosevelt because, "He realizes that any efficiency of organization and delegation of power which is necessary to the promotion of the American national interest must be helpful to democracy."[93] Moreover, unlike Bryan, Roosevelt's ". . . program of reform attaches more importance to a revision of the rules of the game than to the treatment of the winners under the old rules as one would treat a dishonest gambler."[94] Finally, reaching epic proportions in his admiration, Croly declares that Roosevelt ". . . may be figured as a Thor wielding with power and effect a sledge-hammer in the cause of national rightousness . . ."[95]

When Croly was forced to choose between two avowedly Progressive reformers he opted for the most radical. According to Croly, Wilson's "New Freedom" was but an extension of the old negative freedoms.[96] Speaking first of Roosevelt's Progressivism, Croly says,

> Its advocates are committed to a drastic reorganization of the American political and economic system, the substitution of a frank social policy for the individualism of the past, and to this realization, if necessary, by the use of efficient governmental instruments. The progressivism of President Wilson, on the other hand, is ambiguous in precisely this essential respect. ... His version of

progressivism, notwithstanding its immediately forward impulse, is scrupulously careful not to be too progressive, and, like the superseded reform movements, poses as a higher conservatism.[97]

If, as Croly claims, ". . . the essential condition of individual freedom and development . . ." is "the highest possible standard of living"[98] measured in material terms, then what is the proper role of the intellectual? In sum, the philosophers take their place in the social organization as the propagators of the new democratic faith: "In this world faith cannot dispense with power and organization. ... Democracy as a living movement in the direction of human brotherhood has required, like other faiths, an efficient organization . . ."[99] of which the philosopher is an integral member.

> In proportion as political organization gained in prosperity, efficiency, and dignity, special religious associations lost their independence and power. Even the most powerful religious association in the world, the Catholic Church, has been fighting a losing battle with political authority . . . ... Just as formerly the irresponsible and meaningless use of political power created the need of special religious associations, independent of the state, so now the responsible, the purposeful, and the efficient use of physical force, characteristic of modern nations, has in its turn made such independence less necessary . . . A basis of association narrower than the whole complex of human powers and interests will not serve. National organization provides such a basis.[100]

In other words, the nation-state is to become the new Church, the new bearer of the efficacious myth. "The old system must be confronted and superseded by a new system -- the result of an alert social intelligence as well as an aroused individual conscience."[101] The job of the intellectuals is to spread this arousal of consciousness.

Anticipating Benito Mussolini, Croly explicitly
links and applauds the ascendency of human nature,
faith and will over law, reason and knowledge.[102]
Of "the living human will," he explains,

> Its vitality depends, that is, not
> upon knowledge or reason, but the only
> possible substitute for knowledge --
> which is faith. The assurance which
> American progressivism is generally
> acquiring, and of whose necessity it is
> finally becoming conscious, is merely an
> expression of faith -- faith in the
> peculiar value and reality of its own
> enterprise, faith in the power of faith.
> A democracy becomes courageous, progres-
> sive and ascendant just in so far as it
> dares to have faith, and just in so far
> as it can be faithful without ceasing to
> be inquisitive. Faith in things unseen
> and unknown is as indispensabl? to a
> progressive democracy as it is to an
> individual Christian.[103]

Then, to further his point, he quotes Saint Paul to
prove that only faith can transcend the Law which "had
merely an instrumental and educational value."[104]
The implication is that as Christianity was to the old
order, so socialistic nationalism will be to the
present order. Pragmatism, unlike doctrinaire Marxism,
sees the rightly directed will as an instrument of
Progress. In Croly's words,

> A loyal progressive democracy is
> emancipated not merely from the author-
> ity of a legal formulation of social
> rightousness, but from bondage to a
> mechanical conception of social causa-
> tion. The beauty of faith consists in
> the freedom with which it endows the
> faithful. ... The progressive demo-
> cratic faith means a stubborn insistence
> upon the conformity of social facts to a
> social ideal. Those who are to become
> the chosen people must choose themselves
> for the distinction and the work. The
> national will is to make the difference
> between the social present and the
> better social future.[105]

There need be no fundamental
objection taken to the national faith in
the power of good intentions and redistribution of wealth. That faith is the
immediate and necessary issue of the
logic of our national moral situation.
It should be, as it is, innocent and
absolute; and if it does not remain
innocent and absolute, the Promise
of American Life can scarcely be
fulfilled.[106]

Although the logic of the situation or the state of
national development is a necessary prerequisite, in
time of peace the system does not change by itself. It
requires conscious stimulation and reinforcement to
give the teetering old regime the final shove. Faith
and organization reinforce each other. "Only by faith
in an efficient national organization and aggressive
devotion to the national welfare, can the American
democratic ideal be made good."[107]

A Leo Straussian political theorist might argue
that Croly was setting himself up as the Christ or
St. Paul of the new age. Just as St. Paul used
Christianity to emancipate the ancients from the law,
the Straussian would say, so Croly used Jamesian
Pragmatism to spread "progressive democracy." Actually
such speculation is unnecessary. When speaking of the
"democratic fulfillment" Croly told his readers,

If such a moment ever arrives, it
will be partly the creation of some
democratic evangelist -- some imitator
of Jesus will reveal to men the path
whereby they may enter into spiritual
possession of their own individual and
social achievements, and immeasurably
increase them by virtue of personal
regeneration.[108]

The path revealed by Croly was one of ethical Idealism
and ontological Materialism, but entered on by the gate
of epistemological Nominalism.

If the leading and best known editor of the New
Republic was Herbert Croly, the best editor under him
on the original staff was Walter Lippmann (1889-1974).
Lippmann entered Harvard in 1906 and was a member of
the Harvard Socialist Club. His graduating class of
1910 listed Alan Seeger, John Reed, T. S. Eliot, Robert

68

Edmund Jones, and Heywood Broun; the list of his contemporaries at Harvard who did not graduate the same
year is even more startling.

Lippmann also majored in philosophy, taking
courses from conservatives such as Irving Babbitt and
George Santayana. Yet, according to Hari Dam, it was
William James that Lippmann "adored;" he ". . . often
saw him at his home and freely discussed with him
subjects ranging from pragmatism to politics."[109] A
more vivid description of Lippmann's relationship with
James is given by Lippmann's biographer, Ronald Steel:

> Every Thursday morning at eleven
> Lippmann crossed the yard to take tea
> with James and his wife on Irving
> Street. Conversation ranged over
> politics, religion, ethics, whatever
> struck James's fancy. Lippmann re-
> sponded eagerly to the philosopher's
> passion for social reform, commitment
> to experimentation, abhorrence of dogma,
> and deep sense of personal morals. His
> talk with James, he wrote his parents
> after their first meeting, was "the
> greatest thing that has happened to me
> in my college life."[110]

During the course of the First World War Lippmann
got to know Franklin Roosevelt and a number of other
people who would be important contacts for him later
on. In July, 1918 Lippmann was given a special commission as a captain in the Army and sent to Europe
with instructions ". . . to prepare propaganda mater-
ials for dissemination among the German troops."[111]
As a professional propagandist he and his team were
quite successful. The following year, in 1919, he
returned to the editorial board of the New Republic,
but in 1922 he switched to The New York World for the
opportunity to command a larger audience.

Lippmann's first book was A Preface to Politics
(1913); in it his philosophical heroes appear to be
William James, Friedrich Nietzsche, and Georges Sorel.
He praised James's ideal of "The moral equivalent of
war," and declared that "We can use it, I believe, as a
guide post to statesmanship."[112] Instead of fighting
other people, the enemy becomes Nature. For this
purpose he quotes James about the need for ". . .
skilful propagandism, and of opinion-making men
seizing historic opportunities."[113] Then he invoked

Nietzsche to support James in a celebration of the will.[114]

Lippmann believed that thought is not something which understands reality, but something which helps to manipulate it. So also there are no political systems which conform to an unchanging human nature: thus "It is our desperate adherence to an old method that has produced the confusion of political life."[115] Speaking of the relationship between man and nature Lippmann says of man, ". . . the world is something he can make."[116] It is not discovered by the intellect; rather, it is created by the will.

> The type of statesman we must oppose to the routineer is one who regards all social organization as an instrument. Systems, institutions and mechanical contrivances have for him no virtue of their own: they are valuable only when they serve the purposes of men. He uses them, of course, but with a constant sense that men have made them, that new ones can be devised, that only an effort of the will can keep machinery in place. He has no faith whatever in automatic governments. While routineers see machinery and precedents revolving with mankind as puppets, he puts the deliberate, conscious, willing individual at the center of his philosophy.[117]

For Lippmann "even rationality itself is a willful exercise."[118] One sees this nowhere so clearly as in the great systematizers; for instance, "Marx saw what he wanted to do long before he wrote three volumes to justify it."[119] The point is that Marx's system allowed him and others to fulfill the more primary desire to do something. "Belief does not live by logic, but by the need it fills . . . "[120] "Almost all men do require something to focus their interest in order to sustain it. A great idea like Socialism does that for millions."[121] Unfortunately socialism can become misdirected in practice. So, in 1914, Lippmann recommended that "science" be added to socialism as a corrective "discipline."[122] A year earlier he had explained how,

> The prevalent lie is to explain how the new convert, standing upon a

70

mountain of facts, began to trace out the highways that led from hell to heaven. Everybody knows that no such process was actually lived through, and almost without exception the real story can be discerned. A man was dissatisfied, he wanted a new condition in life, he embraced a theory that would justify his hopes and his discontent. For once you touch the biographies of human beings, the notion that political beliefs are logically determined collapses like a pricked balloon. In the language of the philosophers, socialism as a living force is a product of the will -- a will to beauty, order, neighborliness, not infrequently a will to health. Men desire first, then they reason; fascinated by the future, they invent "scientific socialism" to get there.[123]

Then he called upon David Hume to make the point that "reason is itself an irrational impulse."[124] Notice that Lippmann did not say a-rational: apparently he believed that Marx might have gotten more done if he had spent less time thinking. Then again Marx was a rationalist, and ". . . the rationalists are fascinated by a certain kind of thinking -- logical and orderly thinking -- and it is their will to impose that method on other men."[125]

After explaining the socialist myth in detail Lippmann finds that its own determinism has detracted from its ability to promote social action. So, "A new philosophical basis is becoming increasingly necessary to socialism -- one that may not be 'truer' than the old materialism but that shall be more useful."[126] Remember that, for Lippmann, "philosophy" is but a stately word for myth. He clarifies:

I picture this philosophy as one of deliberate choices. The underlying tone of it is that society is made by men for man's uses, that reforms are inventions to be applied when by experiment they show their civilizing value. ... This sense of mastery in a winning battle against the conditions of our life is, I believe, the social myth that will inspire our reconstructions.[127]

71

The result would be a socialism built on willfulness rather than on strict materialism. On the next page the chapter closes with a quote from Nietzsche about the freedom to determine all afresh.[128]

In 1919 Lippmann defined liberty in a characteristically Pragmatic manner;

> There are, so far as I can discover, no absolutes of liberty; I can recall no definition of liberty, which, under the acid test, does not become contingent upon some other social ideal. The goal is never liberty, but liberty for something or other. For liberty is a condition under which activity takes place . . .[129]

For Lippmann any _formal_ definition of liberty

> . . . is an attempt to define liberty of opinion in terms of opinion. It is a circular and sterile logic. A useful definition of liberty is obtainable only by seeking the principle of liberty in the main business of human life, that is to say, in the processes by which men educate their response and learn to control their environment. In this view liberty is the name we give to the measures by which we protect and increase the veracity of the information upon which we act.[130]

The above was written just after ending his stint as a propagandist.

Earlier he was not as concerned with the veracity of the media: "The only rule to follow, it seems to me, is that of James: 'Use concepts when they help, and drop them when they hinder understanding.'"[131] Lippmann's idea of pluralism was a sort of freedom _from_ hindering ideas.

> There are people who flatly refuse to regard Pluralism as a philosophy of life. William James recognized that and spent a large amount of time trying to show that a disorderly world full of variety and spontaneous creation might

still give religious satisfaction. I
doubt whether he succeeded.[132]

Lippmann conceded that "We cannot be absolute pragmatists. But we judge by results as much as we can, as
much as our human limitations allow."[133]

> The men like Nietzsche and James
> who show the wilful [sic.] origin of
> creeds are in reality the best watchers
> of the citadel of truth. For there is
> nothing disastrous in the temporary
> nature of our ideas. They are always
> that. But there may very easily be a
> train of evil in the self-deception
> which regards them as final.[134]

> No creed possesses any final
> sanction. Human beings have desires
> that are far more important than the
> tools and toys and churches they make
> to satisfy them. It is more penetra-
> ting, in my opinion, to ask of a creed
> whether it served than whether it was
> "true."[135]

Thus Lippmann held a grudging admiration for
Niccolo Machiavelli:

> I have always thought that Machi-
> avelli deserves his bad name from a too
> transparent honesty. Less direct minds
> would have found high-sounding ethical
> sanctions in which to conceal the real
> intent. That was the nauseating method
> of nineteenth century economists when
> they tried to identify the brutal prac-
> tices of capitalism with the beneficence
> of nature and the Will of God.[136]

In fact Machiavelli had virtually the same ambition as
modern politicians and financiers:

> Machiavelli's morals are not one
> bit worse than the practices of the men
> who rule the world today. ... His head
> is clearer than the average. He let the
> cat out of the bag and showed in the
> boldest terms how theory became an
> instrument of practice.[137]

73

We find reasons for what we do.
The big men from Machiavelli through
Rousseau to Karl Marx brought history,
logic, science and philosophy to prop
up and strengthen their deepest
desires. ... This amounts to saying
that man when he is most creative is
not a rational, but a wilful [sic.]
animal.[138]

Finally, Lippmann appeals to his favorite contemporary political philosopher in order to set the stage
for his political leader.

What shall we call an idea, objectively untrue, but practically of the
highest importance? The thinker who has
faced this difficulty most radically is
Georges Sorel in the "Reflexions sur la
Violence." His doctrine of the "social
myth" has seemed to many commentators
one of those silly paradoxes that only a
revolutionary syndicalist and Frenchman
could have put forward. ... But he was
not ready to abandon his favorite ideas
because it had been shown to be unrea-
sonable and impossible. Just the
opposite effect showed itself and he
seized the opportunity of turning an
intellectual defeat into a spiritual
triumph.[139]

After praising Sorel for three more pages Lippmann
writes, "We in America might add an example from our
own political life. For it is Theodore Roosevelt who
is actually attempting to make himself and his admirers
the heroes of a new social myth."[140] Lippmann
declares that myths ". . . embody the motor currents in
social life. Myths are judged, as M. Sorel says, by
their ability to express aspiration."[141] Roosevelt
expressed the national aspiration like no one else.
Another three pages later Lippmann cites James's "The
Will to Believe" and Nietzsche's "Beyond Good and Evil"
to support Sorel in this connection.[142]

William Jennings Bryan at least had been able to
articulate mass grievances in a manner that moved the
masses in generally the right direction -- even if
accidentally. Yet, like Croly, Lippmann switches over
to the scientific mode when discussing Bryan, describing him as ". . . a voice crying out in the wilderness,

but a voice that did not understand its own message. ... What we know as the scientific habit of mind is entirely lacking in his intellectual equipment."[143] Yet, ironically, Bryan implicitly is criticized for being too cerebral because Lippmann believed that,

> The attempts of the theorists to explain man's successes as rational acts and his failures as lapses of reason have always ended in dismal and misty unreality. <u>No genuine politican ever treats his constituents as reasoning animals</u>. This is as true of the high politics of Isiah as it is of the ward boss. Only the pathetic amateur deludes himself into thinking that, if he presents the major and minor premise, the voter will automatically draw the conclusion on election day. The successful politician -- good or bad -- deals with dynamics -- with the will, the hopes, the needs and the visions of men.[144] (emphasis added)

He follows with examples from conservatives to radicals, all ultimately appeals to the will. Then, returning to his favorite exemplar: "If you study the success of Roosevelt the point is re-enforced [sic.]. He is a man of will in whom millions of people have felt the embodiment of their own will."[145] Perhaps Lippmann saw Bryan's policies as merely too negative, and Roosevelt's vision as more inspiring; at the least his emphasis on science is suspect in its sincerity. A description given of his "political creator" is rather unintellectual: "He serves the ideals of human feelings, not the tendencies of mechanical things."[146] "For visions alone organize popular passions."[147] ". . . I believe we need offer no apologies for making Mr. Roosevelt stand as the working model for a possible American statesman at the beginning of the Twentieth Century."[148] "Government under him was a throbbing human purpose."[149]

Yet the above was written after Roosevelt's defeat by Wilson. So Lippmann reverted again to the "scientific" criterion to make Wilson look acceptable: "Woodrow Wilson has a talent which is Bryan's chief defect -- the scientific habit . . . ,"[150] even though he ". . . does not incarnate: he has never been a part of the protest he speaks."[151] "Wilson, less complete than Roosevelt, is worthy of our deepest interest because his judgment is subtle where Roosevelt's is crude. He is a foretaste of a more advanced statesmanship."[152] It was Lippmann who persuaded Croly to support Wilson in 1916. Becoming friends with Colonel House and Wilson were two of the best practical moves that the young Lippmann made.

Commentators, such as Hari N. Dam, find Lippmann difficult to categorize, observing that he lived an "intellectual odyssey" similar to his fellow Pragmatist Sidney Hook. Yet, if one allows that Lippmann was even more of a Nominalist than Croly the problem is resolved. Remember that Croly really did believe in systematic determinism in politics, albeit the "exceptional man" determined the system. Lippmann, on the contrary, emphasized that,

> Your doctrine, in short, depends on your purpose: a theory by itself is neither moral nor immoral, its value is conditioned by the purpose it serves. In any accurate sense theory is to be judged only as an effective or ineffective instrument of desire: the discussion of doctrines is technical and not moral. A theory has no intrinsic value: that is why the devil can talk theology.[153]

Thus, without some constraints, there could be a condition of too much freedom; men are capable of evil as well a good. Liberal democracy tends to be a destroyer of myths and authority.

> Yet a stern commander is just what this age lacks. Liberalism suffuses our lives and the outstanding fact is the decay of authority. But this doesn't mean for one minute that we are able to command ourselves. In fact, if a man dare attempt to sum up the spiritual condition of his time, he might say of ours that it has lost authority and retained the need of it. We are freer than we are strong. We have more responsibility than we have capacity.[154]

The preceding quote was penned in 1914. In 1925 Lippmann broke with his old friends at the New Republic. In The Phantom Public (1925) he reputiated the

76

democratic myth of a People which governs in favor
of smaller groups which are interested intensely in
specific affairs. The myth of the People was equally
dangerous as it might be constructive. Later he explained, "In fact demagoguery can be described as the
slight of hand by which a faction of The People as
voters are invested with the authority of The People.
That is why so many crimes are committed in the
people's name."[155] (emphasis Lippmann) At a time
when Herbert Croly was an admirer of Italian fascism
Lippmann was one of the few journalists to speak out
against Mussolini.

Also in 1925 the Scopes Trial in Dayton, Tennessee
bore out Lippmann's apprehension: the prosecutor
Bryan, had the weight of popular opinion on his side,
at least in the vicinity of the trial. Bryan's prose-
cution ". . . did a service to democratic thinking.
For it reduced to absurdity a dogma which had been held
carelessly but almost universally, . . ."[156] the
absolute rule of the majority. Now Lippmann saw
clearly that "The rule of the majority is the rule of
force."[157] Ronald Steel documents Lippmann's turn to
natural law in 1925 when he warned American Catholics
". . . that they should follow Aquinas in holding
natural law above the demands of the state."[158] In
1937, in The Good Society, Lippmann said, "The gradual
encroachment of true law upon willfulness and caprice
is the progress of liberty in human affairs."[159]

In 1955 Lippmann wrote:

> I believe there is a public phi-
> losophy. Indeed there is such a thing
> as the public philosophy of civility.
> ... The public philosophy is known as
> natural law. ... This philosophy is
> the premise of the institutions of the
> Western society, and they are, I be-
> lieve, unworkable in countries that do
> not adhere to it. Except on the pre-
> mises of this philosophy, it is impos-
> sible to reach intelligible and workable
> conceptions of popular election, major-
> ity rule, representative assemblies,
> free speech, loyalty, property, corpor-
> ations and voluntary associations. The
> Founders of these institutions . . .
> were all of them adherents of some one
> of the various schools of natural
> law.[160] (emphasis Lippmann)

Interestingly, in the same book he declared, "What is necessary to continuous action is that it shall be believed to be right. Without that belief, most men will not have the energy and will to persevere in the action."[161] (emphasis Lippmann) Apparently he never gave up being a Pragmatist, only, like Sidney Hook, Lippmann's Pragmatism was stronger than his commitment to liberalism. If the public philosophy of natural law is, at bottom, an efficacious myth, then it appears to have a higher cash value than the other competing myths.

What is significant from the standpoint of the present work is that during the Progressive period two of the most influential journalists can be seen sharing the assumptions of Pragmatism as it applies to society. Both Lippmann and Croly found their intellectual coherence in the philosophy of William James. As editors they were in a position to pick and choose whatever articles that furthered their vision -- regardless of whatever the particular authors took to be reality. In this sense, like all the Progressives, they were eminently political. Again, their hero incarnate was Theodore Roosevelt.

FOOTNOTES FOR CHAPTER 3

[1] Forcey, Charles. The Crossroads of Liberalism: Croly, Weyl, Lippmann and the Progressive Era, 1900-1925. New York: Oxford University Press, 1961, p. 11.

[2] Ibid., p. 12.

[3] Ibid., p. 13.

[4] Ibid., p. 12.

[5] Ibid., p. 15.

[6] Ibid., p. 15.

[7] Ibid., p. 41.

[8] Ibid., pp. 16, 18.

[9] Ibid., pp. 18-19.

[10]   Ibid., p. 20.

[11]   Croly, Herbert.   The Promise of American
Life. New York: E. P. Dutton and Company, Inc., 1963
(original, 1909), p. 400.

[12]   Ibid., p. 454.

[13]   Ibid., p. 9.

[14]   Ibid., p. 10.

[15]   Ibid., p. 22.

[16]   Ibid., p. 263.

[17]   Ibid., p. 264.

[18]   Ibid., p. 13.

[19]   Ibid., p. 17ff.

[20]   Ibid., p. 152.

[21]   Ibid., p. 23.

[22]   Ibid., p. 146ff.

[23]   Ibid., p. 147.

[24]   Ibid., p. 147.

[25]   Ibid., p. 149.

[26]   Ibid., p. 150.

[27]   Croly,   Herbert.   Progressive   Democracy.
New York: The MacMillan Company, 1914, pp. 48-49.

[28]   Ibid., p. 49.

[29]   Ibid., p. 51.

[30]   Ibid., p. 126.

[31]   Ibid., p. 152.

[32]   Ibid., p. 154.

[33]   Ibid., p. 162.

[34] Ibid., p. 167.

[35] Croly, The Promise of American Life, op. cit., p. 454.

[36] Croly, Progressive Democracy, op. cit., p. 153.

[37] Ibid., p. 203.

[38] Croly, The Promise of American Life, op. cit., p. 21.

[39] Ibid., p. 266.

[40] Ibid., p. 280.

[41] Ibid., p. 280.

[42] Ibid., p. 280.

[43] Croly, Progressive Democracy, op. cit., p. 220.

[44] Ibid., p. 171.

[45] Ibid., pp. 177-178.

[46] Ibid., p. 194.

[47] Ibid., p. 212.

[48] Ibid., p. 202.

[49] Croly, The Promise of American Life, op. cit., p. 207.

[50] Ibid., p. 207.

[51] Ibid., p. 208.

[52] Ibid., p. 208.

[53] Ibid., p. 209.

[54] Ibid., p. 210.

[55] Croly, Progressive Democracy, op. cit., p. 217.

[56] Ibid., p. 219.

[57] Ibid., p. 423.

[58] Ibid., pp. 424-425.

[59] Ibid., p. 427.

[60] Croly, The Promise of American Life, op. cit., p. 273.

[61] Ibid., p. 273.

[62] Ibid., p. 278.

[63] Ibid., p. 286.

[64] Ibid., p. 407.

[65] Ibid., p. 284.

[66] Ibid., p. 411.

[67] Ibid., p. 412.

[68] Ibid., p. 418.

[69] Ibid., p. 418.

[70] Ibid., p. 413.

[71] Ibid., p. 417.

[72] Croly, Progressive Democracy, op. cit., p. 13.

[73] Ibid., p. 14.

[74] Ibid., p. 145.

[75] Croly, The Promise of American Life, op. cit., p. 441.

[76] Ibid., pp. 443-444.

[77] Ibid., pp. 444-445.

[78] Ibid., p. 447.

[79] Ibid., p. 454.

[80] Croly, Progressive Democracy, op. cit., p. 202.

[81] Croly, The Promise of American Life, op. cit., p. 250.

[82] Ibid., pp. 250-251.

[83] Ibid., p. 252.

[84] Ibid., p. 255.

[85] Ibid., p. 256.

[86] Ibid., p. 259.

[87] Ibid., p. 256.

[88] Ibid., p. 264.

[89] Ibid., p. 259.

[90] Ibid., p. 261.

[91] Ibid., p. 160.

[92] Ibid., p. 142.

[93] Ibid., p. 169.

[94] Ibid., p. 173.

[95] Ibid., p. 174.

[96] Croly, Progressive Democracy, op. cit., pp. 16-17.

[97] Ibid., p. 15.

[98] Croly, The Promise of American Life, op. cit., p. 206.

[99] Ibid., p. 282.

[100] Ibid., p. 283.

[101] Croly, Progressive Democracy, op. cit., pp. 10-11.

[102] Ibid., pp. 167-168.

[103] Ibid., p. 168.

[104] Ibid., p. 169.

[105] Ibid., p. 174.

[106] Croly, The Promise of American Life, op. cit., p. 402.

[107] Ibid., p. 270.

[108] Ibid., pp. 453-454.

[109] Dam, Hari N. The Intellectual Odyssey of Walter Lippmann: A Study of His Protean Thought, 1910-1960. New York: Gordon Press, 1973, p. 3.

[110] Steel, Ronald. Walter Lippmann and the American Century. New York: Vintage Books, 1981, p. 17.

[111] Dam, op. cit., p. 6.

[112] Lippmann, Walter. A Preface to Politics. New York: Mitchell Kennerley, 1913, p. 48.

[113] Ibid., p. 49.

[114] Ibid., p. 52.

[115] Ibid., p. 23.

[116] Ibid., p. 12.

[117] Ibid., pp. 8-9.

[118] Ibid., p. 216.

[119] Ibid., p. 214.

[120] Lippmann, Walter. Drift and Mastery: An Attempt to Diagnose the Current Unrest. New York: Mitchell Kennerley, 1914, p. 201.

[121] Ibid., p. 281.

[122] Ibid., p. 282.

[123] Lippmann, A Preface to Politics, op. cit., pp. 214-215.

[124] Ibid., p. 215.

[125] Ibid., p. 216.

[126]   Ibid., pp. 242-243.

[127]   Ibid., pp. 243-244.

[128]   Ibid., p. 245.

[129] Lippmann, Walter. Liberty and the News.
New York: Harcourt and Brace, 1920 (original, 1919),
pp. 21-22.

[130]   Ibid., p. 68.

[131] Lippmann, Drift and Mastery: An Attempt to
Diagnose the Current Unrest, op. cit., p. 295.

[132]   Ibid., pp. 202-203.

[133]   Ibid., p. 262.

[134] Lippmann, A Preface to Politics, op. cit.,
p. 236.

[135]   Ibid., p. 225.

[136]   Ibid., p. 211.

[137]   Ibid., p. 212.

[138]   Ibid., p. 213.

[139]   Ibid., pp. 226-227.

[140]   Ibid., p. 230.

[141]   Ibid., p. 230.

[142]   Ibid., p. 233.

[143]   Ibid., pp. 100, 101.

[144]   Ibid., pp. 216-217.

[145]   Ibid., p. 220.

[146]   Ibid., p. 9.

[147]   Ibid., p. 221.

[148]   Ibid., p. 100.

[149]   Ibid., p. 99.

[150]   Ibid., p. 101.

[151]   Ibid., p. 102.

[152]   Ibid., p. 103.

[153]   Ibid., pp. 224-225.

[154] Lippmann, Drift and Mastery: An Attempt to Diagnose the Current Unrest, op. cit., p. 206.

[155] Lippmann, Walter. Essays in the Public Philosophy. Boston, Massachusetts: Little, Brown and Company, 1955, p. 34.

[156] Lippmann, Walter. The Essential Lippmann: A Political Philosophy for Democracy. eds. Rossiter and Lare. New York: Random House, 1963, p. 7.

[157]   Ibid., p. 11.

[158]   Steel, op. cit., p. 242.

[159] Lippmann, Walter. The Good Society. London, England: George Allen and Unwin Ltd., 1937, p. 348.

[160] Lippmann, Essays in the Public Philosophy, op. cit., p. 101.

[161]   Ibid., p. 180.

CHAPTER 4

JOHN DEWEY AND SIDNEY HOOK:
A PARALLELISM WITH CROLY AND LIPPMANN

What distinguishes most American socio-economic determinists from the Marxists is a rejection of dialectical materialism and a rejection of the dictatorship of the proletariat. "Hegelianism" is still present in the notion of conflict and progress. What distinguishes Pragmatism among the naturalistic philosophies is its emphasis upon action together with its rejection of "metaphysics." All ideas are but probabilities to be tested in action.

When Dewey accepted the idea that the underlying cause of social change was neither human nor divine will, it made a profound change in his politics. Dewey's known voting record up until the Great Depression was the following: 1896 for Bryan; 1912 for Theodore Roosevelt's Bull Moose ticket; 1916 for Wilson; 1924 for La Follette; and in 1928 for Al Smith.[1] Dewey made his break with Idealism in graduate school in the early eighties. Merle Curti finds evidence of Dewey's social radicalism in his writings as early as 1894.[2]

Dewey always advocated "social change;" a term which may be translated as using government action to improve the conditions of those less fortunate. In terms of the Depression it is significant that he advocated _organic_ change (change from within and by the existing system) up until the stock market crisis. He voted Progressive, but not for radical restructuring.

In lectures given in 1926 (reprinted as _The Public and Its Problems_, 1929) Dewey's tone was pedantic and uninspiring. He never spoke any better than he wrote, and at that time he did not convey a sense of urgency for his social position. Rather, the lectures consisted of a dry analysis with an occasional tone of "wouldn't it be nice if . . ." Judging by his later writings the following remarks from those lectures may have been directed at the Republican administration:

> No government by experts in which the masses do not have the chance to inform the experts as to their needs can be anything but an oligarchy managed in the interests of the few. And the

enlightenment must proceed in ways which force the administrative specialists to take account of the needs.[3]

The point is that it is impossible to tell if he meant the Republican administration. Now contrast this with his position five years later:

> I speak as one who as far back as 1912 hoped for the resurrection of the Republican party, as one who has at times in national elections hoped for a revival within the Democratic party. But at last I am disillusioned; I am humiliated at the length of time it has taken me to pass something like political maturity. For, I submit, it is an infantile cherishing of illusions, a withdrawal from the realities of economic and political facts, to pin one's hopes and put one's trust on the possibilities of organic change in either of the major parties.[4]

Dewey's reaction to the Depression was most noticeable in his work for The League for Independent Political Action and in his articles in the New Republic. George Dykhuizen has given a good account of his personal letters at this time:[5] he condemned Hoover's lack of action, advocated a planned economy, and saw no real promise in the election of Roosevelt.

The 1928 election of Herbert Hoover distressed Dewey because he saw it as anathema to progress. He considered the old liberalism which Hoover represented to be based upon a fallacy, the notion that freedom is something expressed negatively (freedom from) and its consequent embodiment in laissez-faire capitalism:

> But the course of historic events has proved that they emancipated the classes whose special interests they represented rather than human beings impartially. In fact, as the newly emancipated forces gained momentum, they actually imposed new burdens and subjected to new modes of oppression the mass of individuals who did not have a privileged economic status.[6] (emphasis Dewey)

Rather, Dewey saw liberty as something both positive and concrete:

> Well, in the first place, liberty is not just an idea, an abstract principle. It is power, effective power to do specific things. There is no such thing as liberty in general; liberty, so to speak, at large. If one wants to know what the condition of liberty is at a given time, one has to examine what persons can do and what they cannot do. The moment one examines the question from the standpoint of effective action, it becomes evident that the demand for liberty is a demand for power...[7] (emphasis Dewey)

Eventually he came to state his conclusion that politics is basically a struggle for power. He defined politics as, ". . . the struggle for possession and use of power to settle specific issues that grow out of the country's needs and problems. . . .[P]olitics is the struggle for power to achieve results . . ."[8] Thus he holds the Marxist position in so far as dividing freedom into two categories, formal and factual,[9] puts by far the most emphasis on the factual, sometimes exclusively as above, and draws the conclusion that this requires social(ist) economic planning. He writes:

> If we employ the conception of historic relativity, nothing is clearer than that the conception of liberty is always relative to forces that at a given time and place are increasingly felt to be oppressive. ... Today, it signifies liberation from material insecurity and from the coercions and repressions that prevent multitudes from participation in the vast cultural resources that are at hand. The direct impact of liberty always has to do with some class or group that is suffering in a special way from some form of constraint exercised by the distribution of powers that exists in contemporary society. Should a classless society ever come into being the formal concept of liberty would lose its significance . . .[10] (emphasis Dewey)

Dewey's other reason for attributing success to the Republicans was the fear on the part of the public that another party might upset things. The Republicans, the party of business, supposedly knew how to manage and run affairs in a businesslike way: Hoover, after all, was an engineer. For Dewey this had the ironic effect of proving that the public wanted federal economic management. It was proven again when the public held Hoover accountable for the Depression.

Dewey's reaction to the Depression went through a cycle starting with "Fabian" socialism (he never used the term) prior to the stock market crash. Then, after the crash, he opted for a radical socialism calling for a constitutional convention and ignoring the gains of the New Deal. Finally, as the effects of drastic social engineering in Europe became apparent, he drifted back to a low keyed evolutionary socialism. Like Croly, he was a slow learner.

The first period is best represented by the founding of the League for Independent Political Action (L.I.P.A.) and from Dewey's Individualism Old and New (1930), a collection of essays drawn from his contributions to the New Republic the preceding year. The L.I.P.A. was founded in 1928 as a reaction to Hoover's election. The League's basic contention was that politics and economics had to be squared, and its beacon light was the British Labor Party. The vice president of the League at its inception was Thomas Maurer, Norman Thomas' running mate. Dewey showed up occasionally as a "sympathetic onlooker" but he was not a founding member. With the stock market crash in October of 1929, Dewey thought the time was right for change, and became a member; his reputation immediately propelling him to its presidency. With Dewey as president the major task of the L.I.P.A. became the "education" of the American people concerning economics. Here, their faith in public education was such that they hoped to elect someone with their views to the White House by 1940.

To do this they advocated the formation of a third party, and Dewey asked Senator George W. Norris of Nebraska, a liberal Republican, to head the new party. Norris politely refused. His refusal had two consequences: first, it deepened Dewey's suspicions of the collaboration between the old parties and; second, it gained Dewey the animosity of Norman Thomas and the avowed socialists. The press was also harsh on Dewey, both giving the League bad notices and never allowing

90

Dewey column space for interviews. Both the press and the other minor parties considered the League a group of intellectuals, whereas both the major parties considered it a threat to be defused. Dewey himself may have been partly to blame: he was seventy years old the year of the crash, had lived through previous depressions, and at the start did not express the sense of urgency which is needed in politics.

However, it was soon apparent that the Depression was worse than anything in memory -- so bad, in fact, that it threatened to be the beginning of the total economic collapse expected by the most radical social-ists. By the time of the 1932 elections the League had drawn up a specific platform of eighty-four recommenda-tions, including: a quarter-billion dollars in federal funds for jobs; three to five billion for public works; an end to prohibition at the federal level; an immedi-ate twenty-five percent reduction in the tariff; a situation of complete free trade within twenty years; U.S. membership in the League of Nations; recognition of Soviet Russia; an immediate fifty percent cut in the military budget and a constitutional convention. It was as thorough a socialist program as could be sub-mitted at that time, hedged with words like "eventual" public ownership and recommending an income tax up to seventy-five percent on the highest earning indivi-duals. Dewey warned that the progressive radicals should do as he did and hedge their socialism in evolutionary terms; i.e., not advocating it as a forthright political policy. This was because it might play into the hands of the Facists, whom he was afraid might be in position to compete for power if the whole system collapsed.[11]

Unfortunately, Dewey was a bad political tacti-cian. The Socialists had held their convention four months ahead of his and had stolen much of his thunder. Norman Thomas was calling for most of the same things as Dewey and even admitted the same gradualism in practice. Thomas had the advantage of being an experi-enced candidate with a pre-existing party, one with its ideology and platform already worked out. Also, the pressure was on for a united front.

Dewey had two objections to Thomas. First, Thomas was an acknowledged socialist; he was identified with socialism. In 1931 Dewey wrote:

> I think a new party will have to adopt many measures which are now

91

labeled socialistic -- measures which
are discounted and condemned because of
that tag. But while support for such
measures in the concrete . . . will win
support from American people, I cannot
imagine the American people supporting
them on the ground of Socialism, or any
other sweeping ism, laid down in advance. The greatest handicap from which
special measures favored by the Socialists suffer is that they are advocated
by the Socialist party as Socialism.
The prejudice against the name may be a
regrettable prejudice . . . [12]

Rather, he imagined that the majority of reformers,
". . . all but the most dogmatic Socialists . . . ,"
would enlist in the new party. As Harold Laski said of
Sidney and Beatrice Webb, the left wing founders of the
British Labor Party, they were "pragmatists at bottom,"
and "Their word did more than that of anyone else to
give the doctrine of socialism its necessary pragmatic
roots in the English scene."[13] Dewey felt that it
was only by being such Fabian socialists that the
intellectual elite had a practical chance at achieving
reform. Through education the solutions would suggest
themselves to the voting public. Ironically, there is
an element of Platonism in Dewey's brand of Pragmatism:
to know the good is to do the good, and Dewey depended
upon education to make it known.

Dewey's second objection was that Thomas was an
ideological socialist rather than a practical one.
Dewey believed that men would cooperate for the common good -- once they were properly educated to know
what that common good was. Thomas, on the other
hand, looked at society in terms of the Marxist class
struggle. In responding to Thomas' charge of being a
group of do-nothings, late-comers, and utopian intellectuals, Dewey said:

It has been a constant aim of the
L.I.P.A. to find labor groups which
believe in independent political action,
to bring them together, and to carry on
education among these labor groups which
have not yet seen the light. We are
opposed to the defeatest policy which
assumes that there can be no effective
radical political action in the country
until the majority of the population

have sunk into the "proletariat."
We are not yet convinced that the
Socialist Party has taken the latter
position . . .[14] (emphasis Dewey)

Whereas Thomas had charged that Dewey's League holds "an intellectualized version of a watered-down social- ism," Dewey responded that he was making decisions without regard for dogma. Dewey turned the tables and showed that Thomas' brand of socialism was as watered- down as his own by pointing out that Thomas was only calling for nationalization of the principal means of production and distribution. In practice, the Social- ist Party admitted to the same gradualism that Dewey had recommended in theory. Moreover, Dewey charged the other radicals with alienating the middle class and thus creating an unnecessary handicap. This was, perhaps, his best point.

As can be expected, virtually all the doctrinaire radicals disagreed with Dewey's cooperativism. Even Sidney Hook, his most distinguished convert to Pragma- tism and admirer lamented:

Dewey's idea is a socialized America. In terms of his own position, the
only quarrel one can have with him is
his failure to appreciate the instrumental value of class struggle rather
than class collaboration in effecting
the transition from Corporate America
to Collective America.[15] (emphasis
Hook)

Hook saw nothing wrong with being a Pragmatic Marxist, but neither could he give up the instrumental notion of class struggle completely. Actually Dewey would agree since he was trying to unify the lower and middle classes for an attack (at the polls) on the upper. That was one instance where Dewey was a better tacti- cian than the professionals. He explained, "In spite of the disparaging tone in which 'bourgeois' is spoken, this is a bourgeois country; and an American appeal couched in the language which the American people understand must start from this fact."[16]

With other socialists Dewey was a sort of friendly enemy. He voted for Norman Thomas in 1932. With the Marxists, however, he had more fundamental differences. He had been to Russia and was among the first to advocate diplomatic recognition. He had personally

93

inspected their school system and was impressed with their dedication and their goals of doing so much with so little. Again and again he held up the Russian five year plans as examples of "scientific social planning" which should be instituted in the United States.[17] However, he also considered it a fact that orthodox communists took their orders from Moscow rather than operating directly for the good of human kind. This conclusion was reinforced in 1935 when New York Local No. 5 of the American Federation of Teachers, the teachers' union which he had helped to organize and of which he was a charter member, was brought to a standstill by the Communist Party. Their immediate aim was destructive. Dewey fought back as chairman of the grievance committee and this took much of his time away from the League. (By the time the Communist Party sided with Russia in its attack on Poland and Finland it was too late to affect further Dewey's position on either the Depression or the New Deal.)

Secondly, Dewey held an opposing metaphysics or explanation of change. Even though he had an inclination for explaining change dialectically he did not consider it absolutely necessary, nor even desirable in some cases. The preordained acceptance of violence was especially repugnant to him. He noted:

> Insistence that the use of violent force is _inevitable_ limits the use of available intelligence, for whereever the inevitable reigns intelligence cannot be used. Commitment to inevitability is always the fruit of dogma . . .[18] (emphasis Dewey)

Rather, like the consensus historians, he held that more change and progress comes about through cooperation than through conflict and violent revolution.[19] Although both Marxists and (Catholic) Thomists consider Pragmatism a philosophy of expediency, Dewey believed that the ends are always inherent in the means, and that violent means would always corrupt the ends. The _only_ passage in which Dewey ever advocated force in order to gain his ends was written in 1935:

> . . . when society through an authorized majority has entered upon the path of social experimentation leading to great social change, and a minority refuses by force to permit the method of intelligent action to go into effect. Then

> force may be intelligently employed to
> subdue and disarm the recalcitrant
> minority.[20]

Even then he qualified it to the point of meaning-
lessness.

Lastly, Dewey considered Marxism to be a religion.
He once confided to Bertrand Russell (another friendly
enemy) that since he had gotten over one religion
(Hegelianism) he had no intention of accepting another.
On this point they both agreed.

Dewey prided himself on being undogmatic. Even
so, many Marxists considered that he and they had much
in common. They saw Dewey as representing a progressive evolutionary step in American thought. For
instance, Jim Cork was able to cite nine similarities
between Marx and Dewey:

> 1. Both find a common heritage in
>   Hegel . . . Each in his own way
>   emancipated himself from the
>   idealistic insights of Hegel
>   without sacrificing the great
>   insights of the German philosopher.
>
> 2. Both consider philosophy as not
>   'outside' this world and above
>   common human practices, but a very
>   important part of the general
>   culture of any epoch, reflecting
>   its common experiences, problems
>   and needs. ...
>
> 3. The strong secular, naturalistic
>   note in both philosophers. ...
>
> 4. Both are in the materialistic tra-
>   dition of philosophic thought . . .
>
> 5. Both are opposed to atomism,
>   a-priorism, sensationalism, Pla-
>   tonic essences, and the extremes of
>   both organism and formalism in
>   understanding culture.
>
> 6. Both are opposed to the traditional
>   philosophies of dualism (Descartes,
>   Kant, etc.).

7. Both are opposed to absolute
    truths in favor of relative and
    provisional truths dependent for
    verification (and possible fur-
    ther extension) upon future
    inquiry . . .

8. Both have a deep appreciation of
    the facts of biology and accept the
    philosophical implications of
    Darwinism . . .

9. Both epistemological theories are
    practically identical. Both
    stress the unity of theory and
    practice.[21]

What bothered the Marxists principally was that Dewey
did not adhere to their plan for revolution, calling
instead for mass education rather than class conflict.

Yet Dewey still can be charged with dogmatism. By
the election of 1932 there was no package of mere
reform that he was willing to accept -- not even if it
worked. Beginning in 1929 his political statements
kept getting stronger, until they reached their most
radical and uncompromising form in 1935. It may be
speculated that the "success" of the German National
Socialists had as much to do with his return to caution
as his fear of aiding domestic reactionaries -- he
considered the Union Party (the Coughlin-Lemke-Smith-
Townsend coalition) to be a group of fascists.

In 1930 he blamed the private profit system for
the country's ills: "There lies the serious and fundamental defect of our civilization, the source of the
secondary and induced evils to which so much attention
is given."[22] He declared that economic causes are
"fundamental." The traditional kind of rugged and
competitive individual had his place in the pre-machine
age. The old individualist had created the industrial
state. However, its time is past and we live in a
"collective age."[23] As a former Hegelian himself
he found it easy to accept the Marxist substructure-
superstructure explanation. Again, he accepted it
without the encumbrance of a formal theory of
dialectics:

        Our material culture . . . is
    verging on the collective and corporate.
    Our moral culture, along with our

96

ideology, is, on the other hand, still structured with ideals and values of an individualism derived from the prescientific, pretechnological age.[24]

A new individualism can be achieved only through the controlled use of all the resources of science and technology that have mastered the physical forces of nature.

They are not now controlled in any fundamental sense. Rather they control us.[25]

He accepted both the Marxist theory of alienation and the basic tenant of Marxist psychology, that consciousness itself is a social product:

. . . the relationship of the economic structure to the political operations is one that actively persists.

Indeed, it forms the only basis of present political questions. ... Wealth, property and the process of manufacturing and distribution -- down to retail trade through the chain system -- can hardly be socialized in outward effect without political repercussion. It constitutes the ultimate issue which must be faced by new or existing political parties.[27]

He went on to say that "Socialism" is thought of as a bad word by the old individualists, thus seriously handicapping any party by that name: "But in the long run, the realities of the situation will exercise control over the connotations which, for historical reasons, cling to the word."[28] The inference is that socialism conforms with <u>reality</u>.

In terms of his own theory of Pragmatism this may be criticized as "faith." His own theory, if consistently applied, would not allow him to know any aspect of reality until after it was tested in practice. <u>As a Pragmatist</u> all he had a right to say was that <u>laissez-faire</u> capitalism had been tried and failed. Politically speaking, Dewey was more than just a Pragmatist by 1930: he appeared committed to a <u>truth</u> which had not yet withstood the test of action, one which was not Pragmatically verified and was more than an instrumental myth. There were other alternatives which might have proved workable, such as the measures of controlled and regulated capitalism offered by the New Deal. However, Dewey maintained that, "We are in for some kind of socialism . . . Economic determinism is now a fact, not a theory."[29]

By 1931 his tone had become more vicious. The "economically privileged" had become his target rather than the private profit system, and he had begun to call them the enemy instead of the problem: "The enemy is one, for its elements are combined to maintain economic privilege in control of government."[30] He called Hoover's "engineering mind," ". . . the servant of capital employed for private profit."[31] He charged that, "The deadlocks and impotence of Congress are definitely the mirror of the demonstrated incapacity of the captains of industry and finance to conduct the affairs of the country prosperously as an incident to the process of feathering their own nests."[32] His criticism had become more specific, directed at particular classes and individuals rather than at the more abstract level. He charged also that the Democrats had accepted all the same basic assumptions as the Republicans and had "committed themselves to the policy of alliance with big business." Thus there was no hope for basic change to come out of either party; their self-interest made them intransigent. Property interests always came before human interests. His economic determinism also grew stronger that year. He said, "For it is the pressure of necessity which creates and directs all political change."[33] Logically speaking, he should not have blamed both the individual culprits and the system that determined their behavior.

This trend continued until 1935 when it climaxed in his advocating what amounted to censorship[34] and the limited sanction of violence (see above). His emotion and his authoritarianism grew together. Dewey's "Hegelianism" showed up again that year in his statement that an individual's freedom is realized through acquiescence to collective regimentation: "Regimentation of material and mechanical forces is the only way by which the mass of individuals can be released from regimentation and consequent suppression of their cultural possibilities."[35]

All the evidence points to the fact that Dewey was fully aware of emotionalizing the issues. Consistent with Pragmatism, he remarked:

Here we come to the nub of the matter. Intelligence has no power per se. In so far as the older rationalists assumed that it had, they were wrong. Hume was nearer the truth . . . when he said 'reason is and always must be the slave of passion' of interest.[36]

Pragmatism itself hinges upon a modification of the behaviorist theory of mind; thinking occurs only when unthinking or habitual behavior is blocked. It is a form of problem solving behavior, driven by desire and directed by whatever constructs succeed in fulfilling one's desires. In 1931 Dewey stated:

Again, no movement gets far on a purely intellectual basis. It has to be emotionalized; it must appeal to social imagination. ...

Everything points to a simple conclusion. The only way to achieve any lasting reform is to find the one great issue on which all others converge.[37]

Dewey's one great unifying factor was: "Recovery of the agencies of the government by the national community for the service of the nation . . ."[38] He stated that this was not rigid or dogmatic, but that it would provide an identifiable enemy. It even provided the sense of conflict needed for a movement. Furthermore, he could satisfy his own Pragmatic theory at the same time by saying, "No commitment to dogma or fixed doctrine is necessary. The program can be defined in terms of direct social needs and can develop as these change."[39] In the next breath he advocated nationalization of the power companies and regulation of the stock market.

Of course there is a contradiction between the dogma of socialism itself and the avowed Pragmatic dogma of having no dogma, but former Hegelians have only rarely been stopped by contradictions. After all, logic itself is but a creation of the will. The actual tool of transfer that Dewey did propose was taxation:

Since private control of national resources of the land with its mines, mineral deposits, water power, oil, [and] natural gas, is the stronghold of

> monopolistic privilege, it must be
> attacked at its fortress. . . .[T]axa-
> tion of land values, which are due to
> the requirements of society, is the only
> adequate method. ... They must . . .
> pass into the hands of the public.[40]

In 1931 when this was written he still could be called
a "Fabian" or evolutionary socialist, even though a
hurried one. Within another two years he was calling
for a constitutional amendment that would outlaw all
absentee ownership.

Dewey was not embittered because Roosevelt won in
1932. He expected it. However, he was discouraged by
the fact that not even the New Republic took his third
party movement seriously. A few years later the League
died of neglect.

Dewey was committed to socialism, and nothing that
Roosevelt could have done short of nationalizing the
economy would have pleased him. Supposedly unlike a
good Pragmatist, his mind was already made up ahead of
time. He had predicted that anything good which either
of the old parties did while in office would be undone
if the emergency ended. So, ironically, his estimation
of Roosevelt agreed with that of the conservative,
Peter Viereck: both considered Roosevelt to be a
crypto-conservative, a harmonizer of the old system
while talking as if he represented the new. Whereas
Viereck approved, Dewey wrote:

> The gigantic Roosevelt experiment
> of 'relief, reform and recovery' showed
> a definitely new bias, to a controlled
> and humanized capitalism as contrasted
> to the brutality of laissez-faire. But
> the necessary conclusion seems to be
> that no such compromise with a decaying
> system is possible.[41]

He said, "And now in its second summer, the Roosevelt
experiment is being generally admitted a failure."[42]
As totalitarian elements gained both at home and abroad
many liberals began to swing back to Roosevelt, yet
Dewey never found much that was good in the New Deal.
He wanted strong government and "social control" but
could say almost nothing positive about how it should
work, except to the point to the Russian five year
plans.

After 1935 he began to mellow. When asked a month
before the 1936 election how he intended to vote he
replied:

> I intend to vote for Norman Thomas
> as President. It was a disappointment
> that no genuine mass third party was
> organized, especially in view of the
> fact that the so-called Union Party is a
> union of inflationists and semi-fascist
> elements. I realize that fear of
> reactionary Republicanism will lead many
> to vote for Roosevelt who have no faith
> in the Democratic Party; but I do not
> believe that the actual difference
> between the policies of the old parties
> will be great, whoever is elected. I
> think the Republican Party is conducting
> a campaign under false pretenses.[43]

After that time the rise of totalitarianism abroad
reached alarming proportions. Dewey always referred to
himself as a "social democrat" and believed wholeheartedly in democracy. However, he never did manage
to answer the question of what there is in Pragmatic
social control that ensures that it will be used for
good purposes. How, for instance, is a dialectic of
ideas possible when the government owns the press?

It may be speculated that Dewey's total commitment
to socialism reflected his Hegelian background and his
deep seated optimism. For Hegel, Marx and Dewey, man's
freedom was to be in harmony with his role in a strong
state; a state which was responsive to the reasonable
general will of its people. However, it can be shown
that Dewey's actions were in perfect harmony with
James's Pragmatism. The Pragmatist is free to hold any
belief or myth that gives him comfort. As mentioned
below, there was no national experience to demonstrate
that socialism "worked," only evidence that no system
in the world at that time was living up to its expectations. Yet, believing that socialism would improve
things might make a difference.

After the 1936 election Dewey went back to writing
on logic and education. Then he went off to Mexico to
defend Leon Trotsky. When asked in 1940 how he would
vote he responded: "Shall vote for Norman Thomas. See
no permanent hope from either of the old parties."[44]
At that time he was eighty-one. In 1944 he voted for
Roosevelt and in 1948 cast his last ballot for Truman.

Had Dewey lived only a few more months it is probable that he would have voted the Democratic ticket again in 1952. His actions conceded the fact that he believed the Democratic Party to inspire the most efficacious myths.

There is a distinct parallelism between the lives of Herbert Croly and Walter Lippmann, on the one hand, and John Dewey and Sidney Hook, on the other. In each case the second man in the pair was the more consistent Pragmatist.

What biographical material there is about Sidney Hook (1902-   ) is sketchy and shallow. No one has undertaken his biography at book length. The longest single biography of Hook is to be found in the 1952 edition of Current Biography: Who's News and Why;[45] nearly three pages. Considering that this piece was written during the McCarthy era there is no wonder that it refers to Hook as a philosopher, educator, a friend of John Dewey's and as one who has always been concerned with "the working class movement," but avoids mention of him as a one-time Communist. Rather, it is filled with the chronology of his education, publications, marriages and children. The most that one can do from this biography is to speculate that Hook may have named his first son John Bertrand because of his admiration for John Dewey and Bertrand Russell. A more concise picture of Hook is given in the editor's preface to his 1933 classic, Towards the Understanding of Karl Marx: A Revolutionary Interpretation:

> Sidney Hook was born in New York City. He received his B.S. from College of the City of New York in 1923; his M.A. from Columbia in 1926, and his Ph.D. from Columbia in 1927. He has studied in Berlin, Munich, and done research at the Marx-Engels Institute in Moscow. Mr. Hook has twice been awarded a Guggenheim Fellowship.[46]

Hook's first publication was "The Philosophy of Non-Resistance" in a now hard to find periodical called Open Court in January, 1922, while he was still an undergraduate. His first major publication was his doctoral dissertation, The Metaphysics of Pragmatism: With an Introductory Word by John Dewey[47] (1927). On the whole it is an exceptionally positive treatment and defense of Pragmatism -- the Pragmatism of C. S. Peirce and John Dewey, but not that of William James (who popularized Pragmatism by using it to justify religious faith). Initially, Hook saw no contradiction in being a Pragmatist and a Marxist at once.

In 1928 Hook published an article called "The Philosophy of Dialectical Materialism" in The Journal of Philosophy. Opposite the first page of the article was a half page advertisement for The Metaphysics of Pragmatism, to which Dewey had offered a further quotation in admiration of the book. In this article, Hook called attention to Marx's Theses on Feurbach, saying, "We find here a striking anticipation of the instrumentalist theory of knowledge."[48] (Emphasis Hook) He quotes the eighth thesis, again with added emphasis: "All social life is essentially practical."[49] In analyzing Marx's early views he says, "It is clear that like scientific pragmatism which came long after him, he was struggling against two opposed tendencies -- sensationalistic empiricism and absolute idealism."[50] One may judge that Hook was testing Marx by Pragmatic standards -- the tacit implication being that Pragmatism (the tester) ran deeper than his Marxism (the testee).

In the 1928 article, Hook also offered a criticism of the then current Marxists, saying: "The term 'dialectical' has become a pious epithet upon their lips instead of a clearly defined concept in their heads."[51]

Indeed Hook claimed that he was independent of orthodox Russion Communism as early as 1932.[52] His conversion came about as a result of having served, beginning in 1931, as treasurer for a group which aided exiled Russian Communists. He says that by the time of the Moscow Show Trials in 1936, "I was then ideological Enemy Number One of the Communist party . . ."[53] He had begun his interest in Marxism in 1918 at age sixteen, believing Soviet Russia to be the model for the future, and by 1932 he was a well-known Marxist.

In 1930, in an article for the New Republic, Hook had taken the traditional Marxist stand that earlier American philosophy was, ". . . a prop for political conservatism and religious tradition . . ."[54] His major criticism of contemporary American philosophers was that they did not get involved in politics as did European philosophers, they were not adequately involved socially. Also they did not recognize the importance of class struggle in the realm of ethics. In a 1931 article in the same periodical, titled "John

Dewey and His Critics," Hook vigorously defended Dewey from the charge of being the spokesman of contemporary capitalism while, at the same time, making explicit their differences.

> Dewey's idea is a socialized America. In terms of his own position, the only quarrel one can have with him is his failure to appreciate the instrumental value of <u>class struggle</u> rather than class collaboration in effecting the transition from Corporate America to Collective America.[55] (emphasis Hook)

At this time, Hook was the activist and critic for which he is remembered by Depression-era liberals. In July of 1931, he said, "Prolonged study has convinced me that genuine Marxism is not a science of social evolution but a philosophy of social revolution; that it is not a dogmatic method of predicting history but a critical method of making it."[56] This differs from Dewey's then-current Fabian socialism, as well as from Hook's later interpretation, which bitterly criticized the Soviet Union for using Marxism to make history. He advocated the theory of revolution over the theory of evolution. As for international relations, Hook, like Dewey, advocated formal recognition of the Soviet Union. Hook also felt sorry for the German <u>people</u> because of what was happening to them, socially and economically, as a result of a great war between <u>capitalists</u>, and he advocated that the terms of the Treaty of Versailles be softened.

After his conversion from orthodoxy, he began a new historical study of Marx, which culminated in the aforementioned <u>Towards the Understanding of Karl Marx</u> (1933). Repulsed by Stalin's dictatorship, Hook formed what he now considered to be a "revolutionary" interpretation of Marx's "dictatorship of the proletariate." "<u>Its opposite is not 'democracy' but the 'dictatorship of the bourgeoisie'.</u>"[57] "<u>Whenever we find a state, there we find a dictatorship.</u> Whoever believes in a <u>proletarian</u> state, believes in a <u>proletarian dictatorship</u>. This is Marx's meaning."[58] (All emphasis Hook) He felt called upon to return to this position again and again, continually clarifying it and distinguishing Marx's position from Marxism. For Hook, Marx's word "dictatorship" was a sociological term, rather than a formal or political one. Virtually any form of government is a dictatorship in the sense that one group of people dictates its tastes and interests upon the rest of society. The dictatorship of the proletariate exists under any form of government where the majority rules. It is a government by and for the majority, fading away only when interests become so similar that there are no major clashes of interests. It had the ring of Dewey's cooperative conflict, as opposed to ruthless competition and repression. It was Marxism coupled with Populism-Progressivism and Dewey's faith in democracy. Also, perhaps because of what was happening in the Soviet Union, it was more internationalist and anti-Leninist. Although both Hook and Dewey remained "radicals," their positions began to drift apart. Whereas Dewey kept the faith that Roosevelt's diplomatic recognition of the Soviet Union would turn it into a cooperative member of the world community, Hook perceived that there was something wrong fundamentally -- although he was, as yet, unable to express just what it was.

Max Eastman once gave a critical review of Hook's 1933 book on Marx (quoted from above) under the title, "What Karl Marx Would Have Said If He Had Been a Student of John Dewey." Hook and the Marxists were becoming alienated from each other. When Hook decided to drop the term "Marxist" in 1947 he said,

> For the last twenty years I have presented an interpretation of Marx which has run counter to customary views and conceptions of his fundamental doctrines. "Orthodox Marxism" . . . seems to me to be an elaborate series of myths, confused in idea and vicious in consequence. It would appear that if I were justified in my interpretation of Marx's meaning, I would be perhaps the only Marxist left in the world. This is too much for my sense of humor, and so I have decided to abandon the term as a descriptive epithet of my position . . .[59]

In 1959 Hook said, "In one form or another I have been discussing what is living and what is dead in Marxism for nearly forty years (starting when I was sixteen). Depending on how Marxism was defined, I would characterize myself either as a Marxist of a non-Marxist."[60] He went on to say that if more than one person were present, reaching the definition became impossible and he could never characterize himself. He said,

In writing independently, however,
I often used to refer to myself as a
Marxist on the basis of my interpretation of Marx's ideas. But I gave that
up some time ago because critics told me
that if I were right, it made me the
only Marxist extant in the entire
world -- indeed the only one who had
lived in all history. This seemed
improbable. However, let us not be
rash! The improbable sometimes is true.
... A weightier reason for ceasing to
refer to myself as a Marxist was the
apparent immodesty of being the only
one who really understood Marx -- even
if it were true.[61]

It was always a consolation to Hook to remember that
even Marx had declared that he was not a Marxist.

In the 1936 introduction to From Hegel to Marx
(not published until 1950) Hook makes a defense of
Marx's intellectual honesty,[62] but declines to extend
his defense to the truth of Marx's assertions.

In 1937 Hook questioned whether the Marxist dialectic was capable of moral guidance, as well as
scientific explanation:

For the possession of knowledge is
compatible with diametrically opposed
modes of conduct. Granted, for example,
that the tendency of capitalist production to increase the number of unem-
ployed and unemployable is objectively
verifiable, and universally confirmed by
all investigators; we can no more deduce
from this a universally acceptable
program of action than we can determine
from the objective properties of steel
whether to build tanks or tractors.[63]

He solved the problem through Dewey's Pragmatic method
of objectifying values as a given of the subject
matter, giving most of the credit to Marx in this
instance.

Later the same year, Hook attacked the inconsistency by which the Stalinist maintained the right-wing
Hegelianism for their own side (what is, is right)
while they found no difficulty in applying severe

judgments to Fascism. At this time, he was involved
with Dewey in coming to Leon Trotsky's aid in defense
against the Moscow Trials. Hook's ultimate denunciation
of Russia at this time was to call her system one of
state capitalism.

> If the analysis of the evidence
> reveals the Moscow trials to be shabby
> frauds, what is the real meaning of the
> whole performance? Even conservative
> opinion holds that the Moscow trials
> marked the final departure of Russia
> from ideals of revolutionary socialism
> and an orientation towards state
> capitalism.[64]

In 1940, in <u>Reason</u>, <u>Social</u> <u>Myths</u> <u>and</u> <u>Democracy</u>,
Hook equated Hitlerism and Stalinism as "twin forms of
totalitarianism."[65] Neither was capitalism spared.
He found that, "The perennial source of strength of all
socialist movements is the inequities and inequalities
of capitalist economy."[66] After listing capitalism's
shortcomings, he draws the logical conclusion that in
themselves they do not constitute an argument for
socialism. Rather, they constitute evidence of the
need for something better. For Hook in 1940, the value
of Marxism was its economic criticism of capitalism;
one which "proved" that capitalism could do no better
than it had, that all its evils were a necessary
product of the system itself. Profits, employment and
an adequate standard of living were antithetical. All
mere reforms were bound to fail because they cut into
the capitalists' profits (still a dirty word for Hook),
which was the system's driving force. All that could
be said for capitalism by 1940, was that it was better
than totalitarianism. Even capitalism under Czarism
was better than that. He said, "As far as real wages
is concerned, the worker under Czarism was better off
than he is under Stalin."[67] Hook was convinced that
a capitalist Russia would have progressed as fast as it
did under Soviet communism. The Revolution had per-
verted a natural, and thus progressive, evolution.

The war years saw a decline in Hook's politically
oriented publications. This is not surprising considering that he showed a tragic sympathy for Germany,
an enemy power, and continued his hostility toward
Russia, an Allied power. His position regarding
Germany was all the more remarkable considering the
fact of his Jewish background.

In an early 1943 issue of the _Partisan Review_, he expressed doubt about his Deweyite optimism that the future would be guided "scientifically." He was staunchly against emotion as a justification for action, and regarded the cult of sincerity as justifying Hitler.[68] Like Hitlerism, he considered that "orthodox Marxism is bankrupt"[69] when it came to creating a positive scientific philosophy to rally around. In a sarcastic footnote to a sentence about how all sides in the war posited the presence of God on their side, he says, "For Stalin the dialectic takes the place of Providence. And since June 22, 1941, the Soviet Radio has discovered that Nazism is a movement which seeks to destroy Christianity."[70]

Hook returned to the same themes in the next issue of the same magazine, this time with more force. He said that the Communist Party of the U.S.A. ". . . is little more than the American section of the G.P.U."[71] He felt that the majority of left-wing politicians, including both open revolutionaries and those in Roosevelt's camp ". . . have succumbed to the metaphysical approach to politics."[72] This was to believe that the basic cause of social and political troubles was "sin," that good was fighting evil, instead of understanding that economic circumstances were working themselves out in the ways they must -- and that intelligent social planning could prevent the chaos which is blamed on evil. ("Good" and "evil" were considered to be meaningless metaphysical clutter by the most popular pre-war Anglo-American philosophers. At best they were subjective emotional statements, not capable of scientific analysis. The Pragmatists had great respect for the logical positivists' linguistic theory, and tended to assume that the "good" meant no more than "what worked.")

In this regard, Hook found Norman Thomas and the Socialist Party to be confused and contradictory with regard to the war. Their greatest concern was to assign moral responsibility for the war, rather than to dwell upon its objective consequences. Hook took the long range and somewhat tragic view, concluding that "in varying degrees, everybody" was responsible for the war.[73] Long before the war he had been a critic of the Treaty of Versailles, realizing that economic imbalances would have to be corrected, rather than imposing punishment upon a nation, a people, in order to expiate its collective guilt.

Hook's cynicism, and his skepticism towards
morality in the political sphere in particular, led
him to consider Franklin Roosevelt to be a crypto-
conservative -- again taking a position similar to
Dewey's. Hook said,

> Roosevelt will not hesitate to
> jettison more New Deal cargo and change
> course if his party machine can still
> get that kind of political support from
> the progressive bloc in the name of
> patriotism, which it could not get from
> any other social group without paying
> for it. In order to keep what it has,
> the progressive bloc must organize
> itself independently. Otherwise its
> aspirations will be taken no more
> seriously in Washington than the repre-
> sentations of the Jews on Palestine are
> taken by Downing Street . . .[74]

Like Dewey a decade earlier, Hook hinted at the need
for what amounted to a third political party, but
which, for pragmatic reasons, should stay within the
Democratic organization.

That same year, 1943, Hook published The Hero in
History: A Study in Limitation and Possibility, which
was more critical of the Soviet Union than of Nazi
Germany. In it he said, "Marx's doctrine that no
ruling class ever voluntarily surrenders its power
turned out to be true for the dictatorship of the
Bolshevik Party, too."[75] The real purpose of the
Communist International was the protection of the
Soviet Union. For this reason it could not tolerate
independent socialist movements which were possible
threats to its authority. Taking this line of reasoning to its extreme, Hook concluded,

> The greatest triumphs enjoyed by
> the Bolsheviks outside Russia were not
> the overthrow of any capitalist state
> but the destruction of working-class and
> socialist unity in all countries where
> affiliated sections of the Communist
> International could gain a foothold.
> ... The net effect was the weakening of
> powers of resistance to the forces of
> domestic reaction particularly to the
> large industrialists and land-owners as
> well as the dispossessed middle class

subject to the growing Fascist influence, who were uncompromisingly hostile to the Soviet Union.[76]

Without the Russian Revolution, there would have been a Hitler movement anyway but it would not have triumphed. The worst alternative realizable in Germany would have been a period of reaction similar to other conservative swings of the past. But in time, unable to overcome the crisis endemic to capitalism, a conservative regime would have had to make way for German social democracy . . . or it would have had to pit itself against the overwhelming mass of the German people in open revolt.[77]

In effect, Hook blamed the Soviets for the rise of Hitler: "The destruction of the labor movement which, if it has been unified . . ., could have stopped Fascism in its tracks or, at least, put up so strong a resistance that Germany would have been as exhausted as Spain."[78] Hitler was not the result of German evil: his rule was the consequence of the pressure of the Treaty of Versailles on one side, and the pressure of the Soviet Union on the other.

Hook blamed Lenin, the true event-making individual, for distorting true Marxism, saying: "Lenin was a Marxist who interchanged the 'dictatorship of the proletariat' -- which for Marx was a broader democracy of the working class counterposed to the narrow democracy of capitalist society -- with the outright dictatorship of a minority Communist Party over the proletariat."[79] (Emphasis Hook) This led to the gross perversion that any element of dissent from the party was a voice of the objective enemies of mankind. He began his final chapter with the pessimistic conclusion that, "If the hero is defined as a event-making individual who redetermines the course of history, it follows at once that a democratic community must be eternally on guard against him."[80] Even well-intentioned men were apt to do more harm than good if there were no checks upon their power. At other times, Hook gave signs of being concerned that Roosevelt was the potential hero to worry about in the United States.

By 1947, Hook had regained some of his optimism. In an article called "The Future of Socialism" he said,

> I am a democrat. I am a socialist. And I am still a Marxist in the sense which one may speak of a modern biologist as still a Darwinian. ... I am willing to call myself a Marxist because I believe that Marx's leading ideas, as I interpret them, and revised in the light of the scientific method which he himself professed to follow, are better guides to achieving socialism -- if it can be achieved -- than any other alternative set of ideas known to me.[81] (emphasis Hook)

He also gained a greater acceptance of capitalism, saying:

> It was a mistake to conceive of a socialist economy as planned in its entirety. There is good reason now to believe that some form of mixed economy can more reliably secure the goals of democracy without the inefficiency, bureaucracy, and evasion of responsibility that seem attendant upon a completely planned system of production.[82]

He conceded that Marx had failed to account for two major factors in his scheme: the relative autonomy of a science and technology capable of creating the atom bomb, and the assumption that the workers would act decisively, responsibly, and at the right moment. Rather, when the time was right for socialism, Hitler and Mussolini came to power. "The rise of totalitarian states and the advance in military technology have produced a new historical situation in which the whole Marxist strategy of achieving democratic socialism must be revised."[83] In 1947, he saw British socialism as the light of the future, as Dewey had two decades earlier.

A decade later, Hook was an exponent of American globalism. In 1957, even Norman Thomas felt prompted to say, "I am deeply anti-communist."[84] In the same magazine, New Leader, the same year, Hook said that, "We must defend the free world: That is an 'inflexible principle'."[85] There was nothing philosophically inconsistent in Hook's stand. His position had been one of democratic socialism since 1932. When he talked

111

about the Soviet Union he invoked the image of Hitler and appeasement.

Hook and his old friend Bertrand Russell became bitter opponents over this issue. In 1948, Russell (who had been a pacifist as far back as World War One) had advocated nuclear war as a justifiable defense against the Soviet Union. (Hook finally insisted that the letter upon which this was based be reprinted in the New Leader L, No. 21, October 23, 1967.) After Russia had gained the bomb, Russell advocated unilateral disarmament. He believed that anything was better than destruction. Hook, on the other hand, said, ". . . there are some things that are riskier and more undesirable than war -- totalitarian bondage, for example."[86]

Whereas Russell would have disarmed and made the whole world come under Russian domination, Hook would have intervened in order to free those then under Russian control. In 1957, he said,

> Those who, like Mr. George Kennan, proclaimed that "There is a finality, for better or worse, about what has now occurred in Eastern Europe" -- and proclaimed this before Poznan, before the Polish October and the Hungarian November -- were much too hasty in their judgment and their finality. And unfortunately such judgment itself had an enormous influence on the response to these events. (emphasis Hook)
>
> I am one of those who believe that at the time of the Hungarian Revolution a firm and direct intervention by the United States and the West in response to the appeal of the Nagy government would probably have led to the withdrawal of Soviet troops. The Kremlin will not be slow, we can be sure, to learn the lesson of Hungary. It is now clear that it will use force sufficient to suppress any popular revolt against a Soviet puppet regime . . .[87]

In that same year, far from looking to British socialism, Hook said,

> . . . we have achieved the greatest of
> all welfare states in the history of
> mankind. If the marriage of welfare and
> freedom be considered the principle of
> socialism, there is more socialism in
> the United States than in most countries
> which call themselves socialist.[88]

Of official Marxist philosophy he said, ". . . it is a
premise for the most ruthless suppression of free
inquiry . . . that the world has ever seen. ... This
metaphysics has been a rationalization for intellectual
terror."[89] He sees this as opposed to the traditional spirit of a pluralistic liberalism which invites
inquiry and the conflict of ideas.

The next year, Hook significantly enlarged his
criticism from orthodox Marxism to socialism in
general. After defining the meaning of the word
"socialism" he said:

> But it does not follow that exploi-
> tation is impossible in a socialist
> society. It may simply take another
> form. Exploitation may arise as much
> from the decisions made by the bureau-
> crat or manager of a Party cell repre-
> senting the state on the conditions,
> wages and tempo of work as from an
> individual owner. Indeed, where the
> worker is protected by a free trade
> union and has the right to strike, he
> may be far less exploited in a mixed
> welfare economy or a democratic capi-
> talist economy than in a socialist
> economy if he does not enjoy the rights
> of a free trade unionist. The state,
> because of its monopoly of all economic
> power under socialism, can, by the use
> of the bread-card and work-book as
> instruments of coercion, crush the
> worker far more completely than in a
> democratic welfare economy in which he
> can profit from the competition among
> capitalists. ... The mode of political
> decision is at least as important and
> may sometimes be even more important
> than the mode of economic production.

> If the rulers of a socialist
> economy are not responsible to the

113

> workers, . . . in effect, these poli-
> tical rulers "own" the instruments of
> production. Since power over things
> is power over men, . . . it follows
> that socialism without democracy is
> slavery.[90]

He also declared it to be false that capitalism could
not exist without wars, and unfounded to assert that
any socialistic government (e.g., state capitalism)
would necessarily be warless. Still, he remained
committed to being a democratic socialist. Like Dewey,
he accepted the notion that class cooperation was at
least as important as class struggle.

Hook's final change in the late fifties was to
make greater use of the distinction between Marxism and
Communism. The former was a philosophy, open to
interpretation and revision, whereas the latter was an
orthodox religion. (John Dewey and Bertrand Russell
also considered communism to be a religion.) In 1959,
Hook said, "Marxism is one of the best standpoints from
which to criticize Communism."[91] It is significant
that he was not optimistic about the Sino-Soviet
split -- it just created two orthodoxies rather than
one, and both with the goal of conquering the West.

Hook entered the sixties in the full spirit of the
Cold War. In 1962, while discussing the possibility of
nuclear destruction he said,

> Whatever the costs, they will be
> tragic. But mankind has often paid a
> heavy cost in defense of freedom. The
> cost of submission to tyranny is some-
> times equally high. Six million Jews
> went to their death submissively without
> humanizing their tormentors. The Jews
> who went down fighting in the Warsaw
> Ghetto in a desperate resistance died
> nobly.[92]

The key words here are "tragic" and "noble;" they
pointed to a new vein in Hook's thought. He changed
from his World War Two position or moral cynicism, to
basing his arguments on moral grounds. In response to
Bertrand Russell's defeatism he declared, "The difficulty with the position of absolute pacifism is that it
makes the pacifist morally responsible for the evils
which an intelligent use of force may sometimes prevent."[93] He continued:

But surely any reasonable grounds
offered for believing the war against
Hitler just would apply to some other
wars, too. If it is admitted that
resistance against Hitler and other
tyrants was justified why should
resistance against Communism be considered wicked . . .? Budapest was as
bad as Warsaw; the Soviet concentration
camps hardly better than the Nazi
camps -- for the millions who perished
there. ... To respond to this with
talk about the justice of war against
Hitler and at the same time to urge
capitulation to the Kremlin is to mock
the dead.[94]

The Vietnam war made the breach between Hook and
Russell even more bitter. Whereas Russell considered
the war to be planned genocide, Hook carefully distinguished between accidental and freak atrocities, on
the one hand, and the official terrorist policy of the
Vietcong on the other. Hook concluded that the American involvement in Vietnam was a just one for the sake
of maintaining South Vietnam's independence, and cited
Adlai Stevenson's blessing as evidence to the fact.[95]
Hook compared Ho Chi Minh with Hitler, saying,

The practices closest to the
genocidal behavior of the Nazis have
been the extermination by Ho Chi Minh's
regime of members of socially dangerous
classes, and the wanton slaughter, by
the Vietcong of men, women and children
in South Vietnamese villages refusing to
support them.[96]

By the late sixties, Hook began to see the entire
New Left as the opposition. He implied that C. P.
Snow, author of The Two Cultures, was a Stalinist
(based upon the fact that Snow wrote a biography of
great Twentieth-Century leaders, wherein he gave the
most space to Stalin).[97] He characterized others who
worked for the immediate redress of past social wrongs,
as calling for the punishment of the living for the
sins of the dead. For Hook, the Civil Rights Movement
had gone over to the mountain. In 1968, he said,

Contemporary rhetoricians of
violence find it easy to draw up an
indictment of a whole race. They accept

without qualms the very doctrines of collective guilt and guilt by association that have done so much mischief in the past. They fail to see that morally human beings are guilty only for those consequences which their actions or failure to act have caused. Whatever the crimes of the past may have been; they do not justify any crimes in the present. Otherwise we may as well hang a man today because his grandfather was a horse thief! No nation, no people, no race is free of guilt in the perspective of the past. But this is not relevant to the present.[98] (emphasis Hook)

He took the position that perfection is unattainable and that even the pursuit of perfect social justice is likely to lead to more harm than good.[99] The quest for perfect justice and harmony in international relations is, as evidenced by the experiences of Woodrow Wilson at Versailles, naive at best.

In 1974, Hook published Pragmatism and the Tragic Sense of Life. Once again he attacked the cult of sincerity as he had thirty years earlier:

Today science and the scientific attitude are under attack; intelligence and reason are at a discount on the grounds that they do not serve mankind properly, that they impoverish human life instead of enriching it. The slogans with which the loudest voices in the younger academy seek to rally their followers are "commitment," "engagement," and "subjectivity," while intellectual "neutrality," "disinterestedness," and "objectivity" are unmasked as deceptive claims for special interest.[100]

Here, Hook finds himself supporting tradition against the younger moral idealists, and dangerously close to holding the position for which he attacked Mortimer J. Adler and the Thomists thirty years earlier. For both Hook and the Thomists, this is the view that there is an objective material and moral order -- a view that science is objectively normative, not merely descriptive. Hook first began to argue against subjectivity in response to Fascism (albeit in

116

1922 Benito Mussolini had credited The Will to Believe by the famous Pragmatist, William James, as being the inspiration of his Fascism). Hook's consistency lies in holding that the dispassionate method of science and Pragmatism is the objective way to find truths, whereas the Thomists hold their axioms to be objective and knowable before being put to the test.

In this last major work, Hook's confession of greatest disappointment and disillusionment in his life, was the discovery that knowing the good did not necessarily lead to doing the good.[101] This is especially disturbing to the assumptions of Pragmatism -- a philosophy which holds that the function of the brain is to enable the organism to accomplish what it perceives as good for it. It calls into question the method which Dewey and, later, Hook relied upon to reform the world -- i.e., education, based upon the assumption that it was ignorance, not "evil" which is responsible for most social misfortunes. If the cause is neither evil nor ignorance, then what is left, and how can one pose as a reformer?

In conclusion, Sidney Hook has been a consistent Pragmatist throughout his life rather than a Marxist or even a socialist. Like Dewey, his social(ist) Pragmatism was, at bottom, the result of his humanism and faith in progress. Unlike Dewey, the events of the middle and late twentieth century caused him to lose faith in the inevitability of progress, and to stress the tragic and the heroic in life. Hook has been a more consistent Pragmatist than Dewey. Whereas Dewey wholeheartedly believed that socialism would be the most Pragmatic instrument of human progress, Hook looked at the record and decided that socialism often had been worse in practice than was American capitalism. The same held true when idealism was made the first principle of international relations. According to Dewey's own logic, this is the Pragmatic use of history; however, Dewey always maintained his faith (literally, as if a legacy of his mentor, William James) that the socialist future would be better than the past.

On the other hand, Hook would ask whether it was worth the possibility of accelerated progress to put all power (thus including the press) into the hands of a Woodrow Wilson, a Lyndon Johnson or a Richard Nixon. Hook's 1932 conversion was the result of the pragmatic vindication of Lord Acton's phrase that power tends to corrupt. Also, in a bureaucracy it is the most ruth less, not the morally good, who have the advantage in gaining power and rising to the top. Finally, it is only the capitalist segment of the economy which can support a "free" press, one not owned by the government or a political party. Thus, Pragmatically speaking, a mixed economy, for all its inequities, is preferable to a fully socialist one. On the international level, a high regard for the status quo is more likely to produce good effects than is the quest for the millennium. Disenchantment with radicalism at home went hand-in-hand with the rejection of radicalism abroad. There was no Promised Land whose system made it the obvious moral alternative. Hook's intellectual odyssey ended in what was for him a tragic discovery: the world is not perfectable. It is the world as described by Martin Wight, Hedley Bull, and Hans Morgenthau.

FOOTNOTES FOR CHAPTER 4

[1] Novack, George. Pragmatism Versus Marxism: An Appraisal of John Dewey's Philosophy. New York: Pathfinder Press, 1975, p. 263.

[2] Curti, Merle. The Social Ideas of American Educators. New York: Charles Scribner's Sons, 1935, pp. 502-503.

[3] Dewey, John. The Public and Its Problems. New York: Henry Holt and Company, 1927 (from lectures given in 1926), p. 208.

[4] Dewey, John. "Who Might Make a New Party?" New Republic, LXVI (April 1, 1931), p. 177.

[5] Dykhuizen, George. The Life and Mind of John Dewey. Carbondle and Edwardsville, Illinois: Southern Illinois University Press, 1973, pp. 251ff.

[6] Dewey, John. "Philosophies of Freedom" (1928). The Moral Writings of John Dewey. ed. J. Gouinlock. New York: Hafner Press, 1976, p. 193.

[7] Dewey, John. "Liberty and Social Control" (1935). Problems of Men. New York: Philosophical Library, 1946.

[8] Dewey, John. "The Future of Radical Political Action." The Nation, CXXXVI (January 4, 1933), p. 8.

[9] Dewey, John. Liberalism and Social Action. New York: G. P. Putnam's Sons, 1935, pp. 34-35.

[10] Ibid., p. 48.

[11] Dewey, John. "Correspondence: A Third Party Program." New Republic, LXX (February 24, 1932), pp. 48-49.

[12] Dewey, New Republic, LXVI, op. cit., p. 178.

[13] Laski, Harold J. "The Founders of the Fabians." New Republic, LXXVI (October 25, 1933), p. 313.

[14] Dewey, The Nation, op. cit., p. 9.

[15] Hook, Sidney. "A Communication: John Dewey and His Critics." New Republic, LXVII (June 3, 1931), p. 74.

[16] Dewey, New Republic, LXVI, op. cit., p. 178.

[17] Dewey, John. "Surpassing America." New Republic, LXVI (April 15, 1931); see also, John Dewey, "Social Science and Social Control" New Republic, LXVII (July 29, 1931).

[18] Dewey, Liberalism and Social Action, op. cit., p. 78.

[19] Ibid., pp. 80-81.

[20] Ibid., p. 87.

[21] Cork, Jim. "John Dewey and Karl Marx." John Dewey: Philosopher of Science and Freedom. ed. Sidney Hook. New York: The Dial Press, 1950, pp. 338-340.

[22] Dewey, John. Individualism Old and New. New York: Minton, Balch and Company, 1930, p. 31.

[23] Ibid., p. 33.

[24] Ibid., p. 74.

[25] Ibid., p. 93.

[26] Ibid., pp. 55-56.

[27] Ibid., pp. 103-104.

[28] Ibid., p. 104.

[29] Ibid., p. 119.

[30] Dewey, John. "Policies of a New Party."
New Republic, LXVI (April 8, 1931), p. 203.

[31] Dewey, John. "The Need for a New Party; The
Present Crises." New Republic, LXVI (March 18, 1931),
p. 115.

[32] Dewey, John. "The Need for a New Party:
II." New Republic, LXVI (March 25, 1931), p. 150.

[33] Dewey, New Republic, LXVI (March 18, 1931),
op. cit., p. 115.

[34] Dewey, "Intelligence as Social" (1935), The
Moral Writings of John Dewey, op. cit., pp. 213-214.

[35] Dewey, Liberalism and Social Action, op.
cit., p. 90.

[36] Dewy, John. "Intelligence and Power." New
Republic, LXXVII (April 25, 1934), p. 307.

[37] Dewey, New Republic, LXVI (April 8, 1931),
op. cit., p. 203.

[38] Ibid., p. 203.

[39] Ibid., pp. 203-204.

[40] Ibid., p. 204.

[41] Dewey, John. "Introduction." Challenge to
the New Deal. eds. Bringham and Rodman. New York:
Falcon Press, 1934, p. vi.

[42] Ibid., p. v.

[43] Dewey, John. A letter in New Republic,
LXXXVII (October 7, 1936), p. 249.

[44] Dewey, John. "How They Are Voting." New
Republic, CIII (September 23, 1940), p. 412.

[45] _Current Biography; Who's News and Why_, 1952. eds. Roth and Lohr. New York: The H. W. Wilson Company, 1953, pp. 269-271.

[46] Hook, Sidney. _Towards the Understanding of Karl Marx; A Revolutionary Interpretation_. New York: The John Day Company, 1933, p. vi.

[47] Hook, Sidney. _The Metaphysics of Pragmatism: With an Introductory Word by John Dewey_. Chicago, Illinois: The Open Court Publishing Company, 1927.

[48] Hook, Sidney. "The Philosophy of Dialectical Materialism, I." _The Journal of Philosophy_, XXV, No. 5 (March 1, 1920), p. 118.

[49] Ibid., p. 119.

[50] Ibid., p. 119.

[51] Ibid., pp. 148-149.

[52] Hook, Sidney. "Dear Editor." _New Leader_, LII, No. 8 (April 28, 1969), p. 34.

[53] Ibid., p. 9.

[54] Hook, Sidney. "Contemporary American Philosophy." _New Republic_, LXIII, No. 815 (July 16, 1930), p. 238.

[55] Hook, Sidney. "A Communication: John Dewey and His Critics." _New Republic_, LXVII, No. 861 (June 3, 1931), p. 74.

[56] Hook, Sidney. "Correspondence: Marx and Darwinism." _New Republic_, LXVII, No. 869 (July 29, 1931), p. 290.

[57] Hook, _Towards the Understanding of Karl Marx; A Revolutionary Interpretation_, op. cit., p. 299.

[58] Ibid., p. 300.

[59] Hook, Sidney. "The Future of Socialism." _Partisan Review_, SVI, No. 1 (January-February, 1947), p. 25.

[60] Hook, Sidney. "What's Left of Karl Marx." _Saturday Review_, LXII, No. 23 (June 6, 1959), p. 12.

[61] Ibid., p. 12.

[62] Hook, Sidney. From Hegel to Marx: Studies in the Intellectual Development of Karl Marx. New York: The Humanities Press, 1958, p. 11.

[63] Hook, Sidney. "Marxism and Values." Marxist Quarterly, I (1937), in Greenwood Reprint Corporation: New York, 1968, p. 41.

[64] Hook, Sidney. "Liberalism and the Case of Leon Trotsky." The Southern Review, 3, No. 2 (Autumn, 1937), pp. 281-282.

[65] Hook, Sidney. Reason, Social Myths and Democracy. New York: Harper Torchbooks, 1966 (original 1940), p. 93.

[66] Ibid., p. 110.

[67] Ibid., p. 144.

[68] Hook, Sidney. "The New Failure of Nerve." Partisan Review, X, No. 1 (January-February, 1943), p. 2.

[69] Ibid., p. 8.

[70] Ibid., p. 23n.

[71] Hook, Sidney. "The Failure of the Left." Partisan Review, X, No. 2 (March-April, 1943), p. 166.

[72] Ibid., p. 166.

[73] Ibid., p. 170.

[74] Ibid., p. 177.

[75] Hook, Sidney. The Hero in History; A Study in Limitation and Possibility. New York: The Humanities Press, 1950 (original, 1943), p. 188.

[76] Ibid., pp. 190-191.

[77] Ibid., p. 200.

[78] Ibid., p. 199.

[79] Ibid., p. 223.

[80] Ibid., p. 229.

[81] Hook, "The Future of Socialism," op. cit., p. 24.

[82] Ibid., p. 25.

[83] Ibid., pp. 26-27.

[84] Thomas, Norman. "An Open Letter to Bertrand Russell." New Leader, XL, No. 1 (Jan. 7, 1957), p. 16.

[85] Hook, Sidney. "Abraham Lincoln, American Pragmatist." New Leader, XL, No. 11 (March 18, 1957), p. 18.

[86] Hook, Sidney. "The Atom and Human Wisdom." New Leader, XL, No. 22 (June 3, 1957), p. 8.

[87] Hook, Sidney. "Socialism and Liberation." Partisan Review, XXIV, No. 4 (Fall, 1957), p. 498.

[88] Hook, Sidney. "The Old Liberalism and the New Conservatism." New Leader, XL, No. 27 (July 8, 1957), p. 7.

[89] Ibid., p. 8.

[90] Hook, Sidney. "Socialism and Democracy." New Leader, XLI, No. 40 (November 3, 1958), p. 17.

[91] Hook, "What's Left of Karl Marx," op. cit., p. 58.

[92] Hook, Sidney. "The Cold War and the West." Partisan Review, XXIX, No. 1 (Winter, 1962), p. 24.

[93] Ibid., p. 25.

[94] Ibid., p. 26.

[95] Hook, Sidney. "Lord Russell and the War Crimes Trial." New Leader, XLIX, No. 21 (October 24, 1966), p. 11.

[96] Hook, Sidney. "Dear Editor." New Leader, XLIX, No. 25 (December 19, 1966), p. 28.

[97] Hook, "Dear Editor" (1969), op. cit., p. 16ff.

[98]   Hook, Sidney, et al. _Social Justice and the Problems of the Twentieth Century_. North Carolina State University, North Carolina: The William D. Carmichael Lecture Series, Spring, 1968, p. 22.

[99]   Ibid., p. 22.

[100]   Hook, Sidney. _Pragmatism and the Tragic Sense of Life_. New York: Basic Books, Inc., 1974, p. x.

[101]   Ibid., p. xvi.

CHAPTER 5

PROGRESSIVES AS PRESIDENTS:
THEODORE ROOSEVELT AND WOODROW WILSON

The Progressive Era saw the United States blessed with two scholars for Presidents. This is significant because they exemplify how Progressives thought and acted when, in fact, they were elevated to the position of highest political authority. With these Presidents Progressivism was tested at the highest level of practice. Theodore Roosevelt (1858-1919) was a well established writer and historian long before he became famous for leading the Rough Riders up San Juan Hill during the Spanish American War. In his spare time as a law student at Harvard Roosevelt researched and wrote the definitive history of the War of 1812; his books on the American frontier and wilderness still are classics. The only figure of the period to hold the office of President who was more academically qualified than Roosevelt was Woodrow Wilson (1856-1924). Wilson held a doctorate in political science and, before seeking elective office, was the president of Princeton. Thus the Progressive Presidents were more than capable of articulating the philosophical underpinnings of their respective platforms. Although they represented different political parties, and in spite of the fact that they were bitter enemies, it will appear that their common adherence to the Progressive label will be prefaced by a number of assumptions that they shared in common and with the Pragmatists.

In the opinion of Robert Wiebe, Theodore Roosevelt was motivated primarily by his own interest in power and glory. In this interpretation Roosevelt was a Progressive simply because he and the Progressives could use each other symbiotically; for instance, the demand for strong "public management" was emphasized by both.[1] What Wiebe fails to understand is that Roosevelt appears to have accepted and believed in a large part of the Progressive ideology. At one point Wiebe notes that Progressivism was expansive mainly because of its optimism and ". . . even more from its faith in method."[2] Yet, without citing the name, the description that Wiebe gives of the method is that of Pragmatism.

Theodore Roosevelt combined practicality with a deep sense of duty. The emphasis on duty is shot all through his works; for instance in an article of

August, 1890 in the _Atlantic Monthly_ he stated that
educated people have a positive duty to go into public
life.[3] They have more ability than others to improve
society. Four years later he echoed James's moral
equivalent of war, saying "A politician who really
serves his country well, and deserves his country's
gratitude, must usually possess some of the hardy
virtues which we admire in the soldier who serves his
country well in the field."[4] Yet, after noting that
ideals are necessary for progress, he moved on to
explain that

> The actual advance must be made in
> the field of practical politics among
> the men who represent or guide or
> control the mass of voters, the men who
> are sometimes rough and coarse, who
> sometimes have lower ideals than they
> should, but who are capable, masterful,
> and efficient.[5]

In 1890 Roosevelt cited approvingly Frederick the
Great's musing ". . . that if he wished to punish a
province, he would allow it to be governed by the
philosophers."[6] Yet Roosevelt held strong philosophical positions -- all in the negative: he found
it easy to _reject_ most formal philosophical systems.
For example, in an 1895 review of Benjamin Kidd's
theory of social evolution Roosevelt took issue with
Spencerianism or social Darwinism, writing:

> . . . progress results not from the
> crowding out of the lower classes by the
> upper, but on the contrary from the
> steady rise of the lower classes to the
> level of the upper, as the latter tend
> to vanish, or at most barely hold their
> own. In progressive societies it is
> often the least fit who survive; but on
> the other hand, they and their children
> often tend to grow more fit.[7]

Roosevelt was a compassionate Darwinian. In 1900 he
had written approvingly of the fact that ". . . the
professors of the different creeds themselves are
beginning tacitly to acknowledge that the prime worth
of a creed is to be gaged by the standard of conduct it
exacts among its followers toward their fellows."[8]
In 1899 he declared, "One thing I believe that we are
realizing more and more, that is the valuelessness of

126

mere virtue that does not take a tangible and efficient shape."[9]

The explanation behind Roosevelt's seeming contradiction of a devotion to duty coupled to a repudiation of philosophy was a sort of practical humanism. As mentioned above, education produces a different kind of person, one so greatly advanced that he has a duty to his fellow human beings. Roosevelt belonged to an elite that expected to overcome ethnocentrism -- at least on the national level. Not only did he claim that the educated "do not really form a class at all,"[10] he also asserted that their political duty must be "disinterested."[11] If he had an objective marker of value it was health or well-being, usually measured in material terms, but adapting whatever was needed to achieve it. He said, "Fellow-feeling, sympathy in the broadest sense, is the important factor in producing a healthy political life."[12]

One of Roosevelt's foremost tools for producing the healthy political life was the myth of the People. During an address to the convention of the Progressive Party in Chicago on August 6, 1912 he shouted, "We Progressives stand for the rights of the people."[13] "The first essential of the Progressive programme is the right of the people to rule."[14] In fact, he was running in order to rule in their name. So he explained, "The administrative officer should be given full power, for otherwise he cannot do the people's work; and the people should be given full power over him."[15] Remember that Roosevelt exempted himself from being a member of, much less a spokesman for, any particular class or faction. In an address on September 14 of the same year he told his audience, "Our proposal is to increase the power of the people themselves and to make the people in reality the governing class."[16] In fairness Roosevelt did back the initiative, the referendum, and the recall when applied to "representatives" of the people -- although not to the President who was their spokesman. These representatives should be "experts" who thereby can "formulate a policy for our betterment."[17] His example in 1912 was Germany: "What Germany has done in the way of old-age pensions or insurance should be studied by us, and the system adapted to our uses . . ."[18]

Roosevelt exhibited jealousy toward anyone else who claimed to be the spokesman of the People. Although he gave addresses in Milwaukee, even praising the Wisconsin Progressives for showing the nation how politics should be carried on,[19] he never mentioned Robert La Follette by name. As for Woodrow Wilson, as early as 1890 Roosevelt called his ideal of parliamentary democracy a "queer freak;"[20] explaining that,

> The English, or so-called "responsible" theory of parliamentary government is one entirely incompatible with our own governmental institutions. It could not be put into operation here save by absolutely sweeping away the United States Constitution.[21]

The irony here is that Roosevelt came to accept Charles Beard's economic interpretation of the Constitution. After his defeat in 1912 he said, "The doctrine of the divine right of judges to rule the people is every whit [sic.] as ignoble as the doctrine of the divine right of kings; and this doctrine is now chiefly and powerfully upheld by the legal and financial representatives of privilege."[22] "We also hold with Abraham Lincoln -- and we and only we are the heirs of Lincoln's principles -- that the people are the masters of the constitution."[23] America's most famous Nominalist, John C. Calhoun, might have agreed with Roosevelt's 1912 campaign statements about the Supreme Court.

Yet, by today's standards -- or those of Herbert Croly and the young Walter Lippmann -- Roosevelt was not a radical. He accused Wilson of asserting only a "Platonic devotion to the purposes of the Progressive party"[24] because Wilson's notion of freedom was too negative -- freedom _from_ legal restraint. According to Roosevelt, when it comes to Wilson's "New Freedom," "The worth of any such phrase as this of our scholarly and well-intentioned President lies in its interpretation."[25] Still, what Roosevelt's economic program amounted to was regulation, not ownership of business. In the 1912 campaign he declared, "Our aim is to control business, not to strangle it . . ."[26] He anticipated the direction that Pragmatism would take with the analytic school of linguistic philosophy: after all, if "ownership" is the power to use and dispose of something, then what is "regulation" but a correlative of the presupposition of co-ownership by the government. Words are defined by their use or interpretation.

The above can be clarified by reference to a speech which Roosevelt delivered at the Sorbonne, Paris in 1910, where he took issue with Marxism:

> Character must show itself in the man's performance both of the duty he owes himself and the duty he owes the state. The man's foremost duty is owed to himself and to his family; and he can do this only by earning money, by providing what is essential to material well-being; it is only after this has been done that he can hope to build a higher superstructure on the solid material foundation; it is only after this has been done that he can help in movements for the general well-being. He must pull his own weight first, and only after this can his surplus strength be of use to the general public. . . . [C]ontempt is what we feel for the being whose enthusiasm to benefit mankind is such that he is a burden to those nearest him; who wishes to do great things for humanity in the abstract, but who cannot keep his wife in comfort and educate his children.[27]

Notice that, in criticism, he was quite capable of subordinating the myth of the People, "humanity in the abstract," to concrete individuals. Continuing,

> My position as regards the moneyed interests can be put in a few words. In every civilized society property rights must be carefully safeguarded; ordinarily, and in the great majority of cases, human rights and property rights are fundamentally and in the long run identical; but when it clearly appears that there is a real conflict between them, human rights must have the upper hand, for property belongs to man and not man to property.[28]

Again emphasizing language Roosevelt said, "Much of the discussion about socialism is entirely pointless, because of the failure to agree on terminology."[29] Speaking of the capitalism-socialism debate in general he elucidated,

It is quite impossible, and equally
undesirable, to draw in theory a hard
and fast line which shall always divide
the two sets of cases. This everyone
who is not cursed with the pride of the
closet philospher will see, if he will
only take the trouble to think about
some of our commonest phenomena. ...
Much of the discussion about socialism
and individualism is entirely pointless,
because of the failure to agree on
terminology. It is not good to be the
slave of names.[30]

In the November 18, 1914 issue of The Outlook
Roosevelt reviewed Croly's Progressive Democracy and
Lippmann's Drift and Mastery. He agreed that the
conservative Supreme Court had created ". . . a system
as emphatically undemocratic as government by heredi-
tary aristocracy,"[31] and joined Croly in attacking
the "theory of government by litigation."[32]

In practice the equal protection of
the laws meant unequal opportunity to
bring lawsuits, and government by law
was turned into government by corpora-
tions and political bosses. This
continued until observers of vision
finally became convinced that democracy
and legalism were incompatible.[33]

Still, one can speculate that had he seen the end
of the Twentieth Century, Roosevelt probably would
have agreed with Theodore Lowie's call for juridical
democracy and administration by experts. The difference is that Roosevelt was surrounded by conservative
judges.

Switching to Lippmann to compliment, Roosevelt
said,

Mr. Lippmann sees clearly, as does
Mr. Croly, that democracy cannot possibly be achieved save among a people fit
for democracy. There can be no real
political democracy unless there is
something approaching an economic
democracy. ... As Mr. Lippmann says,
the first item in any rational programme
for a democratic State must be the
insistence on a reasonably high minimum

130

standard of life, and therefore of pay,
for the average worker.[34]

This, of course, could be done with no more than some
regulation, such as minimum wage laws.

Roosevelt's criticism of Croly and Lippmann, as if
borrowed from Frederick Taylor, is that they do not go
far enough in emphasizing economic efficiency.

We cannot pay for what the highest
type of democracy demands unless there
is a great abundance of prosperity. A
business that does not make money
necessarily pays bad wages and renders
poor service. Merely to change ownership of the business without making it
yield increased profits will achieve
nothing. In practice this means that
when the nation suffers from hard times
wage-workers will concern themselves,
and must concern themselves, primarily
with a return to good times, and not
with any plan for securing social and
industrial justice.[35]

The justification he gives is that immediate betterment
always will persuade the average voter before the
seemingly non-Pragmatic question of the general good.
Roosevelt did not think of human beings as being perfectable. Moreover,

. . . only a wealthy state can spend
money sufficient to embody the reform
into law. There is no point in having property unless there can be an
equitable division of property. But
there can be no equitable division of
property until the property is there to
divide.[36]

The emphasis was on the notion that economic efficiency
simply had to take precedence over moral reform --
similar to Taylor's Pragmatic model of proper
administration.

After the Revolution in Russia Roosevelt called
Bolshevism an "evil phenomenon"[37] and publically
criticized the New Republic for supporting it.[38]
Obviously he never lived up to Croly's expectations.
Roosevelt was a Pragmatist of the will, but they saw

131

differently with regard to science. In many ways Croly and Wilson were closer philosophically, and yet Wilson was to give him even less to be happy about.

Woodrow Wilson went from advocating parliamentary government to seeing the Presidency as the voice of the people, all the people. According to Wiebe, "In a microcosm, he underwent the intellectual migration of his generation."[39] Still, one can agree that he was predisposed to accept several of the assumptions of Pragmatism. First, even more than Croly, he shared the view that an individual's freedom lies in knowing what will be the consequences of his actions. This was the message that he preached to his students. Then too like Croly, he applied Darwinism to politics, believed that laws lagged behind the advance of society, emphasized the importance of nationalism, and criticized the notion of mechanical government or Madisonian pluralism. Ultimately, Croly and Wilson shared the proposition which not even Roosevelt could accept -- to whit the denial of original sin, the belief that perfection is possible here on Earth. The difference between Croly and Wilson is that Wilson, like Roosevelt, put less emphasis upon the substructure or economic system and more emphasis on slow, gradual change. According to Wilson in 1912, "Now, the problem is to continue to live in the house and yet change it."[40] This, he said, will take "a generation or two," and then ". . . man can live as a single community, cooperative as in a perfected, coordinated beehive . . ."[41]

Wilson made explicit his Darwinian outlook in his Constitutional Government in the United States (1908: not his dissertation) when arguing against the structure of checks and balances:

> The trouble with the theory is that government is not a machine, but a living thing. It falls, not under the theory of the universe, but under the theory of organic life. It is accountable to Darwin, not to Newton. It is modified by its environment, necessitated by its tasks, shaped to its functions by the sheer pressure of life. No living thing can have its organs offset against each other as checks, and still live. ... This is not theory, but fact, and displays its force as fact, whatever theories may be thrown across its track. Living political

132

constitutions must be Darwinian in
structure and in practice.[42]

His commitment to gradualism was evident as early as
1898 when, in The State, he wrote:

> In politics nothing radically novel
> may safely be attempted. No result of
> value can ever be reached in politics
> except through slow and gradual develop-
> ment, the careful adaptations and nice
> modifications of growth. Nothing may be
> done by leaps. More than that, each
> people, each nation, must live in the
> lines of its own experience. Nations
> are no more capable of borrowing exper-
> ience than individuals are.[43]

Notice, like John Dewey, Wilson's emphasis upon
growth." (On the other hand, growth came so slowly for
Wilson that with his blessing racial segregation was
reintroduced to Washington, D.C. for the first time
since the Civil War.) Moreover, in the same work,
Wilson displayed the Pragmatists' characteristic of
having thought lag behind material circumstances:

> . . . the most ardent reformers have had
> to learn that too far to outrun the more
> sluggish masses was to render themselves
> powerless. Revolution has always been
> followed by reaction, by a return to
> even less than the normal speed of
> political movement. Political growth
> refuses to be forced; and institutions
> have grown with the slow growth of
> social relationships; have changed in
> response, not to new theories, but to
> new circumstances.[44]

Thus, in 1912 when Wilson identified himself as a
Progressive it was because circumstances demanded it.
In the past law had applied to business as done by
individuals, but now business was carried on by cor-
porations. Thus the law must change.

> I am . . . forced to be a progres-
> sive, if for no other reason, because we
> have not kept up with our changing
> conditions, either in the economic field
> or in the political field. ... We have
> not kept our practices adjusted to the

133

facts of the case, and until we do, and unless we do, the facts of the case will always have the better argument; because if you do not adjust your laws to the facts, so much the worse for the laws, not for the facts, because law trails along after the facts.[45]

If, in the quote above, one changes the word "law" to "theory" it reads almost exactly like a quote from James in defense of his Pragmatism. Continuing,

If your laws do not fit facts, the facts are not injured, the law is damaged; because the law, unless I have studied it amiss, is the expression of the facts in legal relationships. Laws have never altered the facts; laws have always necessarily expressed the facts; adjusted interests as they have arisen and have changed toward one another.[46] (emphasis added)

Making use of the myth of the People in the same argument Wilson defined "tyranny" as control of the law by entities other than the people:

By tyranny, as we now fight it, we mean control of the law, of legislation and adjudication, by organizations which do not represent the people, by means which are private and selfish. We mean, specifically, the conduct of our affairs and the shaping of our legislation in the interest of special bodies of capital . . . We mean the alliance, for this purpose, of political machines with selfish business.[47]

In a one sentence paragraph Wilson summed up his position as a Progressive: "All that progressives ask or desire is permission . . . to interpret the Constitution according to the Darwinian principle; all they ask is recognition of the fact that a nation is a living thing and not a machine."[48] Wilson, like Roosevelt, was more consistent as a Pragmatist than was Croly. After all, the liberation from the contemporary "Newtonian" or automatic theory of government did not imply acceptance of the idea that socialism automatically would be either more productive or more humane.

134

In order to distance himself from Roosevelt, Wilson stressed evolution over radicalism: "Now, movement has no virtue in itself. Change is not worth while for its own sake. If a thing is good today, I should like to have it stay that way tomorrow."[49] "I am not one of those who wish to break connection with the past; I am not one of those who wish to change for the mere sake of variety."[50] In what was certainly a successful act of damning an opponent by caricature, Wilson claimed that other politicians were those ". . . whose conception of greatness was to be forever frantically doing something."[51] Whereas he said of himself, "If I did not believe that to be progressive was to preserve the essentials of our institutions, I for one could not be a progressive."[52]

It is apparent that Wilson's campaign strategy in 1912 was both to be a Progressive and to capture the electorate that was put off by radicalism. Yet philosophically he was even more of a Pragmatist than Roosevelt. His gradualism had <u>perfection</u> as its goal, and his <u>faith in his mission</u> was what he used to sustain both his own efforts and those of his followers. As such, he was the embodiment of Progressivism. Even if Wilson lacked direct contact with James at Harvard he was still swept along by the current that carried the new intellectuals.

Although he is outside the focus of this dissertation, one might argue that Franklin Roosevelt was the President who most incarnated the principles of Pragmatism. The second Roosevelt graduated from Harvard in 1904 -- taking no psychology, and dropping out of his only philosophy class in the third week. Yet, according to James MacGregor Burns, "Wilson was Roosevelt's kind of Democrat -- clean, cultivated and progressive but not too progressive."[53] "While Wilson talked about following 'the vision,' about 'destiny,' about 'lifted eyes,' about America's duty, about Americans' dreams, Roosevelt was more pragmatic, more experimental."[54] This Roosevelt, as Burns sees it, became a Progressive because he was an "'original Wilson man,'"[55] and after Wilson's demise "He was still a Wilson man."[56]

Perhaps the best Pragmatists are not intellectuals. Like Nietzsche's heroes, they require a forgetful streak, an ability to discard theories and doctrinal limitations. In Burns's words, Franklin "Roosevelt was a nonintellectual -- a man who lived and thought on the skin of things."[57]

> Roosevelt distrusted the kind of doctrinaire and systematic thinking that was implicit in intellectual radicalism. Roosevelt, in fact, was an eminently "practical" man. He had no over-all plans to remake America but a host of projects to improve this or that situation. ... What excited Roosevelt was not grand economic or political theory but concrete achievements that people could touch and see and use.[58]

Perhaps without even being aware of it, he was the heir of the tradition of his cousin and of Wilson. For Roosevelt even the Great Depression could be lifted if only the country would dispel the myth of its own fear and have faith in its own ability. His programs were only experiments, but he was <u>doing</u> something. One more time in the words of Professor Burns:

> Roosevelt was too much of an opportunist and pragmatist to be catalogued neatly under any doctrinal tradition, no matter how broad it might be. ... His mind, open to almost any idea and absolutely committed to almost none, welcomed liberal and radical notions as well as conservative.[59]

When ruling ideas are fully accepted they often are not perceived as such -- they are seen for reality.

Perhaps also when Presidents govern Pragmatically they must be studied quantitatively: Which specific groups are benefited and how much? Another reason for such Nominalism, or emphasis on the individual parts of society, may be found in the administrative and economic advice given to the Presidents.

FOOTNOTES FOR CHAPTER 5

[1] Wiebe, Robert. <u>The Search for Order 1877-1920</u>. New York: Hill and Wong, 1967, p. 190.

[2] Ibid., p. 198.

[3] Roosevelt, Theodore. <u>The Works of Theodore Roosevelt, National Edition</u>, Vol. XIII, ed. H.

Hagedorn. New York: Charles Scribner's Sons, 1926, p. 36ff.

[4]   Ibid., p. 33.

[5]   Ibid., p. 29.

[6]   Ibid., p. 44.

[7]   Ibid., p. 227.

[8]   Ibid., p. 369.

[9]   Roosevelt, Vol. XIV, op. cit., p. 309.

[10]   Roosevelt, Vol. XIII, op. cit., p. 37.

[11]   Ibid., p. 46.

[12]   Ibid., p. 355.

[13]   Roosevelt, Vol. XVII, op. cit., p. 277.

[14]   Ibid., p. 258.

[15]   Ibid., p. 259.

[16]   Ibid., p. 310.

[17]   Ibid., p. 260.

[18]   Ibid., p. 269.

[19]   Ibid., pp. 327-328.

[20]   Roosevelt, Vol. XII, op. cit., p. 42.

[21]   Ibid., p. 43.

[22]   Roosevelt, Vol. XVII, op. cit., p. 354.

[23]   Ibid., p. 355.

[24]   Ibid., p. 306.

[25]   Ibid., p. 380.

[26]   Ibid., p. 272.

[27]   Roosevelt, Vol. XIII, op. cit., p. 514.

[28]   Ibid., pp. 515-516.

[29]   Ibid., p. 520.

[30]   Ibid., p. 520.

[31]   Roosevelt, Vol. XII, op. cit., p. 234.

[32]   Ibid., p. 234.

[33]   Ibid., p. 234.

[34]   Ibid., p. 237.

[35]   Ibid., p. 238.

[36]   Ibid., p. 239.

[37]   Roosevelt, Vol. XIX, op. cit., p. 350.

[38]   Ibid., p. 351.

[39]   Wiebe, op. cit., p. 217.

[40]   Wilson, Woodrow. The New Freedom: A Call for the Emancipation of the Generous Energies of a People. New York: Doubleday, Page and Company, 1914 (from the campaign speeches of 1912), p. 51.

[41]   Ibid., p. 51.

[42]   Wilson, Woodrow. Constitutional Government in the Unite States. New York: Columbia University Press, 1947 (original, 1908: not his dissertation), pp. 56-57.

[43]   Wilson, Woodrow. The State: Elements of Historical and Practical Politics. New York: D. C. Heath and Company, 1918 (original, 1898), p. 68.

[44]   Ibid., p. 534.

[45]   Wilson, The New Freedom: A Call for the Emancipation of the Generous Energies of a People, op. cit., p. 34.

[46]   Ibid., p. 35.

[47]   Ibid., pp. 49-50.

[48]   Ibid., p. 48.

[49]   Ibid., p. 38.

[50]   Ibid., p. 39.

[51]   Ibid., p. 39.

[52]   Ibid., p. 44.

[53]   Burns, James MacGregor. <u>Roosevelt</u>: <u>The</u> <u>Lion</u> <u>and</u> <u>the</u> <u>Fox</u>. New York: Harcourt, Brace and World, Inc., 1956, p. 47.

[54]   Ibid., p. 70.

[55]   Ibid., p. 48.

[56]   Ibid., p. 71.

[57]   Ibid., p. 243.

[58]   Ibid., p. 244.

[59]   Ibid., p. 238.

CHAPTER 6

ADMINISTRATORS AND ECONOMISTS:
FREDERICK W. TAYLOR AND THORSTEIN VEBLEN

The history of public administration in the United
States goes back at least as far as Thomas Jefferson.
Usually the first modern work to be cited in the area
is Woodrow Wilson's 1887 essay, "The Study of Administration," wherein the intention was to separate
partisan politics from the day to day questions of
management and organization. Although Wilson's essay
preceded the popularity of Pragmatism, given an intermediate step it may be said to have set the stage for
Pragmatists such as Luther Gulick who were advisors to
Franklin Roosevelt. The intermediate step was supplied
by Frederick Winslow Taylor (1856-1915), the pioneer of
time and motion studies who generally is referred to as
"the father of scientific management," or the founder
of the classical school. Here any particular system of
production takes precedence over the quality of personal leadership; in fact Taylor makes "leadership"
obsolete, only quantitative concepts are meaningful.

No one can best Taylor when it comes to maintaining that truth is the cash value of an idea. In
the 1911 edition of his Shop Management (1903) he
wrote,

What the workmen want from their
employers beyond anything else is high
wages, and what employers want from
their workmen most of all is a low labor
cost of manufacture. These two conditions are not diametrically opposed
to one another as would appear at first
glance. On the contrary, they can be
made to go together in all classes of
work, without exception, and in the
writer's judgment the existence or
absence of these two elements forms the
best index to either good or bad management. This book is written mainly
with the object of advocating high
wages and low labor costs as the foundation of the best management ... [1]
(emphasis original)

In 1912 in testimony before a committee of the
U.S. House of Representatives, Taylor accepted the

141

notion that science itself is defined as "classified or organized knowledge of any kind."[2] Theories as to how it should be organized were subordinated to practical concerns. His paradigm case of scientific management was simple enough for the average Representative to grasp: "the management of a first-class American baseball team."[3]

Of course in other speeches and writings Taylor was more subtle. In a speech of 1915 he revealed one of his methodological principles: his concrete example was the making of pig-iron, and the assumption was that whatever applies to such a simple case will apply also to something more complex. In Taylor's words, ". . . the presumption is that it can be applied to something better."[4] In sum, Taylor was a mechanical reductionist: complexity was only a matter of quantity.

More still, reductionism was a psychological principle for Taylor. After delivering a glowing report about how his time and motion studies had improved the output of the concrete trade, he claimed that the same methods could be applied to the more complex operations of a machine shop.

> After a few years . . . someone will be ready to publish the first book giving the laws of the movements of men in the machine shop -- all the laws, not only a few of them. Let me predict, just as sure as the sun shines, that is going to come in every trade. Why? Because it pays, for no other reason. . . . Any device which results in an increased output is bound to come in spite of all opposition, whether we want it or not.[5]

Notice that he is an optimistic epiphenomenalist. Modern society is internally driven to optimize itself. It is a felicitous "Marxism" without impoverization or the specter of revolution. It is peacefully and progressively evolutionary.

> Scientific management at every step has been an evolution, not a theory. In all cases the practice has preceded the theory, not succeeded it. In every case one measure after another has been tried out, until the proper remedy has been found. That series of proper

eliminations, that evolution, is what is
called scientific management.[6]

Every scientifically managed system of production
is under the controlling principle of mechanical
efficiency, not the thoughts of the workmen. From
Taylor's perspective, ". . . even the highest class of
mechanic cannot possibly understand the philosophy of
his work, cannot possibly understand the laws under
which he has to operate."[7] For this he gives a
number of illustrations to

> . . . make it clear that in almost all
> the mechanic arts the science which
> underlies each workman's act is so great
> and amounts to so much that the workman
> who is best suited actually to do the
> work is incapable (either through lack
> of of education or through insufficient
> mental capacity) of of understanding
> this science.[8]

In a sentence in 1911 that marked the great transition
from the old concept of leadership to the new concept
of management Taylor decreed, "In the past the man has
been first; in the future the system must be first."[9]
Leadership or motivation based upon character, even
great character, could not compete over the long run
with directions based on mechanical efficiency.
Workers were recognized for being but extensions of the
tools they operated.

Taylor often made the claim that his system elimi-
nated labor strikes. Strikes and disharmony had been
caused because the profit margin in industry never
had been enough to give both labor and management all
that they wanted. Basically, labor alienation amounted
to a dissatisfaction with the distribution of the
fruits of any particular section of manufacturing.
Taylor, however, solved the problem through abundance:

> The new outlook that comes under
> scientific management is this: The
> workmen, after many object lessons, come
> to see and the management come to see
> that this surplus can be made so great,
> provided both sides will stop pulling
> apart, will stop their fighting and will
> push as hard as they can to get as cheap
> an output as possible, that there is

no occasion to quarrel. Each side can get more than ever before.[10]

Thus, "There will never be strikes under scientific management."[11] (Of course any instance to the contrary merely proves that the management in that particular case was not really scientific.) After all,

> Every one of the complaints of the men have to be heeded, just as much as the complaints from the management that the workmen do not do their share. This is characteristic of scientific management. It represents a democracy, cooperation, a genuine division of work which never existed before in the world.[12]

Marx might not have envied such a managerial revolution because of the continued division of labor, but it appealed to Americans -- especially those with some higher education.

To his credit Taylor did not believe in human perfectibility, not even through his system -- just infinite amelioration. Like a good Pragmatist he admitted, "There is nothing in scientific management that is fixed."[13] "Scientific Management [sic.] makes no pretense that there is any finality in it. We merely say that the collective work of thirty or forty men in the trade through eight or ten years has gathered together a large amount of data."[14] The emphasis was on quantity, on what could be measured. Darwinian necessity would force industrialists to make use of that data, and the process would go on improving itself forever at a steadily increasing rate.

The father of scientific management was, of course, like most Pragmatists a great optimist. The noted exception to all that optimism was to come from the dismal science in the person of Thorstein Veblen (1857-1929). Veblen received his doctorate in philosophy at Yale in 1884 and, starting in the mid-1890's, served as an original member of the newly founded (and now famous) department of Economics at the University of Chicago. There he taught courses on agricultural economics, the history of economic theory, and socialism. Also, he edited The Journal of Political Economy. Needless to say, he was influential.

After the turn of the century the University of Chicago became a stronghold for the Pragmatists, and Veblen led the crusade to shift the reference of study from "spiritual" features such as natural laws to more measurable entities. In 1899 his paradigm of science was chemistry:

> In the modern sciences, of which chemistry is one, there has been a gradual shifting of the point of view from which the phenomena which the science treats of are apprehended and passed upon; and to the historian of chemical science this shifting of the point of view must be a factor of great weight in the development of chemical knowledge. Something of a like nature is true for economic science; . . .[15]

Veblen thought that economics had gone wrong largely due to Jeremy Bentham's pleasure-pain psychology[16] (wherein pleasures and pains are thought to be the sources or causes of human behavior), and that the better alternative was to be found in James's theory of acquired habits. Value is a "spiritual" notion and, according to Veblen, "The post-Bentham economics is substantially a theory of value."[17] Yet the Utilitarians got cause and effect backwards: "With Adam Smith, value is discussed from the point of view of production. With the utilitarians, production is discussed from the point of view of value."[18] The values of pleasures and pains do not cause production; rather, the modes of production and distribution cause pleasures and pains.

As are all Pragmatists, Veblen was a Darwinian. In his famous 1898 essay, "Why is Economics Not an Evolutionary Science?" he stated, "Economic action must be the subject-matter of the science if the science is to fall into line as an evolutionary science."[19] Again, a major reason why this change had not occurred earlier was because economists conceived of human beings in terms of fixed natures such as rationalistic maximizers or the hedonistic calculus. Instead, for Veblen, in the light of "the later psychology" ". . . it is the characteristic of man to do something, not simply to suffer pleasures and pains . . ."[20] "According to this new view . . . the activity is the substantial fact of the process . . ."[21] Thus, ". . . . an evolutionary economics must be the theory of a process of cultural growth as determined by the

145

economic interest, a theory of a cumulative sequence of economic institutions stated in terms of the process itself."[22]

Yet Veblen was not content to create a science of society. In fact in Veblen's special terminology "science" was to "technology" as "business" (useless money-making activity of the kept classes) was to "industry" (genuine productive activity). Moreover, it was business that, through the combined parasitic and predatory nature of its class, held industry back from achieving its potential. Like James and, indeed, with his help, Veblen pushed reductionism to its limit: Science itself was reduced to myth.

In 1906 Veblen asserted that modern "science" (as he used the term) is not distinguished even by its quantity of learning: for instance, "Among the savage and lower barbarian peoples" (he dripped sarcasm) there is a great deal of learning, especially myths, which has "no pragmatic value."[23] There, even when there is learning with true moral or pragmatic value ("industry"), there is no advance, no progress. At least in the West science and technology did reinforce each other somewhat, though nowhere enough. However Veblen witnessed that primacy "has passed from pragmatism to disinterested inquiry."[24] For Veblen, "disinterestedness" was a feature of the doings of the useless leisure class. it had no productive or industerious purpose.

At this point Veblen directed the reader to a footnote in James's Psychology (II, p. 640). Veblen did not bother to quote James directly, but turning to the great work it reads, "The aspiration to be 'scientific' is such an idol of the tribe to the present generation," claiming that ". . . it was invented but a generation or two ago. In the middle ages it meant only impious magic"[25] and it still means that in much of the world today. A span of sixteen years had passed since James had reduced science to magic (at least in Veblen's interpretation) to the time when Veblen could use this citation for political purposes. Given Veblen's many references to the new psychology it is clear that James was among his intellectual mentors.

Continuing, Veblen substitutes the word "pragmatism" for "technology:" "Pragmatism creates nothing but maxims of expedient conduct. Science creates nothing but theories. It knows nothing of policy or utility, or better or worse."[26] Veblen's sarcasm is so thick that he is difficult to interpret. Still, his opinion of the role of science and other myths comes through clearly; ". . . scientific inquiry proceeds on the same general motive of idle curiosity as guided the savage myth-makers, though it makes use of concepts and standards in great measure alien to the myth-makers' habit of mind."[27] "The name of science is after all a word to conjure with. So much so that the name and the mannerisms, at least, if nothing more of science, have invaded all fields of learning and have overrun territory that belongs to the enemy."[28]

In Veblen's mind pure science is destructive to the productive forces, as are the other myths of the leisure class. Science, for Veblen, is like what German philosophy was for Nietzsche, a deleterious fantasm causing German intellectuals to be born old with long grey beards. When applied to what should be acts of changing the world, "Scientifically speaking, these quasi-scientific inquiries necessarily begin nowhere and end in the same place; while in point of cultural gain they commonly come to nothing better than spiritual abnegation."[29] "But there is no intrinsic antagonism between science and scholarship, as there is between practical training and scientific inquiry. Modern scholarship shares with modern science the quality of not being pragmatic in its aim. Like science it has no ulterior end."[30] In other words, only production and its "technology" (or description) is objective, while all else -- theory, theoretical science, witchcraft, etc. -- are but the delusions and rationalizations of men who don't have to work for a living. Humans are capable of objective understanding only of what they themselves create.

The irony of Veblen's positon is that, in point of fact, he did hold a _theory_ of society and -- if only by strong implication -- a theory of the good society. For instance, speaking of science he concludes that "The normal man" will be "restive under its domina-tion."[31] As much as Veblen might like to hide behind his sarcasm, that was a value statement.

In 1919 in the preface to _The Vested Interests and the Common Man_ he wrote,

> The aim of these papers is to show how and, as far as may be, why a dis-crepancy has arisen in the course of time between those accepted principles of law and custom that underlie business

147

enterprise and the businesslike management of industry, on the one hand, and the material conditions which have now been engendered by that new order of industry that took its rise in the late 18th century, on the other hand; together with some speculations on the civil and political difficulties set afoot by this discrepancy between business and industry.[32]

The exposition of his philosphical position regarding law runs as follows: "It is evident that these principles and standards of what is right, good, true, and beautiful will vary from one age to another, in response to the varying conditions of life . . ."[33] The reason principles and standards vary is because they were of practical value in the settings in which they were generated. Although it is the common belief that they are "fundamentally and eternally good," in reality "they are of an institutional character and they are endowed with that degree of perpetuity only that belongs to any institution."[34] Unfortunately for most members of society, the social institutions tend to lag behind the more rapidly changing economic circumstances which produced them, and therefore come up against "the compulsion of a new range of circumstances."[35] "So soon as the conditions of life shift and change in any appreciable degree, experience will enforce revision of the habitual standards of actuality and credibility, because of the habitual and increasingly obvious failure of what has before habitually been regarded as an accepted fact."[36] Note his use of the epiphenomenal theory of mind. It used to be that horoscopes, witchcraft, the efficacy of prayer, and the divine right of kings were perceived as objectively real. So it is today with property rights. For Veblen, ". . . the axioms of law and custom that underlie any established schedule of rights and perquisites . . .," although stemming from "the material circumstances of the community" are always in themselves "of the nature of make-believe,"[37] or instrumental myths. Perhaps it was the fact that he saw through the myths of his society that Veblen was marginal man, the idols of the tribe were only impediments to him.

Yet there is a trace of optimism in the way that Veblen combines James with Marx. Veblen held with James that "History teaches that men, taken collectively, learn by habituation rather than by precept or reflection . . . "[38] The "matter of fact logic of

148

the machine industry and the mechanical organization of life" now forces men to see laws and customs in terms of their efficiency.[39] The "kept classes" are but an impediment to efficiency: "Such a vested right to free income . . . does not fall in with the lines of that mechanistic outlook and mechanistic logic which is forever gaining ground as the new order of industry goes forward."[40] Soon the "mechanistic conception of things" that goes with modern production will alter the "established system of rights, duties, properties and disabilities . . . to bring it all more nearly into congruity with that matter-of-fact conception of things that lies at the root of the late-modern civilization."[41] Thus the new order is on the verge of replacing the late-modern one.

Veblen's model for the future was for a time the Soviet Union, and he felt that the World Revolution had been suppressed by America's entry into the Great War. In 1919 he argued that "Bolshevism is revolutionary. It aims to carry democracy and majority rule over to the domain of industry. Therefore it is a menace to the established order and to those persons whose fortunes are bound up with the established order."[42] ". . . Bolshevism is a menace to the vested interests, and to nothing and no one else."[43] The "kept classes" everywhere hated the Soviets because they no longer could collect on their contracts with the Czar's government. In 1922 Veblen emphasized his belief that American participation in the Great War had been a conservative conspiracy, ultimately preserving the role of the "kept classes" instead of letting the war take its course and forever discrediting them: "The American intervention saved the life of the German Empire as a disturber of the peace, by saving the German forces from conclusive defeat, and so saving the rule of the kept classes in Germany."[44] Of course he was factually wrong, American forces turned the tide when Russia had collapsed and the Allies were exhausted, but Veblen's interpretation fit well with Veblen's theory of society. For Veblen the fear of Bolshevism was a result of a conspiracy of business interests to keep the workers disciplined and from facing their true situation.[45]

Veblen's Pragmatic Marxism comes across in his review of John Maynard Keynes's The Economic Consequences of the Peace in the September, 1920 issue of The Political Science Quarterly (XXXV). The Pragmatic criticism is that the language of the Treaty of Versailles does not reflect its consequences. Veblen found Keynes's analysis to be superficial, "His discussion, accordingly, is a faithful and exceptionally intelligent commentary on the language of the Treaty, rather than on the consequences which follow from it or the uses to which it is lending itself."[46] In the following paragraph Veblen explains how

> . . . the central and most binding provision of the Treaty (and of the League) is an unrecorded clause by which the governments of the Great Powers are banded together for the suppression of Soviet Russia . . . ... Of course, this compact for the reduction of Soviet Russia was not written into the text of the Treaty; it may rather be said to have been the parchment upon which the text was written. ... So this difficult but important task of suppressing Bolshevism, which faced the Conclave from the outset, has no part in Mr. Keynes's analysis of the consequences to be expected from the conclave's Treaty.[47]

Apparently Veblen viewed Marxism as a technology for the enhancement of industry, rather than as merely a (scientific) theory held by certain economists and intellectuals. Marxists were men of "technology" and "industry" as opposed to "science" and "business:" They were producers.

Veblen praised Woodrow Wilson for having the courage to pit morality against the international capitalist structure. Yet the strength of the economic system also accounted for why Wilson failed, and why so few people understood what a difficult task he had.

> Therefore, regretfully and reluctantly, but imperatively, it became the part of wise statesmanship to save the existing order by serving absentee ownership and letting the Fourteen Points go in discard. Bolshevism is a menace to absentee ownership; and in the light of events in Soviet Russia it became evident, point by point, that only with the definite suppression of Bolshevism and all its works, at any cost, could the world be made safe for that Democracy of Property Rights on

150

which the existing political and civil
order is founded. So it became the
first concern of all the guardians of
the existing order to root out Bolshevism at any cost, without regard to
international law.[48]

Still, Veblen's emphasis on the make-believe, on
words to conjure with, and on myths, is characteristic
of his intellectual environment and would have made him
suspect to orthodox Marxists. He was sarcastic in his
treatment of the status quo because he believed that
Utopia was physically possible, but he was pessimistic
because he was the first Pragmatist to see that the
ultimate human tool of language could be used quite
efficiently for nonproductive purposes. What he des-
perately longed for was a day when the myths of culture
would give way to the true rationality of technology
and industry, the day when he no longer would feel
alienated and restive. He appeared to dismiss the
notion that Bolshevism would produce its own myths.

What Veblen and Taylor shared in common was a
striving for industrious perfection, both mediated by
an avowedly Pragmatic denigration of theory. The
implication for those who followed them was to concen-
trate on a Nominalistic methodology, one that stressed
quantification and technique over understanding. The
great historians of the Progressive Era labored under
many of the same constraints.

FOOTNOTES FOR CHAPTER 6

[1] Taylor, Frederick Winslow. Shop Management.
New York: Harper and Brothers Publishers, 1911 (original, 1903), p. 22.

[2] Taylor, Frederick Winslow. "Scientific
Management" in Classics of Public Administration. eds.
Shafritz and Hyde. Oak Park, Illinois: Moore Publish-
ing Company, Inc., 1978, p. 18.

[3] Ibid., p. 20.

[4] Taylor, Frederick Winslow. "The Principles
of Scientific Management" in Classics of Organization
Theory. eds. Shafritz and Whitbeck. Oak Park, Illinois: Moore Publishing Company, Inc., 1978, p. 17.

[5]   Ibid., p. 15.

[6]   Ibid., p. 12.

[7]   Ibid., p. 20.

[8]   Taylor, Frederick Winslow. The Principles of Scientific Management. New York: Harper and Brothers, 1911, p. 41.

[9]   Ibid., p. 7.

[10] Taylor, Classics of Organization Theory, op. cit., p. 13.

[11] Ibid., p. 16.

[12] Ibid., p. 16.

[13] Ibid., p. 12.

[14] Ibid., p. 23.

[15] Veblen, Thorstein. What Veblen Thought; Selected Writings of Thorstein Veblen. ed. W. C. Mitchell. New York: The Viking Press, 1936, p. 41.

[16] Ibid., p. 93ff.

[17] Ibid., p. 95.

[18] Ibid., p. 96.

[19] Veblen, Thorstein. The Place of Science in Modern Civilization and Other Essays by Thorstein Veblen. New York: B. W. Huebsch, 1919, p. 72.

[20] Ibid., p. 74.

[21] Ibid., p. 74.

[22] Ibid., p. 77.

[23] Ibid., p. 7.

[24] Ibid., p. 19.

[25] James, William. The Principles of Psychology, Vol. II. New York: Dover Publications, 1950 (a reprint of the 1890 original by Henry Holt and Company), p. 640n.

[26] Veblen, The Place of Science in Modern Civilization and Other Essays by Thorstein Veblen, op. cit.,
p. 19.

[27] Ibid., p. 26.

[28] Ibid., p. 27.

[29] Ibid., p. 28.

[30] Ibid., p. 28.

[31] Ibid., p. 31.

[32] Veblen, Thorstein. The Vested Interests and
the Common Man ("The Modern Point of View and the New
Order"). London, England: George Allen and Unwin,
1919 (originally published as separate articles in The
Dial, 1918-1919), Preface: not numbered.

[33] Ibid., p. 3.

[34] Ibid., p. 4.

[35] Ibid., p. 5.

[36] Ibid., p. 7.

[37] Ibid., p. 33.

[38] Ibid., p. 15

[39] Ibid., p. 178.

[40] Ibid., p. 178.

[41] Ibid., pp. 11-12.

[42] Veblen, Essays in Our Changing Order. ed.
Leon Ardzrooni. New York: The Viking Press, 1934,
p. 400 (copyright renewed in 1962, reprinted here by
permission).

[43] Ibid. p. 402.

[44] Ibid., pp. 424-425.

[45] Ibid., pp. 446, 449.

[46] Ibid., p. 464.

[47] Ibid., p. 464.

[48] Ibid., p. 467.

CHAPTER 7

PRAGMATISM AND THE NEW HISTORIANS

Many researchers of the Progressive Movement in the United States assume that there is a connection between Pragmatism and Progressivism. Yet few are willing to make the connection explicit, other than acknowledging that they were contemporaneous. For instance, A. S. Link and W. M. Leary have compiled an extensive bibliography, The Progressive Era and the Great War, 1896-1920,[1] without a single mention of either Pragmatism or William James. Their only mention of John Dewey is Sidney Hook's 1935 biography. In The Pragmatic Revolt in American History (1959), Cushing Strout asserted that Pragmatism "stimulated"[2] both Charles Beard and Carl Becker, that Beard defended his undertakings in "characteristically pragmatic tones,"[3] and that Beard and Becker would have agreed with Dewey's factual-contextual relativism if they had read works such as his new logic. Strout uses the term "Pragmatic" in his title in a technical sense, one which he explicitly defines as a form of relativism.[4] Then, of course, he equivocates with the now common usage of the term in his work. Although Strout's Pragmatic Revolt is otherwise a good work, his treatment of the connection between Pragmatism and the historians of the Progressive Movement may be taken as typical: the family resemblance is taken for granted, influences are hinted at, but little is made explicit and no causal relations are established.

Both the Pragmatists and the Progressive historians shared an explanation of history. However, the best attempts to show the connection between the Pragmatists and Progressives have come from those who do not share their view of history.

George Novack is a Marxist philosopher and historian who, when discussed among other Marxists, is labeled a "Trotskyist." In 1937 he joined with Dewey in forming and carrying out The International Commission of Inquiry into the Moscow Trials for the purpose of clearing Trotsky's name. It was Leon Trotsky himself who suggested that Novack research and write a Marxist critique of Dewey's philosophy. In 1975 he published Pragmatism Versus Marxism; An Appraisal of John Dewey's Philosophy, the second chapter of which is titled, "Dewey and the Progressive Movement."

155

Novack sees the Populist-Progressive movement as one fifty year phenomenon; the reaction of a squeezed middle class which was seeking to maintain its position, a "loyal opposition" left wing of the capitalist regime. In Novack's eyes:

> The fundamental reason for the failure of Progressivism lay in the fact that it was truly progressive only in its incidental features. At bottom it was a retrograde movement which aspired to turn back the wheel of history and reverse the development of modern society.[5]

> Dewey belongs wholly to this movement. He was a foremost participant in many of its most important enterprises. In time he became the supreme and unchallenged theoretical head of the legions like Weaver or La Follette. He was rather the leader of the advanced intellectuals, those who worked out the theoretical premises and formulated the views and values corresponding to the mass movement in their various spheres of professional activity.[6]

In Novack's work Dewey and his brand of Pragmatism assume the position of highest intellectual importance. Novack tacitly accepts the position that the "defection of the intellectuals" (not his term) precedes a revolution and holds the Marxist position that it will be led by those who have been squeezed down from high positions in the capitalist power struggle. Thus Pragmatism, the American philosophy, was (and still is for Novack) a conservative force, bent upon upholding the crumbling system through reforms. A nation's philosophy is its ultimate distilled consciousness; hence, Novack alternatively sees Pragmatism as the tragedy of the middle class or as the instrument of class repression wielded by the upper class.

Novack fails to take account of Dewey's own periods as a socialist, his spirited defense of Trotsky and his view of the class nature of society. On this Dewey says, "The direct impact of liberty always has to do with some class or group that is suffering in a social way from some form of constraint exercised by the distribution of powers that exist in contemporary society."[7] Dewey also was noted for such statements as:

> The liberals of more than a century
> ago were denounced in their time as
> subversive radicals, and only when the
> new economic order was established did
> they become apologists for the status
> quo or else content with social patch-
> work. If radicalism is defined as
> perception of need for radical change,
> then any liberalism which is not also
> radicalism is irrelevant and doomed.[8]

Throughout the Thirties Dewey repeatedly called for the abolition of monopoly capitalism and the substitution of a planned economy in its place. Perhaps what Novack cannot forgive is that Pragmatism, as personified in Dewey, does not hold Marxism as the ultimate philosoph- ical truth, but as an option to be considered and evaluated in practice.

The Pragmatists and the New Historians were bound together in an attempt to break the grip of natural law philosophy on the U.S. judicial system. For instance, Holmes's Lochner dissent fits perfectly into the Pro- gressive Movement. In Lochner vs. New York (1905 -- 198 U.S. 45) a five to four decision of the U.S. Supreme Court held unconstitutional a New York law limiting bake shop hours to a maximum of ten hours a day. Holmes, who was a legal historian, countered:

> This case is decided upon an
> economic theory which a large part of
> the country does not entertain. If it
> were a question whether I agreed with
> that theory, I should desire to study it
> further and long before making up my
> mind. But I do not conceive that to be
> my duty, because I strongly believe that
> my agreement or disagreement has nothing
> to do with the right of a majority to
> embody their opinions in law. It is
> settled by various opinions of this
> court that state constitutions and state
> laws may regulate life in many ways
> which we as legislators might think as
> injudicious, or if you like as tyran-
> nical, as this, and which equally with
> this, interfere with the liberty to
> contract. ... The 14th Amendment does

not enact Mr. Herbert Spencer's Social Statics . . ., a Constitution is not intended to embody a particular theory, whether of paternalism and the organic relation of the citizen to the state or of laissez-faire. It is made for people of fundamentally differing views, and the accident of our finding certain opinions natural and familiar, or novel and even shocking, ought not to conclude our judgment upon the question whether statutes embodying them conflict with the Constitution of the United States.[9]

Three years later, in Muller vs. Oregon (1908: 208 U.S. 412), Louis D. Brandeis defended a similar statute before the U.S. Supreme Court. This time the dispute was over the constitutionality of an Oregon law prohibiting women in certain industries from working more than ten hours a day. In an abrupt turnabout the Court unanimously upheld the Oregon statute. Brandeis' approach was designed to minimize legal precedents and to stress the results of ruling one way or the other. He had no other choice since the major precedent, the Lochner case, was against him. So, in reality, his brief consisted of a sociological argument, and the "Brandeis brief" was to set a precedent for future appeals. In 1917 in Bunting vs. Oregon (1917: 243 U.S. 426) the Court in effect overturned the Lochner opinion by allowing the state of Oregon to apply the ten hour law to men.

Eight years before his Lochner dissent Holmes revealed his basis for it in his "bad man" or predictive theory of law. He said, "If you want to know the law and nothing else, you must look at it as a bad man, who cares only for the material consequences which such knowledge enables him to predict . . ."[10] "The prophecies of what the court will do in fact, and nothing more pretentious, are what I mean by the law."[11]

Morality (and natural rights) are not to be confused with law for Holmes, as evidenced by the fact that there are bad laws. "Manifestly, therefore, nothing but confusion of thought can result from assuming that the rights of man in a moral sense are equally rights in the sense of the Constitution and the law. ... No one will deny that wrong statutes can be and are enforced, and we should not all agree as to which were the wrong ones."[12] It is also worth noting that in some cases the statutes are, or will be, disregarded. Here he cites an example given by Louis Agassiz where the force of custom was so strong that no enforceable law could be made against it.[13]

Holmes believed that moral intent, or the state of mind of a defendant, is not actually a part of a legal decision.[14] Rather, it is the objective consequences of the defendant's actions that are in question.

Holmes says:

> The primary rights and duties with which jurisprudence busies itself again are nothing but prophecies. One of the many evil effects of the confusion between legal and moral ideas . . . is that theory is apt to get the cart before the horse, and to consider the right or the duty as something existing apart from and independent of the consequences of its breach, to which certain sanctions are added afterward. But, as I will try to show, a legal duty so called is nothing but a prediction that if a man does or omits certain things he will be made to suffer in this or that way by judgment of the court; and so of a legal right.[15]

The Pragmatic emphasis upon action and results is obvious.

In 1933 Morris R. Cohen wrote,

> It is a curious fact that while critics and reformers of the law formerly used to take their stand on self-evident truths and eternal principles of justice and reason, their appeal now is predominantly to vital needs, social welfare, the real or practical need of the times, etc. . . .
>
> The seed of the protest against the overemphasis of the logical element in the law was planted by Jhering and Justice Holmes over a generation ago.[16]

159

Cohen describes Holmes's view of the law as "an anthro-pological document"[17] and says that it could be attached to any modern "ism" such as functionalism or behaviorism. He says, "Holmes's position is, I judge, in perfect agreement with that of a logical pragmatist like Peirce: Legal principles have no meaning apart from the judicial decisions in concrete cases that can be deduced from them, and principles alone (i.e., without knowledge or assumption as to the facts) can not logically decide cases."[18] He could have made a better comparison of Holmes's theory to James's epiphenomenalism or spectator theory of motivation.

There are other historians, such as Richard Hofstader, who agree that the Progressives were orderly reformers, not revolutionaries. Reformers work within the given system. Hofstader says:

> The Progressive movement, then, may be looked upon as an attempt to develop the moral will, the intellectual in-sight, and the political and administra-tive agencies to remedy the accumulated evils and negligences of a period of industrial growth. Since the Progres-sives were not revolutionaries, it was also an attempt to work out a strategy for orderly change.[19]

Hofstader's appraisal of the origin of the Progressive Movement is similar to Novack's, but that in no way leads him to the same conclusions. One must believe that the basic system itself must be changed drastic-ally if he is not to agree with reform. For but one example of the orthodox historians George Mowry con-fronts the Marxist historians directly, saying, "The bald confident assertion of the New Left historians that big business shaped the Progressive program to its own interests seems highly erroneous . . ."[20] He substantiates his claim by going on to catalogue the struggles that took place between the Progressives and big business. Regarding the possibility of the over-throw of the whole system, he says:

> One other question raised by the New Left historians remains -- that revolving around their wistful, might-have-been statement that Progressive reforms drew off the necessary popular support for and therefore obstructed the growth of a viable democratic socialist

> party. To me, at least, that seems to
> be one of the more impossible fantasies
> of American history.[21]

The institutions of private property are too strong and ingrained, and the Great Depression and two world wars have not been cataclysmic enough to do what the Progressives were supposed to have only set back. It is apparent that the doctrinaire Marxists are wrong.

Another contemporary historian who sees a strong tie between the Progressive Movement and Pragmatism is David Noble. He writes, "It is my thesis that the point of view of the modern American historian is directly related to the world view of the English Puritans who came to Massachusetts."[22] This is the notion that the poeple made a pact with God (later changed to Nature and Nature's God, Reason) to remain simple and, thus, virtuous. This is a sort of natural harmony which, as long as it is preserved from artificial "alien complexities," will keep America safe from the sort of strife experienced by the rest of the world, especially Europe. The major historians of each generation are, thus, philospher-prophets, "Jeremiahs," crying out warnings. Since all history was that of artificial institutions, not of humanity itself which changes not at all, these historians could be termed as being "against history." As such, the historians within the Progressive Movement were concerned to help Americans to regain their lost virtue or to reground virtue with better knowledge. They were popular because the American people believed in their own virtuousness. History is written and used instrumentally.

Noble pointed out that in a 1913 essay of Carl Becker's, "Some Aspects of the Influence of Social Problems and Ideas upon the Study and Writing of History," Becker mentions Dewey and Pragmatism by name as a justification for the historian to select what he considers to be the important facts from the almost limitless chaos of facts.[23] Unlike Novack, Noble views the Progressives as using the Pragmatists, rather than being led by them. This is very similar to Strout's "skeptical relativism" (another technical term) which he uses to describe Becker. Strout says:

> Becker's answer to the problem of
> synthesis led him to the skeptical
> relativism that has made him such a
> controversial figure. He urged the

161

historian to accept for his own field
the implications of pragmatism, which
made truth and reality subject to
change. Did not pragmatism, he
asked, undercut the Olympian ideal of
objectivity . . .? It was necessary,
he felt, to analyze the process of historical reconstruction in the light of
this new outlook.[24]

Strout goes so far as to say that Becker substituted
will for objectivity. He says, "If thought and will
are identified, the pursuit of truth is debased by
practical aims, and action deprived of the necessary
guidance of knowledge. In giving such dangerous
primacy to the practical will, Becker was even more
pragmatic than pragmatism itself . . ."[25]

At this point it is worth reviewing what Dewey had
to say about the writing of history twenty-five years
later, in 1938.

> The formation of historical judg-
> ments lags behind that of physical
> judgments not only because of greater
> complexity and scantiness of the data,
> but also because to a large extent
> historians have not developed the habit
> of stating to themselves and to the
> public the systematic conceptual struc-
> tures which they employ in organizing
> their data to anything like the extent
> in which physical inquirers expose their
> conceptual framework. ...

> The slightest reflection shows that
> the conceptual material employed in
> writing history is that of the period in
> which a history is written. There is no
> material available for leading prin-
> ciples and hypotheses save the historic
> present. As culture changes, the
> conceptions that are dominant in a
> culture change. Of necessity new
> standpoints for viewing, appraising and
> ordering data arise. History is then
> rewritten.[26]

> Recognition of change in social
> states and institutions is a precon-
> dition of the existence of historical

162

judgement. ... Annals are material for history but are hardly history itself. Since the idea of history involves cumulative continuity of movement in a given direction toward stated outcomes, movement. History cannot be written en mass.[27]

　　All historical construction is necessarily selective. ... Further-more, if the fact of selection is acknowledged to be primary and basic, we are committed to the conclusion that all history is necessarily written from the standpoint of the present, and is, in an inescapable sense, the history not only of the present but of that which is contemporaneously judged to be important in it.[28] (emphasis Dewey)

He goes on to give as an example the fact that Herodotus wrote selectively what the Athenians wanted to hear. Dewey claims that historiographers must posit principles for guiding the selection of facts to emphasize and, in so doing, "The selection is truly a logical postulate as those recognized as such in mathematical propositions."[29] He says:

　　The notion that historical inquiry simply reinstates the events that once happened "as they actually happened" is incredibly naive. ... For historical inquiry is an affair (1) of selection and arrangement, and (2) is controlled by the dominant problems and conceptions of the culture of the period in which it is written.[30]

It would seem that during the quarter century since Becker cited Pragmatism Dewey found time to learn from Becker. The Instrumental use of history was just what Dewey, Becker and Beard had in mind. Dewey said: "A further important principle is that the writing of history is itself an historical event. ... The acute nationalism of the present era, for example, cannot be accounted for without historical writing."[31] He continues to say that Marxist history has significantly influenced history in the present also. Dewey held that, "Intelligent understanding of past history is to some extent a lever for moving the present into a certain kind of future."[32] He said:

History cannot escape its own process. It will, therefore, always be rewritten. As the new present arises, the past is the past of a different present. Judgment in which emphasis falls upon the historic or temporal phase of redetermination of unsettled situations is thus a culminating evidence that judgment is not a bare enunciation of what already exists but is itself an existential requalification.[33]

Thus, for Dewey, Becker was not substituting will for either logic or objectivity. For Dewey, the will is always an essential principle of any logical situation. Without going into a discussion of their truth or falsity, it can be seen that the relationship between the Pragmatists and the Progressives was a two-way affair. In this case William James had proposed a theory of perception and action, John Dewey had expanded it, Carl Becker had acted upon it and Dewey had come back to his rescue.

One of the most obvious characteristics shared by both Pragmatism and Progressivism is the notion of evolutionary progress. The Progressive historian James Harvey Robinson (1863-1936) had done advanced work in biology at Harvard and had studied under William James. He approached psychology from the standpoint of evolutionary biology as James did. Dorothy Ross says that, "Among all the social sciences, it was psychology that suggested to Robinson the central question the historian should ask: 'the great and fundamental question of how mankind learns and disseminates his discoveries and misapprehensions . . .'"[34] Robinson accepted the idea that the brain -- and thought -- was an instrument of adaptation.

However, evolution was more than just adaptive, it was progressive. Robinson added "faith" to evolution:

. . . I, for one, have faith that if we gave it a show, mere human intelligence, based upon our ever increasing knowledge, would tend to remedy or greatly alleviate many forms of human discontent and misery. This is a matter of faith, I admit. But holding this faith, the chief end of education seems to me to be

164

                    the   encouragement   of   a   scientific
          attitude of mind . . .[35]

His age had witnessed such amazing breakthroughs in
technology as to make his generation noticably different from the preceding one. Perhaps this can throw
light on his extravagant appraisal of science: "Science, in short, includes all the careful and critical
knowledge we have about anything of which we can come
to know the fundamental conception that controls
determination of subject-matter as historical is that
of a direction of something about."[36] (emphasis
Robinson) Like F. W. Taylor's, it was a quantitative
definition. Robinson sought to make history into a
science, thus actually helping in the progress of
history. He accepted the later Pragmatists' instrumental explanation of mind. The task was now to find
out what laws governed between man and nature that
insured causal patterns of adaptation. Then man might
control his history as he did his physical environment.
He said:

          Hitherto writers have been prone
          to deal with events for their own sake;
          a   deeper   insight   will   surely   lead
          us . . . to reject the anomalous and
          seemingly   accidental   occurences   and
          dwell rather on those which illustrate
          some   profound   historical   truth.   And
          there is a very simple principle by
          which the relevant and useful may be
          determined and the irrelevant rejected.
          Is the fact or occurence one which will
          aid the reader to grasp the meaning of
          any great period of human development
          or the true nature of any momentous
          institution?[37]

Robinson observes that there have been many sorts of
histories, "But the one thing that it ought to do, and
has not effectively done, is to help us understand
ourselves and our fellows and the problems and pros-
pects of mankind."[38] He calls this the most significant form of history. More important, the present
human condition is a result of past history, and does
not change as rapidly as it could if it were adequately
understood. The understanding is an instrument for
desired change or action. Robinson used the example of
an individual's history, which is responsible for what
he is doing at the present, to suggest that the collective consciousness of societies functions in the

same manner. This constituted a perfect instance of applying the Pragmatic view of mind -- the very heart of Pragmatism -- to history. Reform can only take place when the process that produced the present is understood. He explained:

> We must develop historical-mindedness upon a far more generous scale than hitherto, for this will add a still deficient element in our intellectual equipment and will promote rational progress as nothing else can do. The present has hitherto been the willing victim of the past; the time has now come when it should turn on the past and exploit it in the interests of advance.

> The "New History" is escaping from the limitations formerly imposed upon the study of the past. It will come in time consciously to meet our daily needs; it will come in time to avail itself of all those discoveries that are being made about mankind by anthropologists, economists, psychologists and sociologists -- discoveries which during the past fifty years have served to revolutionize our idea of the origin, progress and prospects of our race.[39]

Robinson cites Karl Marx as being among the earliest who ". . . denounced those who discover the birthplace of history in the shifting clouds of heaven instead of in the hard, daily work on earth."[40] Although Robinson denied that Marx's economic theory accounted for everything, he was greatly impressed by the fruits of his new method as well as its origin, and considered it a great advance over all past methods. Like Marx, Robinson saw that the historian should be the one who studies all knowledge as a whole, he advocates becoming the historian-philosopher: ". . . specialization would lead to the most absurd results if there were not some one to study the process as a whole; and that some one is the historian."[41] In effect, such an historian becomes the only legitimate philospher, taking a God's-eye-view of the results of all knowledge. The fact is that the specialist, by his nature as a specialist, is unable to trace all the effects and interrelations of his particular discipline. This faith in progress

166

becomes even stronger in Charles Beard. Beard defines progress:

> Briefly defined, it implies that mankind, by making use of science and investigation, can progressively emancipate itself from plagues, famines, and social disasters, and subjugate the materials and forces of the earth to the purpose of the good life -- here and now.[42]

> In substance, it is a theory that the lot of mankind on this earth can be continually improved by the attainment of exact knowledge and the subjugation of the material world to the requirements of human welfare. Associated with it are many subsidiary concepts. Its controlling interest is in this earth, in our own time, not in a remote heaven to be attained after death. It assumes an indefinite future and plans for greater security, health, comfort, and beauty in the coming years. While a philosophy of history, it is also a gospel of futurism.[43]

He goes on to make the Hegelian move of identifying progress with rationality itself.[44] This Hegelian strain becomes even more evident as he uses art and architecture to illustrate the Zeitgeist from culture to culture, saying, "All branches of civilization mirror the dominant idea."[45]

"Hegelianism" was alive and well then as it is today. David Noble makes the remark that, "Our final vision of the frontier is that which came from the Europe of Rousseau and Hegel."[46] From Rousseau came the connection of virtue with naturalism and simplicity, and from Hegel came the notion of an unfolding national destiny. If Noble had followed up this last notion he might have gained a great deal. Pragmatism, like Marxism, can be looked on as a version of Hegelianism, a highly Nominalistic variation. Progress is certain, but its explanation is subject to perpetual revision.

Dewey was a metaphysical Idealist for a good part of his life before he converted, through James, to Pragmatism. His Idealism may be termed "Hegelian" in

167

that it was progressive, and it was not held in order to contemplate a realm of perfect eternal forms. In the 1880's he was busy defining such things as the will as "the self realizing itself."[47] When he converted to Pragmatism he took much of his former psychology with him. Today's "progressive" education's preoccupation with "growth" and "self-realization" is in large part traceable to Dewey's years as a "Hegelian."

Probably the most famous "Hegelian" in the history of thought is Karl Marx. When Marx stood Hegel on his head he merely substituted History or Matter in motion for God. The dialectical interpenetration of opposites, by itself, is no less mysterious without God, Spirit or Reason. After making consciousness an effect of matter in motion, Marx began to search for historical laws, or regularities to explain the progressive movement of history. Of course the best known of these is his dialectical materialism. The key to Marxist psychology is Marx's statement that, "It is not the consciousness of men that determines their existence, but their social existence that determines their consciousness."[48] Man is matter become conscious and, up until Marx, that consciousness was merely an epiphenomenal reflection of that matter. Now that Marx had discovered man's true history he could become "self-knowing" for the first time. For the Marxists only the economist-philosopher and the historian-philosopher can adequately perceive the human estate.

For the Pragmatist the true human state is perceived by the psychologist-philosopher and the historian-philosopher. The conception of mind is basically the same for both the Pragmatist and the Marxist. The basic difference is that whereas Marxism tends to be a form of Continental rationalism in practice, Pragmatism takes its lead from British empiricism: for the Marxist reality must conform to his iron laws; whereas for the Pragmatist his laws must conform to reality, they must "work" in practice. The Hegelian factor in both systems is that they are "progressive." Evolution is not just change and adaptation, it is progress. It goes from the lower to the higher, to the more conscious and rational. This Hegelian faith in progress was common to the vast majority of the reformers of the Progressive Era.

What evidence there is shows that socio-economic determinism in America developed independently of Marx. Stow Persons says:

The materialist interpretation of history, a preoccupation with the economic basis of the class struggle, and the sense that society formed an interacting organic whole were naturalistic ideas independent of the particular formulation that Marx gave to them.[49]

The evolutionary anthropologists, who were historians in the broadest sense, were among the first to indicate the possibilities of a comprehensive interpretation of history.[50]

Lewis Henry Morgan is the perfect example here. His independent discovery of natural, progressive stages of economic evolution was often cited by Friedrich Engels.[51] The fact of Morgan's independent discovery gave Marxists proof that their data was scientific and objective. Beard is another good example. Persons says,

As early as 1916, Charles Beard had listed the names of those whom he regarded as mentors in the tradition of economic interpretation of politics: Aristotle, Machiavelli, Harrington, Locke, Madison, Webster and Calhoun. Marx's name was conspicuous by its absence, and many years later, when someone questioned him on the point, Beard readily conceded that Marx was, like himself, a collateral descendant of these same teachers. The omission of Marx had not been an oversight. The bond that united Simons and the Beards was not a common dependence on Marxism; it was a common participation in the basic presuppositions of naturalism.[52]

W. A. Williams makes the point that, "Beard never attacked private property as such, not even in the heyday of the Progressive movement or the New Deal."[53] Williams continues:

Those who call Beard a Marxian would seem to make the fundamental error of equating economic determinism with Marxism. Economic determinism is an open-ended system of causal analysis.

Marxism, as generally understood and as used by the critics of Beard, is a closed system of utopian prophecy. Beard tried to clarify the difference between these two systems by pointing out that the ancients, from Aristotle to James Harrington, had emphasized economic differences as a source of dynamic conflict and change.[54]

In conclusion, Williams quotes Lenin's statement that, "A Marxist is one who <u>extends</u> the acceptance of class struggle to the <u>dictatorship</u> <u>of</u> <u>the</u> <u>proletariat</u>,"[55] (emphasis his) and then reminds the reader that Beard never did so. This is why it was natural for Beard to look to Madison rather than Marx.

What produced the family resemblance among historians, sociologists, economists, anthropologists, educators and philosophers of the Progressive Era -- the New Academia -- now can be made explicit. It was the materialist-functionalist view of the human mind based on the theory of evolution, combined with a disguised Hegelian theory of progress. The philosophy of man -- what it is to be human -- is primarily a theory of mind. Virtually all the new social sciences and philosophy had converted from the view of mind as a changeless spirit which was capable of intuiting eternal truths, to one of mind as a tool of adaptation, itself still changing and in the making. The Hegelian idea of inevitable progress had lost its zig-zag dialectical quality in favor of lineal "stages" of development. Terms such as "manifest destiny" and "stages of self-actualization" are testimony to the American materialist adaptation of Hegelianism. The Chicago Pragmatists, Dewey, C. I. Lewis and George H. Mead, are distinguished by the fact that they worked longest and hardest on completing the theoretical aspects, the philosphy, of this view of man and nature. As Darnell Rucker puts it, "If psychology was initially subordinated to philosophy departmentally at Chicago, the tail may have been said to have wagged the dog."[56] T. A. Goudge agrees and adds, "The pragmatists were the first group of philosophers to work out in detail a philosophy of mind based on evolutionary principles. Moreover, since they were familiar with classical ideas in the field, they were able to assess the kinds of changes in those ideas which evolutionary principles required."[57]

The next two chapters document explicitly the changes in logic and the philosophy of mind that were made by the Pragmatists; the Nominalistic changes that succeeded in dropping terms such as "rights," "society," "nation," "mind," and even "concept" from the proper scientific vocabulary.

FOOTNOTES FOR CHAPTER 7

[1] Link, A. S. and Leary, W. M. eds. The Progressive Era and The Great War, 1896-1920. New York: Appleton-Century-Crofts, 1969.

[2] Strout, Cushing. The Pragmatic Revolt in American History: Carl Becker and Charles Beard. New Haven, Connecticut: Yale University Press, 1959, p. 14.

[3] Ibid., p. 100.

[4] Ibid., p. 9.

[5] Novack, George. Pragmatism Vesus Marxism: An Appraisal of John Dewey's Philosophy. New York: Pathfinder Press, Inc., 1975, p. 39.

[6] Ibid., p. 40.

[7] Dewey, John. Intelligence in the Modern World: John Dewey's Philosophy. ed. J. Ratner. New York: The Modern Library, 1939, p. 451.

[8] Ibid., p. 455.

[9] Kelly, A. H. and Harbison, W. A. The American Constitution; Its Origins and Development. New York: W. W. Norton and Company, 1970, p. 529.

[10] Holmes, Oliver W. "The Path of the Law." Harvard Law Review, Vol. X, No. 8 (March 25, 1897), p. 459.

[11] Ibid., p. 461.

[12] Ibid., p. 560.

[13] Ibid., p. 460.

[14]   Ibid., p. 463.

[15]   Ibid., p. 458.

[16]   Cohen, Morris R. Law and the Social Order; Essays in Legal Philisophy. New York: Harcourt, Brace and Company, 1933, p. 165.

[17]   Ibid., p. 203.

[18]   Ibid., p. 213.

[19]   Hofstader, Richard. ed. The Progressive Movement; 1900-1915. Englewood Cliffs, New Jersey: Prentice-Hall, Inc., 1963, pp. 2-3.

[20]   Mowry, George E. The Progressive Era, 1900-1920; The Reform Persuasion. Washington, D.C.: The American Historical Association, 1972, p. 35.

[21]   Ibid., p. 36.

[22]   Noble, David W. Historians Against History: The Frontier Thesis and the National Covenant in American Historical Writing Since 1830. Minneapolis, Minnesota: University of Minnesota Press, 1965, p. 3.

[23]   Ibid., p. 81.

[24]   Strout, op. cit., p. 38.

[25]   Ibid., p. 44.

[26]   Dewey, John. Logic, The Theory of Inquiry. New York: Holt, Rinehart and Winston, 1950 (original 1938), p. 233.

[27]   Ibid., p. 234.

[28]   Ibid., p. 235.

[29]   Ibid., p. 236.

[30]   Ibid., p. 236.

[31]   Ibid., p. 237.

[32]   Ibid., p. 239.

[33]   Ibid., p. 239.

[34] Ross, Dorothy. "The New History and the New Psychology: An Early Attempt at Psychohistory." The Hofstader Aegis; A Memorial. Elkins, S. and McKitrick, B. eds. New York: Alfred A. Knopf, 1974, pp. 220-221.

[35] Robinson, James Harvey. The New Humanizing of Knowledge. New York: George G. Doran Company, 1923, pp. 62-63.

[36] Ibid., p. 57.

[37] Robinson, James Harvey. The New History; Essays Illustrating The Modern Historical Outlook. Springfield, Massachusetts: The Walden Press, 1958 (original 1912), p. 15.

[38] Ibid., p. 17.

[39] Ibid., p. 24.

[40] Ibid., p. 50.

[41] Ibid., p. 67.

[42] Beard, Charles A. "The Idea of Progress." A Century of Progress. ed. C. Beard. New York: Harper and Brothers Publishers, 1933, p. 3.

[43] Ibid., p. 6.

[44] Ibid., p. 18.

[45] Ibid., p. 19.

[46] Noble, op. cit., p. 16.

[47] Dewey, John. The Early Works of John Dewey, 1882-1898, Vol. II. ed. G. E. Axtelle, et al. Carbondale and Edwardsville, Illinois: The Southern Illinois University Press, 1976, p. 357. See also preceding chapters.

[48] Marx, Karl. A Contribution to the Critique of Political Economy. trans. S. W. Ryazanskaya. New York: International Publishers, 1970, p. 21.

[49] Persons, Stow. The American Mind; A History of Ideas. New York: Holt, Rinehart and Winston, 1958, p. 325.

173

[50]   Ibid., p. 325.

[51]   Marx, Karl and Friedrich Engels. "Manifesto of the Communist Party." The Marx-Engels Reader. ed. R. C. Tucker. New York: W. W. Norton & Company, 1972, p. 335, n.b. Engels remarks here that he also dealt with Morgan in The Origin of the Family, Private Property and the State.

[52]   Parsons, op. cit., p. 329.

[53]   Williams, William Appleman. "A Note on Charles Austin Beard's Search for a General Theory of Causation." The American Historical Review; A Quarterly, Vol. LXII, No. 1 (October, 1956), p. 62.

[54]   Ibid., p. 63.

[55]   Ibid., p. 63.

[56]   Rucker, Darnell. The Chicago Pragmatists. Minneapolis, Minnesota: The University of Minnesota Press, 1969, p. 29.

[57]   Goudge, T. A. "Pragmatism's Contribution to an Evolutionary View of Mind." The Monist; An International Quarterly Journal of General Philosophical Inquiry, Vol. 57, No. 2 (April, 1973), p. 133.

CHAPTER 8

THE NEW LOGIC:
JOHN DEWEY AND ARTHUR BENTLEY

There is a controversy over the relationship between John Dewey (1859-1952), Progressivism, and the New Social Sciences. Marxists, such as the Stalinist, Harry K. Wells, claim that "Dewey's assertions are bald lies designed to conceal the fact that he is denying the possibility of a science of society."[1] "Dewey is indeed the high priest of bourgeois apologetics in the United States. He is the head salesman of theology."[2] From another corner Robert Wiebe dismisses the effect of Pragmatism on Progressivism, claiming that James was too much of an aristocrat and a psychologist to have influenced politics,[3] and that Dewey's Pragmatism was more akin to Hegelian Idealism than to anything suitable to pluralistic and bureaucratic politics.[4] On the contrary, the position pursued here is in agreement with Richard Rorty's finding in his Consequences of Pragmatism (1982): "Dewey made the American learned world safe for the social sciences. ... The American academy social order, and American philosophy became a call for reconstruction."[5] Thanks to Pragmatism, "If there is one thing that we have learned about concepts in recent decades it is that to have a concept is to be able to use a word, that to have mastery of concepts is to be able to use a language, and that languages are created rather than discovered."[6]

There is no doubt that Dewey was influenced by Hegel. Dewey's Psychology (1887) preceded James's by three years, and in it he held, "The unity of the self is the will. The will is the man, psychologically speaking."[7] Then in the same paragraph, after discussing self-realization, Dewey declared that "Will we have just seen to be the self realizing itself. ... Here will is seen to be self-determination. The will, in short, constitutes the meaning of knowledge and of feeling; and moral will constitutes the meaning of will."[8] Although it may be over stated, Sidney Ratner gives the generally accepted picture of the effect that James had on Dewey:

> The liberation of Dewey from neo-Hegelian idealism was due in large part to the impact of William James's The Principles of Psychology in 1890 on

175

Dewey's whole way of thinking and his
bedrock presuppositions. Reading James
was intellectually as revolutionary an
experience to Dewey as reading Charles
Renouvier's essay on free will had
been to James twenty years before.
... Dewey found especially congenial
that strain in the Psychology which
emphasized the objective approach to
psychology, based upon a biological
characterization of the psyche, as
against the more subjective view of
psychology as a theory of "consciousness" . . . The behavior-centered
psychological approach worked its way
more deeply into Dewey's ideas and
transformed his basic philosophical
beliefs.[9] (emphasis Ratner)

The overstatement is the impression given that James
caused Dewey to abandon his Hegelianism. It would have
been better to say that James turned it on its head by
giving it a biological basis: the will to "grow" and
to evolve still permeated Dewey's writings for over
half a century to come.

In 1909 Dewey defined "scientific thinking" simply
as "thinking that has proved fruitful in any subject."[10] His emphasis then, and in many articles
for the rest of his life, was to overcome "the magic
of words:"

. . . I would even go so far as to say
that only the gradual replacing of a
literary by a scientific education
can assure to man the progressive
amelioration of his lot. Unless we
master things, we shall continue to be
mastered by them; the magic that words
cast upon things may indeed disguise our
subjection or render us less dissatisfied with it, but after all science, not
words, casts the only compelling spell
upon things.[11]

In the April 6, 1918 issue of Croly's The New
Republic Dewey praised the willpower of British Labor
for not falling for ". . . the development of a lazy
automatism which assumes that as a matter of course
tremendous social changes, all tending to improve the
conditions of wage-earners, are bound to occur after

the war."[12] Labor in Britain and the U.S. will face the same obstacles with one great exception: "Our constitution will presumably be again in force after the war."[13] So, one of the tools which will help to overturn the old order is an education which exposes as "myths" the supposedly scientific principles which underlie that order: "The exposed myth is that the existing social order is a product of natural laws which are expounded in a rational, a scientific, way in the traditional sciences of society."[14] The war

> . . . has shown that our ordinary rationalizing and justifying ideas constitute an essential mythology in their attributions of phenomena to basic principles . . . [The results are,] . . . in short a historic accident. And in turn it appears that any science which pretends to be more than a description of the particular forces which are at work and a descriptive tracing of the particular consequences which they produce, which pretends to discover basic principles to which social things conform, and inherent laws which "explain" them, is, I repeat, sheer mythology.[15]

The present social crisis (1918) destroyed the myth of Laissez-faire and

> . . . reveals how little affairs have been effects of intelligent desire and direction. ... One may doubt whether William James foresaw how soon events would confirm his presentment that a substitution of pragmatic experimental-ism for the reign of rationalistic sciences involves an "alteration in the seat of authority."[16]

Continuing,

> The exigencies have shown that intelligence exists as an operative power. ... A centralized intellectual policy has been demonstrated to be feasible as well as imperatively needed. Empirical description of forces is not, then, the whole of the social science which should replace our rationalized

mythology. What is required is large
working hypotheses concerning the uses
to which these forces are to be put.[17]

Thus, in spite of his avowed Nominalism, Dewey was
calling for new social myths to be taught because
". . . a new social order cannot be built with the help
of a science inherited from an old social order."[18]

For three weeks in Croly's journal, the New
Republic, Dewey published an article titled "Political
Science as a Recluse." Here Dewey revealed his hatred
for the notion of science as knowing and understanding
phenomena. Political science of this nature is
cowardly, conservative, and reclusive. Of this sort
of political scientist: "His own standards (called
rational because they consist in a circle of logically
ordered concepts) expresses in effect only one of his
emotions -- personal aversion to change."[19] Thus
such a political scientist withdraws from society and
"social control becomes a matter of luck."[20] Dewey
shared with Veblen a curious ambivalence toward certitude. He found it impossible to doubt that there
should be "social control," but he had no fixed principles or limits for doing so. As he explained a few
years later, "Morals must be a growing science if it is
to be a science at all . . . because life is a moving
affair in which old moral truth ceases to apply."[21]
Obviously, such a science is an instrument of the will,
a means to attain what at any moment is desired.

For Dewey the pursuit of philosophy was not
engaged in for the discovery of truths or certitude.
Rather, its purpose was to unmask the beliefs of others
through showing their origins. In Context and Thought
(1930) he explained,

Philosophy is criticism; criticism
of the influential beliefs that underlie
culture; a criticism which traces the
beliefs to their generating conditions
as far as may be, which takes them to
their results, which considers the
mutual compatibility of the elements of
the total structure of beliefs.[22]

Thus, ". . . the finally significant business of philosophy is the disclosure of the context of beliefs
. . ."[23] A year earlier, in The Quest for Certainty
(1929) he had made clear his conception of "the true
object of knowledge:" "If we see that knowing is not

the act of an outside spectator but of a participator inside the natural and social scene, then the true object of knowledge resides in the consequences of direct action."[24] In short, ". . . consequences are the object of knowing . . ."[25]

The foregoing leads to Dewey's theory of human freedom, as expressed in Experience and Education (1938). Here, freedom is an intellectual quality, not just a property of movement, but primarily concerned with judgment.[26] Originally, as in the case of every sentient organism, there are "natural impulses and desires," but

> Thinking is stoppage of the immedi-
> ate manifestation of impulse until that
> impulse has been brought into connection
> with other possible tendencies to action
> so that a more comprehensive and coher-
> ent plan of activity is formed. ...
> Thinking is thus a postponement of
> immediate action, while it effects
> internal control of impulse through
> a union of observation and memory, this
> union being the heart of reflection.
> What has been said explains the meaning
> of the well-worn phrase "self-control."
> The ideal aim of education is creation
> of power of self-control.[27]

Impulse is not properly to be identified with purpose. For Dewey. ". . . freedom resides in the operation of intelligent observation and judgment . . ."[28] "The crucial educational problem is that of procuring the postponement of immediate action upon desire until observation and judgment have intervened. Unless I am mistaken, this point is definitely relevant to the conduct of progressive schools."[29] (If B. F. Skinner had come to the some conclusions his system would be a great deal more credible.)

There is a problem, however, in trying to square Dewey's conception of freedom with his notion of langu-age and logic. What is required is a perfect language or logic of discourse, but what standard can one appeal to in order to know that it is so perfected? In his Logic the Theory of Inquiry (1938) Dewey said,

> A sound or mark of any physical
> existence is a part of language only in
> virtue of its operational force; that

179

is, as it functions as a means of evoking different activities performed by different persons so as to produce consequences that are shared by all the participants in the conjoint undertaking.[30] (emphasis Dewey)

In his 1916 work, Essays in Experimental Logic, Dewey argues that in the past men's language biases had severed them from the world of experience. Then came the scientific revolution:

> The significance of experience was . . . that men would not put their trust any longer in things which are said, however authoritatively, to exist, unless these things are capable of entering into specifiable connections with the organism and the organism with them.[31]

The ground of language is experience and as Dewey said in his Studies in Logical Theory (1903), "The general logic of experience can alone do for the region of social values and aims what the natural sciences after centuries of struggle are doing for activities in the physical realm."[32] In 1916 he probably had in mind the philosophy of natural law when he lamented, "A creation of a world of substances or essences which are quite other than the world of natural existences . . ." is responsible for the continuance of social problems;[33]

> That such a cut-off, ideal world is impotent for direction and control of social change of the natural world follows as a matter of course. It is a luxury, it belongs to the "genteel tradition" of life, the persistence of an "upper" class given to a detached and parasitic life. Moreover, it places the scientific inquirer within that irresponsible class.[34]

The problem is that "Words tend to fix intellectual contents and to give them a certain air of independence and individuality."[35] Anticipating Ludwig Wittgenstein's last turn of linguistic philosophy, Dewey saw in 1916 that "There is, in truth, a certain real fact --existent reality -- behind both the word and the meaning it stands for. This reality is social

usage."[36]   Pushing   his   position   only   a   little
farther, Dewey explicitly equates ideas with "customs."[37] The culmination of his Experimental Logic
is an attack on the individual theory of mind and the
logic of the so-called social laws which apply to
creatures possessing such entities. Other minds are
never experienced directly, they are but inferred; and
"The dependence of mind upon inference . . . explains
the theories which, becuase of misconception of the
nature of mind and consciousness, have labeled logical
distinctions physical and subjective."[38] J. S. Mill
made this mistake. Instead,

> That an individual . . . performs
> the acts is to say something capable of
> direct proof through appeal to obser-
> vation; to say that something called
> mind, or consciousness does it is itself
> to employ inference and dubious infer-
> ence.   ...   [S]ave   as   mind   is   but
> another word for the fact of inference
> it cannot be referred to as its cause,
> source, or author.[39]

In his Logic the Theory of Inquiry (1938) Dewey
recapitulated his earlier progress, and then added,
"Personally, I doubt whether there exists anything
that may be called thought as a strictly psychical
existence."[40] (emphasis Dewey)

> The naturalistic concept of logic,
> which underlies the position here taken,
> is thus cultural naturalism. Neither
> inquiry nor the most abstractly formal
> set of symbols can escape from the
> cultural matrix in which they live, move
> and have their being.[41] (emphasis
> Dewey)

Humans learn thought and consciousness as they learn
their native tongues. Language

> . . . permeates both the forms and the
> contents of all other cultural activi-
> ties. Moreover, it has its own dis-
> tinctive structure which is capable of
> abstraction as a form. This structure,
> when abstracted as a form, had a de-
> cisive influence historically upon the
> formulation of logical theory . . .[42]
> (emphasis Dewey)

181

Now,

> . . . we shall consider . . . how a
> logic of ordered discourse . . . was
> taken to be the final model of logic and
> thereby obstructed the development of
> effective modes of inquiry into exist-
> ence, preventing the necessary recon-
> struction and expression of the very
> meanings that were used in discourse.
> For when those meanings in their ordered
> relations to one another were taken to
> be final in and of themselves, they were
> directly superimposed upon nature. . . .
> The result was that the belief that the
> requirements of rational discourse
> constitute the measure of natural
> existence, the criterion of complete
> Being.[43]

Here Dewey crosses the intellectual Rubicon, he unmasks
logic:

> . . . the meanings that were recognized
> were ordered in a gradation derived from
> and controlled by a class-structure of
> Greek society. . . . The scheme of
> knowledge and of Nature became, without
> conscious intent, a mirror of a social
> order in which craftsmen, mechanics,
> artisans generally, held a low position
> in comparison with a leisure class. . . .
> The historic result was to give philo-
> sophic, even supposedly ontological,
> sanction to the cultural conditions
> which prevented the utilization of the
> immense potentialities for attainment
> . . . instead of being subordinated to
> a scheme of uses and enjoyments con-
> trolled by given socio-cultural
> conditions.[44]

> . . . [T]he very fitness of the Aris-
> totelian logical organon in respect to
> the culture and common sense of a
> certain group in the period in which it
> was formulated unfits it to be a logical
> formulation of not only the science but
> even the common sense of the present
> cultural epoch.[45]

The old logic permeates society to the point of being "common sense," and it causes people to see and act upon supposed <u>qualitative</u> differences inherent in things.

> On the other hand, both the history of science and the present state of science prove that the goal of the systematic relationship of facts and conceptions to one another is dependent upon <u>elimination</u> of the qualitative as such and upon reduction to non-qualitative formulation.[46] (emphasis Dewey)

Thus Dewey has made an argument in favor of a strictly quantitative methodology.

In the old logic quantity was constantly changing, ephemeral, whereas the object apprehended by the mind had an immutable species quality. The old logic was based upon epistemological Realism: things had essential features. Seeing reality in this way, even critics and reformers such as J. S. Mill

> . . . have disastrously compromised their case by basing their logical constructions ultimately upon psychological theories that reduced "experience" to mental states and external associations among them, instead of upon the actual conduct of scientific inquiry.[47]

Aristotle still rules "common sense" but, for Dewey, real scientists take notice only of quantitative relations.

Anticipating Skinner's dictum relating behavior to its consequences, Dewey finds that "Reasonableness or rationality is, according to the position taken here, as well as in ordinary usage, an affair of the relation of means and consequences."[48] In 1949 Dewey wrote his last work on logic, co-authored with another man who was searching for a perfect language, Arthur F. Bentley. The two had carried on an extensive correspondence since 1932. In <u>Knowing</u> <u>and</u> <u>the</u> <u>Known</u> they said,

> It is our most emphatically expressed belief that such a jumble of references such as the word "definition" in

the logics has today to carry can not
be brought into order until a fair
construction of human behaviors across
the field is set up, nor until within
that construction a general theory of
language on a full behavioral basis has
been secured.[49]

The above passage was given a footnote which read:

We have already cited Skinner's
view that without a developed behavioral
base modern logic is undependable, and
we repeat it because such a view so
rarely reaches the logicians' ear. ...
Skinner's conclusion is that eventually
the verbal behavior of scientists
themselves must be interpreted, and that
if it turns out that this "invalidates
our scientific structure from the point
of view of logic and truth-value, then
so much the worse for logic, which
will also have been embraced by our
analysis.[50]

Arthur Fisher Bentley (1870-1957) was well known
in his own right as a Pragmatist, a Progressive, a
journalist, and as a political scientist. His The
Process of Government (1908) clearly embodies the
effects of Pragmatism on the Progressive Movement.
Bentley starts his book with the problem inherent in
trying to explain overt behavior by reference to inner
or mental states: e.g. the supposed reason for someone's rescuing a boy from a bully is the rescuer's
"sympathy." Yet sympathy is not observable and, for
Bentley, does not add any true explanatory value -- it
does not even appear to function in other cases which
should call forth more of the same emotion. After
citing several more examples he declares:

Why, in short, are some particular
forms of street and alley torture
suppressed and some immensely larger and
more common forms of public torture
erected into institutions? That pure
innate quality of soul, love, sympathy,
kindness, or whatever you wish to call
it, will have trouble in replying.[51]

Then Bentley poses the question of mind another
way. After enumerating a number of famous persons such

184

as Aristotle and Shakespeare, and then juxtaposing them with menial positions such as peasant and day laborer, he states, "We are apt to forget that all of these scales of valuation are relative; that, with but a sufficiently long sweep, there is no reason to suspect that even our firmest substratum of scientific knowledge would show the same relativity; . . ."[52] and anyone might be esteemed most worthy if judged under the right conditions. The terms "genius" and "ability" are but added after an approved behaviour and do not explain it.

Bentley uses James's terminology of mind and feeling "stuff" to discredit social actions in just the way that James employed it against the explanation of individual actions: "So long as such 'stuff' is used in explanation of the forms of our social actions on no better ground than that we assume changes in the 'stuff' form the mere fact of the changes in the action, then it is no explanation."[53] Bentley devoted 107 pages to his first chapter, "Feelings and Faculties as Causes" in an attempt to prove them to be irrelevant.

Then, in the first paragraph of Chapter II, "Ideas and Ideals as Causes," he stated, ". . . I am engaged simply in showing that the use of specific forms of soul-stuff gives us absolutely no help in interpreting the doings of social men."[54] The problem is to discover the source of ideas:

> When "ideas" in full cry drive past, the thing to do with them is to accept them as an indication that something is happening; and then search carefully to find out what it really is they stand for, what the factors of social life are that are expressing themselves through ideas. The thing to do is to try to become more exact, not to outdo the vagueness of popular speech.[55]

In the following chapter Bentley took another cue from James and located consciousness in the activities accompanying speech, saying ". . . nowhere could feeling and idea factors be located for themselves as apart from the activities they were appealed to to explain -- no where, that is, except in the speech activities of society."[56] Thus, for Bentley, consciousness, like politics, is a social product. The

185

implication now is that no man can hope to know others, or even himself, through his own effort. As Bentley explains,

> Certainly no man has any direct experience of the feelings or other mental states of other men. ... For myself, my observation indicates that so far from having direct knowledge of the soul states of other men, the truth is that I have next to none of my own. I know myself, so far as I have knowledge that is worth while, by observation of my actions, and indeed largely not by my own observations, but by what other people observe and report to me directly or indirectly about my actions.[57]

Notice that during James's lifetime and the Presidency of the first Roosevelt, Bentley set the academic stage for its emphasis on quantification. If men could not know the (natural) laws of the good society, then at least they could record what other men do. At the political level this becomes the study of how power is wielded -- although it is interesting to note that he saw nothing suspicious or spiritual in the notion of power or force. When it came to the concept of <u>power</u> Bentley suddenly became more of an epistemological Realist: the term "power" referred to something or a relationship, that was not just a convention. Bentley dodges this criticism with a smokescreen of words:

> The phenomena of government are from start to finish phenomena of force. ... I prefer to use the word pressure instead of force, since it keeps the attention closely directed upon the groups themselves, instead of upon any mystical "realities" assumed to be underneath and supporting them . . .[58]

Moreover, "pressure" can be measured and, "It is impossible to attain scientific treatment of material that will not submit itself to measurement in some form. Measurement conquers chaos."[59] As every graduate student in the social sciences today knows we have Bentley to thank for pointing out that "the raw material of government" is found only in concrete actions. People other than scientists can be concerned with the telos of government.

However Bentley was not really so stupid and this last implication bothered him greatly. So, from 1918 to 1920 he worked on a manuscript that, as some commentators have it, was designed to overcome the dichotomy between the professional and the philosopher. According to Sidney Ratner, "The significance of Makers, Users, and Masters to political scientists stems in part from its disclosure of Bentley as a person who demonstrated that he could be both a rigorous social scientist and a committed reformer."[60]

Like so many of his friends, Bentley saw the Great War as the beginning of an as yet incomplete Great Revolution. He argued that ". . . we are already far advanced in revolution. ... In short, our industrial government . . . is itself a revolution. It is a revolution not fully completed . . ."[61] Once begun he denied the possibility of a middle road of "palliative measures" which would alleviate the worst features of the current industrial system while leaving it essentially unchanged.[62] "Middle class intervention, no matter how radical, must then be regarded as more counter-revolution than as revolution."[63]

Yet Bentley maintained his identification with the middle class (apparently considering "class" to be a real quantity or force). "This book," he explained, "is, in its way, an attempt to find the heart of the trouble as it may be seen by middle class eyes."[64] "The essential fact about the middle-class man, for the political purposes of the immediate future, is that his interests as a consumer have become superior to his interests as a producer or appropriator."[65] Since the defining characteristic of the middle class is material acquisition, its counter-revolution against both the upper and lower classes must be

> . . . an aggressive but constructive and productive revolution, a peaceful political revolution -- the cure for destructive or throttling revolutions from other quarters. Such a revolution must be aimed directly at the appropriative uses of property and at the powers that have grown out of such uses. ... It must be a revolution that replaces, or, better said, completes political democracy with industrial democracy.[66]

Thus, instead of the Revolution ending in the universalization of the proletariate, it will end in the universalization of the middle class. The alternative is "a day of vengeance" inflicted by a lower class mob which will take down the middle class along with the appropriative class: "If the struggle of industrial autocracy and proletarian revolution runs its course, the middle class will become the trampled battleground of the opposing forces."[67] For this reason of self-interest the middle class is expected to ". . . abandon some of their powers of appropriation, because those very powers in the hands of the strongest appropriators have been elaborated until they overshadowed all our interest."[68]

As expected, Bentley's model was the way that the United States had been run during the Great War. Then the overriding goal was efficiency. As if incorporating F. W. Taylor into socialism, Bentley perceived that "If the essential thing for the nation is the best utilization of resources so as to get the greatest amount of service out of them with the least cost, . . . then the government can give it to us in peacetime as it did through its wartime unification."[69]

In 1924 Bentley led the Indiana section of the Progressive campaign for Robert La Follette. The same year he completed the manuscript for Relativity in Man and Society (1926). His aim was to do for the social sciences that Einstein had done for physics, and his method was to return to the attack on "mind-stuff." Nineteen-twenty-four was the year that Dewey's student, John B. Watson, published his Behaviorism, and Bentley was able to see the behavioral movement in perspective:

> As to mind, in the sense of mind-stuff, the psychologists long ago abandoned it. Likewise in its old categories, such as sensation, feeling, will, it has passed into decay. Through pragmatisms which have accomplished much, into behaviorisms which have accomplished more, the psychologists have come ever more to a study of action, events.[70]

Again speaking of psychology, "It has recently gone far towards identifying language and thought."[71] For Bentley, ". . . language and thought must be taken as one activity . . ."[72] Moreover, "The whole development of the study of society in the last fifty years has been a progressive elimination of the terms of individual consciousness and of all other terms of psychology as agents of interpretation of society."[73] Thus, "Little can be done until our knowledge is recast into explicit terms of activities . . ."[74] Of course he begged the question about who it was who cared or desired to do something.

In 1935, in Behavior Knowledge Fact, Bentley made another attempt to go from James's psychology to social science. In the opening sentence of the preface he said, "Knowledge, whether regarded as the wisdom of the individual or the accumulated intellectual treasure of the many, is always in some sense the behavior of men."[75] Whereas the history of individuality has proceeded from "soul," to "mind," to "person," to "body," all four categories are misdirected;[76] the real source of consciousness is social interaction and the "individual" is but a highly reified abstraction. "'Fact,' for science, is the reference it establishes for the most efficient language it uses. The frame of this language is observability."[77] Thus, for Bentley, "All science is description; we postulate this, and we hold strictly to the postulate."[78]

Given Bentley's ultimate scientific postulate social science would be rather bland. One example that he uses is the "concept of the State:"

> The word 'concept' reveals enough, since it is devoid of scientific signif- icance, and the men who use it have no technically definite understanding of what they mean by it. ... In none of them do we have it before us as an evident 'fact' in the way we have 'a dog' in direct observation and corre- sponding designation . . . ... The State is asserted to be a fact, but it is denied proper observability. ... No matter how elaborate are such discus- sions, the 'State,' about which they all center, is merely a word of confused survival from linguistic antiquity, in its applications primitive and inade- quate except for minor practical pur- poses. ... If the State is not 'factual' in some definite scientific sense, then the sooner we drop it from our direct objects of study, the better.[79]

The State was chosen as an example because it was so easy to make disappear:

> But what is true of the State in this respect is substantially true of the great body of presentations which social research has before it, no matter how vehement a denial may be here or there made. It is true of all the presentations that the science of economics has before it today. ... Or consider the case of 'crime.' ... The 'observational' is lacking throughout the social field; hence the 'factual' is lacking, and the word 'social' remains a word of chaotic reference, with no security of meaning.[80]

Bentley declares that the word "concept"

> . . . must be appraised as without any possibilities at all -- as indeed utterly hopeless for intelligible use. 'Concept' is a convenient word for use where one has no definite attitude as to what he is talking about, and it is a necessary word where the old mind-language is relied upon.[81]

A year later, in 1936, Bentley criticized the Logical Positivists for letting the word "concept" creep into their system. The word "concept" derives from the old language of 'consciousness' and 'mind,'"[82] which, he insisted, should be abandoned altogether. "The part it plays for logical positivists is therefore not unique, but merely sympotomatic of a disease of language, widespread in our era."[83] The significance here is that the Logical Positivists were among the most radical linguistic philosophers of their day: usually they are given credit for inventing the "verifiability principle" as a criterion of meaning-fulness; any sentence that is neither empirically verifiable nor a tautology, as in the case of defini-tions, is literally "non-sense." All ethical state-ments, ipso facto, are excluded -- as for instance, "It is wrong to lynch Blacks or to burn Jews." Needless to say within only a few years Logical Positivism was discredited by history. Yet Pragmatism, which showed itself to be far more radical, survived with but a few name changes.

The following chapter continues to trace the methodology of the famous "Chicago School," especially the linguistic sociology of G. H. Mead and C. I. Lewis.

FOOTNOTES FOR CHAPTER 8

[1] Wells, Harry K. Pragmatism: Philosophy of Imperialism. New York: International Publishers, 1954, p. 160.

[2] Ibid., p. 186.

[3] Wiebe, Robert. The Search for Order 1877-1920. New York: Hill and Wong, 1967, p. 151.

[4] Ibid., p. 152.

[5] Rorty, Richard. Consequences of Pragmatism. Minneapolis, Minnesota: University of Minnesota, 1982, p. 63.

[6] Ibid., p. 222.

[7] Dewey, John. The Early Works, 1882-1898, Vol. 2 (1887). Carbondale and Edwardsville: Southern Illinois University Press, 1967, p. 357.

[8] Ibid., p. 357.

[9] Dewey, John and Arthur F. Bentley. A Philosophical Correspondence, 1932-1951. ed. Sidnay Ratner, et al. New Brunswick, New Jersey: Rutgars University Press, 1964, p. 8 (from the introduction by Sidney Ratner).

[10] Dewey, John. Characters and Events: Popular Essays in Social and Political Philosophy, Vol II. ed. John Ratner. New York: Octagon Books, 1970, p. 774.

[11] Ibid., p. 774.

[12] Ibid., p. 733.

[13] Ibid., p. 734.

[14] Ibid., p. 735.

[15] Ibid., p. 736.

[16] Ibid., p. 737.

[17] Ibid., p. 737.

[18] Ibid., p. 738.

[19] Ibid., p. 731.

[20] Ibid., p. 731.

[21] Dewey, John. Human Nature and Its Conduct: An Introduction to Social Psychology. London, England: George Allen and Unwin, Ltd., 1922, p. 239.

[22] Dewey, John. Context and Thought. Berkeley, California: University of California Press, 1930, p. 221.

[23] Ibid., p. 222.

[24] Dewey, John. The Quest for Certainty: A Study of the Relation of Knowledge and Valuation. New York: Minton, Balch and Company, 1929, p. 196.

[25] Ibid., p. 197.

[26] Dewey, John. Experience and Education. New York: Collier Books, 1972 (original, 1938), p. 61.

[27] Ibid., p. 64.

[28] Ibid., p. 71.

[29] Ibid., p. 69.

[30] Dewey, John. Logic the Theory of Inquiry. New York: Henry Holt and Company, 1951 (original, 1938), p. 48. Reprinted by permission of C.B.S. College Publishing.

[31] Dewey, John. Essays in Experimental Logic. New York: Dover Publications, Inc.; an unabridged reprint of the 1916 edition by the University of Chicago, p. 62.

[32] Dewey, John. Studies in Logical Theory. Chicago, Illinois: The University of Chicago Press, 1903, p. 20.

[33] Dewey, *Essays in Experimental Logic*, op. cit., p. 71.

[34] Ibid., p. 72.

[35] Ibid., p. 186.

[36] Ibid., p. 186.

[37] Ibid., p. 187.

[38] Ibid., p. 419.

[39] Ibid., p. 421.

[40] Dewey, *Logic the Theory of Inquiry*, op. cit., p. 21.

[41] Ibid., p. 20.

[42] Ibid., p. 45.

[43] Ibid., p. 58.

[44] Ibid., pp. 58-59.

[45] Ibid., p. 65.

[46] Ibid., p. 65.

[47] Ibid., p. 81.

[48] Ibid., p. 9.

[49] Dewey, John and Arthur Fisher Bentley. *Knowing and the Known*. Boston, Massachusetts: The Beacon Press, 1949, p. 199.

[50] Ibid., p. 204 n51.

[51] Bentley, Arthur Fisher. *The Process of Government: A Study of Social Pressures*. Bloomington, Indiana: The Principia Press, 1949 (original, 1908), p. 7.

[52] Ibid., p. 7.

[53] Ibid., p. 18.

[54] Ibid., p. 110.

[55]   Ibid., pp. 152-153.

[56]   Ibid., p. 169.

[57]   Ibid., p. 187.

[58]   Ibid., p. 258.

[59]   Ibid., p. 200.

[60]   Bentley, Arthur Fisher. <u>Makers</u>, <u>Users</u>, <u>and</u> <u>Masters</u>. ed. Sidney Ratner. New York: Syracuse University Press, 1969 (manuscript began in 1918, and completed in 1920), p. xxiv (introduction by Sidney Ratner).

[61]   Ibid., p. 186.

[62]   Ibid., pp. 187-188.

[63]   Ibid., p. 186.

[64]   Ibid., p. 189.

[65]   Ibid., p. 190.

[66]   Ibid., p. 192.

[67]   Ibid., p. 223.

[68]   Ibid., p. 193.

[69]   Ibid., p. 231.

[70]   Bentley, Arthur Fisher. <u>Relativity in Man and Society</u>. New York: G. P. Putnam's Sons, 1926 (manuscript completed in 1924, the year he led the Progressive campaign in Indiana), p. 64.

[71]   Ibid., pp. 66-67.

[72]   Ibid., p. 68.

[73]   Ibid., p. 77.

[74]   Ibid., p. 197.

[75]   Bentley, Arthur Fisher. <u>Behavior Knowledge Fact</u>. Bloomington, Indiana: The Principia Press, 1935, p. V.

[76]   Ibid., p. 106.

[77]   Ibid., p. 217.

[78]   Ibid., p. 322.

[79]   Ibid., pp. 218-219.

[80]   Ibid., p. 220.

[81]   Ibid., pp. 305-306.

[82]   Bentley, Arthur Fisher. Inquiry into Inquiries: Essays in Social Theory.   ed. Sidney Ratner.
Boston, Massachusetts: The Beacon Press, 1954, p. 103.

[83]   Ibid., p. 103.

CHAPTER 9

SOCIOLOGY AND THE CHICAGO PRAGMATISTS:
GEORGE HERBERT MEAD AND CLARENCE IRVING LEWIS

World War I took the steam out of the Progressive
Movement in the United States. For a short time almost
the whole world was in philosophic retreat. Paul
Weiss, writing in The New Republic, credits the war for
leading to the final disillusionment with high-minded
speculation and ultimate truths, and for the subsequent
popularity of Logical Positivism. Of the latter he
says:

> This doctrine alone seemed to
> answer adequately to that far flung
> post-war spirit of disillusionment which
> so readily gave up the belief in fixed
> ideals and standards and the possibility
> of knowledge reaching beyond the here
> and now. "The Lost Generation" thought
> it better to strain for present clarity
> than for ultimate truth.[1]

The Pragmatists had moved their center to the
University of Chicago in the decade before the war.
For the next generation of English speaking professional philosophers everything was dominated by
linguistic analysis. Earlier, James had proven than
Pragmatism lent itself to linguistic analysis by
stressing what he had shown terms like the "Absolute"
to mean in practice. What was left for the academic
Pragmatists was to justify the connection between their
evolutionary psychology and a "scientific" way of
talking about the world.

In one respect Pragmatism had an advantage. Since
it is a philosophy of and for action, it could lay
claim to being both scientific and optimistic. In
spite of the fact that both G. H. Mead and C. I. Lewis
considered Josiah Royce to be their best professor at
Harvard they both rejected him in favor of a "scientific" philosphy of action. Now their task was to
upgrade and defend this philosphy against Royce,
Santayana, Russell and others. Mead and Lewis may be
thought of as those who were doing the precision work
for John Dewey, leaving him free to do popular works in
politics and education.

Action is the center around which the entire philosophies of Mead and Lewis revolve. For George Herbert Mead (1863-1931), intelligence is not properly designated as a characteristic of mind because it is merely the adaptation of the organism to its environment.[2] It is found in vegetables and unicellular forms. Rather, mind is an extension of intelligence, the basic ability of an organism to <u>act</u> or adapt for its own good. Mead makes a better example of the inversion of Idealism than Charles Beard does. In a preface to one of Mead's works Dewey says that not only was Idealism the dominant philosophy when Mead began his career, but that he considered Mead's entire philosophical development to be an outgrowth of his problem with the nature of individual consciousness.[3] Again, he had to square it with the fact that reality consisted ultimately of physical matter in motion.

In reaction to Henri Bergson, Mead objected that, "The unit of existence is the act, not the moment. And the act stretches from stimulus to response."[4] Any act is an adaptation of the organism to its environment. For Mead, "Thinking is a certain way of solving problems."[5] It arises only when the action is complex enough that direct or habitual action is blocked. Like John Watson, Mead implies that the organism is passive in its act of adjustment to the environment:

> A living organism has only such an environment as it can respond to in so far as it receives stimulations from it. Its environment, therefore, is bounded by the capacity of the organism to be affected by it through its various sense processes. Furthermore, the objects that exist in that environment are determined by the form of the responses of the organism.[6]

He explains that, "Consciousness is involved where there is a problem, where one is deliberately adjusting one's self to the world, trying to get out of difficulty or pain."[7] Without the possibility of action, thought and sensation are worthless. Mead's solution to the problem of mind-body dualism is to say that, ". . . pragmatism regards cognition as simply a phase of conduct, denying any awareness to immediate experience."[8]

John B. Watson (1878-1958) studied under both Dewey and Mead at Chicago. In his autobiography he states that he learned nothing from either one of them in class, but that he and Mead had a very good relationship when the latter would visit him in his animal laboratory. Mead and Dewey rejected Watson's <u>classical</u> behaviorism of the reflex arc because it did not account for conscious intelligence or planning. Also, it was too individualistic. However both had the highest regard for its "scientific" character of sticking with objective data. Mead said that, "Social differentiation is the function of what we call mental life . . . ; and behavioristic psychology is bringing this highest phase of organization among the members of the species within the pale of scientific contemplation and control."[9] He says that, "The opposition of the behaviorist to introspection is justified. It is not a fruitful undertaking from the point of view of psychological study. ... What the behaviorist is occupied with, what we have to come back to, is the actual reaction itself."[10] Mead explicitly and simply identifies meaning with response.[11]

Mead saw that Watson's animal behaviorism was capable of great extension. He said, "A behavioristic psychology represents a definite tendency rather than a system, a tendency to state as far as possible the conditions under which the experience of the individual arises."[12] Of his own psychology Mead said, "It is behavioristic, but unlike Watsonian behaviorism it recognizes the parts of the act which do not come to external observation, and it emphasizes the act of the human individual in its natural situation."[13] In discussing Watson, Mead claimed that it is impossible to <u>reduce</u> consciousness to behavior, but it is possible to <u>explain</u> it behavioristically. This is Mead's functional approach. He says that, "Mental behavior is not reducible to non-mental behavior. But mental behavior or phenomena can be explained in terms of non-mental behavior or phenomena as arising out of, and as resulting from complications in the latter."[14] He wrote:

> We want to approach language not
> from the standpoint of inner meanings to
> be expressed, but in its larger context
> of cooperation in the group taking place
> by means of signals and gestures. Mean-
> ing appears within that process. Our
> behaviorism is a social behaviorism.[15]

199

If Mead had stopped at that point he might have been known as the father of modern operant conditioning, and the connection between Pragmatism and Behaviorism would be explicit. As things are, B. F. Skinner has never mentioned his indebtedness to Mead. Perhaps this is because of Mead's "Freudian" behaviorism.

Mead was critical of Freud for the latter's excessive emphasis on sex, and found little that was good to say about him. However he accepted the notion that there were general biological reasons behind or governing most specific human actions. Mead says, "The good reasons for which we act and by which we account for our actions are not the real reasons."[16] David L. Miller suggests that Mead's "I" and "Me" are best explained in terms of Freud's Id and Superego.[17] Where Mead differs from Freud is that the "I" could never exist without the "Me," the generalized "other" adapted from Thomas Cooley's looking-glass self (where we learn our identity in terms of what other people tell us about ourselves). Man is strictly a social animal at the psychic level, and language is merely a form of learned behavior. The psyche is not a product of biology.

Also unlike Freud, internal conflicts between the "I" and the "Me" occur only when the structure of society is inadequate to meet the individual's problems. He does not accept Freud's idea that "free" man is necessarily in conflict with a society which is by nature restrictive. What Mead rejected in Cooley was the idea of starting with selves which, later took the attitude of other. Independent conscious entities were abhorent to him.

Mead's conception of the human psyche pivots upon language as the means for cooperation in action. He picked up the idea of the gesture from the physician-psychologist Wilhelm Wundt (1832-1920) while studying in Germany and modified it to suit his system. For Mead, "The Language symbol is simply a significant or conscious gesture."[18] The fundamental characteristic of a significant or conscious gesture is that it affects the speaker in the same way as it affects the one spoken to -- i.e., they both respond the same way and, hence, they share a common meaning. Thus he achieves his purpose and can say that, "The locus of mind is not in the individual."[19] "Psychologically, the perspective of the individual exists in nature, not in the individual. Physical science has recently discovered this and enunciated it in the doctrine of relativity."[20] He finds that relationships and responses are beginning to take the place of consciousness in both science and philosophy.

Language is the means of building the self or generalized other. Mead commented:

> We are, especially through the use of vocal gestures, continually arousing in ourselves those responses which we call out in other persons, so that we are taking the attitude of the other persons into our own conduct. The critical importance of language in the development of human experience lies in the fact that the stimulus is one that can react upon the speaking individual as it reacts upon the other.

> A behaviorist, such as Watson, holds that all our thinking is vocalization. In thinking we are simply starting to use certain words. That is in a sense true.[21]

His criticism of Watson is that Watson does not take into account the full social complexities of language. In short, Watson was a psycho-biologist rather than a socio-psycho-biologist. Vocal stimulation is also self-stimulation: "That is fundamental for any language; if it is going to be a language one has to understand what he is saying, has to affect himself as he affects others."[22]

> Only in terms of gestures as significant symbols is the existence of mind or intelligence possible; for only in terms of gestures which are significant symbols can thinking -- which is simply an internalized or implicit conversation of the individual with himself by means of such gestures -- take place.[23]

Thinking is a matter of talking to one's self, only it is a social product in that it is the individual's "I" which carries on a dialogue with him "Me" or social self, and even the "I" is a social product since it cannot exist without a "Me."

Mead sees clearly that, "It is necessary to pre-suppose a system in order to define the objects that make up that system."[24] Society provides that system through its language. Mead accepts the consequence that this makes reality and rationality a relative matter. He writes: "Now relativity . . . has not only vastly complicated the spatio-temporal theory of measurement, but it has also reversed what I may call the reality reference."[25] Mead used Einstein's theory of relativity in physics to argue to a theory of social relativity in consciousness.[26] He notes:

> Reason is the reference to the re-lations of things by means of symbols.
> . . .
>
> No individual or form which has not come into the use of such symbols is rational. A system of these symbols is what is called language, . . . It always involves, even when language makes thought possible, a cooperative social process. It is society that through the mechanism of cooperative activity has endowed man with reason. It is only through communication that meanings have arisen.[27]
>
> Language is ultimately a form of behavior and calls for the rationally organ ized society within which it can function. It implies common ends, and common ends are ipso facto rational ends.[28]

Striving for common ends -- doing and saying what those around one are doing and saying -- is being rational for Mead. There is nothing more objective than society to appeal to, Nominalism is triumphant. Change soci-eties and one changes realities.

At this point it is worth noting that the philo-logist, Edward Sapir (1884-1939), and his famous student, the linguistic anthropoligist, Benjamin Lee Whorf (1897-1941), were contemporaries of Mead at Chicago. Whorf says that:

> We cut nature up, organize it into concepts and ascribe significances as we do, largely because we are parties to an agreement to organize it in this way --

202

an agreement that holds throughout our speech community and is codified in the patterns of our language. The agreement is, of course, an implicit and unstated one, BUT ITS TERMS ARE ABSOLUTELY OBLIGATORY; . . .

We are thus introduced to a new principle of relativity, which holds that all observers are not led by the same physical evidence to the same picture of the universe, unless their linguistic backgrounds are similar, or can in some way be calibrated.

This rather startling conclusion is not so apparent if we compare only our modern European languages, . . . But this unanimity exists only because these tongues are all Indo-European dialects cut to the same plan, . . . [29]

The Sapir-Whorf hypothesis may be taken as the extreme position of linguistic relativity (at least as derived by social scientists). If they consciously owed any- thing to Mead they did not admit it. However the important point is that once consciousness is no longer seen as an independent entity, it must become relative to something. If one chose the behavioristic position -- either classical or operant -- that thought is accounted for by speech, and that speech is learned behavior, then it follows that thought and conscious- ness is a learned process, relative to the society and language group that teaches it.

B. F. Skinner says that, "Without the help of a verbal community all behavior would be unconscious. Consciousness is a social product."[30] Michael Polanyi writes:

All human thought comes into existence by grasping the meaning and mastering the use of language. Little of our mind lives in our natural body; a truly human intellect dwells in us only when our lips shape words and our eyes read print.[31]

Our native gift of speech enables us to enter on the mental life of man by assimilating our cultural heritage. We

203

come into existence mentally, by adding to our bodily equipment an articulate framework and using it for understanding experience. Human thought grows only within language and since language can exist only in society, all thought is rooted in society.[32]

David Miller claims that Mead,

. . . would agree with Wittgenstein that there can be no private language, that . . . the life of a word is in its use, but language is a social affair involving communication, that language is the vehicle of thought, that thoughts and ideas are not subjective . . .

Parts of The Blue Book, The Brown Book, and the Investigations read as if Wittgenstein had been communicating with the deceased Mr. Mead but had received only Mead's conclusions and not the experimental basis for arriving at them.[33]

Whether or not Whorf, Skinner, Polanyi, or Wittgenstein owe anything directly to Mead, it is obvious that they all arrived at similar conclusions concerning language. They all hold that thought is acquired via speech, that it determines the nature of one's thought and that ultimately it is a learned behavior similar to any other. Mind ultimately is located outside the organism, and the only reality that it can know is social.

C. I. Lewis (1883-1964) also stressed action as the basis for knowing. As Lewis states it, "The ruling interest in knowledge is the practical interest of action."[34] He continues by noting that,

The significance of conception is for knowledge. The significance of all knowledge is for possible action. And the significance of common conception is for community of action. Congruity of behavior is the ultimate practical test of common understanding. Speech is only that part of behavior which is most significant of meanings and most useful for securing human cooperation.[35]

Like Mead, Lewis finds that the key to the evolution of the human mind is the hand. Man's dexterious hands, his opposable thumbs, were better adapted for rearranging the world than anything any of the other animals possessed. All the senses are an extension of the sense of touch. This is what makes Lewis a Pragmatist since touching is used to manipulate the environment. Humans had the fortune of having an adaptive nervous system commensurate with their physical possibilities. Lewis finds the hand-brain situation to be of almost equal importance; he has a preference for viewing evolution as being organic rather than lineal. However he concludes that the hand must have preceded brain development, since men have yet to catch up with their potential for physical manipulation.[36] Thus the unique potential for human action is the genesis of the uniquely complicated human brain.

Also like Mead, Lewis sees that the common world, or common reality, is a social product created by the needs of cooperative action. He says:

> Our common understanding and our common world may be, in part, created in response to our need to act together and to comprehend one another. ...

> Indeed our categories are almost as much a social product as is language, and in much the same sense. It is only the possibility of agreement that must be antecedently presumed. The 'human mind' is a coincidence of individual minds which partly, no doubt, must be native, but partly is itself created by the social process.[37] (emphasis Lewis)

He says, "Our common world is very largely a social achievement -- an achievement in which we triumph over a good deal of diversity in sense experience."[38] One understands or anticipates what others are going to do, what are their wants and habits; and then must coordinate his actions with theirs, especially with regards to ends. He continues, "The sharing of a common 'reality' is, in some part, the aim and the result of social cooperation, not an initial social datum prerequisite to common knowledge."[39] Thus, to a large extent social action precedes and creates social awareness, as with Marx or Beard. After Lewis concedes that there must be some sort of preexisting common reality in order to entertain common action and common concepts, he continues:

> But both our common concepts and our common reality are in part a social achievement, directed by the community of needs and interests and fostered in the interest of cooperation. Even our categories may be, to a degree, such social products; and so far as the dichotomy of subjective and objective is governed by consideration of community, reality itself reflects criteria which are social in their nature.[40]

So far, Lewis sounds in agreement with Mead, Whorf, Skinner and Polanyi. However this is deceptive because Lewis has a different causal sequence. For Lewis social reality is a matter of cooperative action, and the stress is on physical action, not verbal.

For this reason meaning precedes language. The farthest that Lewis ever went in equating thought with language was an aside in which he added, "Also, we largely think in words . . ."[41] His usual position is closer to (early) James's: Lewis says, "Action precedes reflection and even precision of behavior commonly outruns precision of thought -- fortunately for us."[42] For Lewis it is the relationship of actions that are meaningful, rather than responses as with Mead. As if in response to Mead, Lewis retorts:

> Meanings are conveyed by language . . . But it would be doubtful that meaning arises through communication or that verbal formulation is essential. Presumably the meanings to be expressed must come before the linguistic expression of them . . . Also other things than language have meaning . . .[43]

He goes on to stress that certain fixed meanings are necessary to creatures which survive through their own behavior -- regardless of language. As if referring to Sapir and Whorf he argues:

> The linguistic use of symbols is indeed determined by convention and alterable at will. Also what classifications are to be made, and by what criteria, and how these classifications

206

shall be represented, are matters of decision. ... Nevertheless such conventionalism would put emphasis in the wrong place. Decision as to what meanings shall be established, or how those attended shall be represented, can in no wise affect the relations which these meanings themselves have or fail to have.[44]

Even though it is true that one's culture determines what aspects of reality its members will stress and be aware of, the relationships of these parts are objective and independent of human will. The whole system always conforms to rules and, unlike Whorf's formulation, those rules are objective. Action and, therefore, meaning takes place in the objective world of relations. Lewis transcends Nominalism:

The original determinations of analytic truth, and the final court of appeal with respect to it, cannot lie in linguistic usage, because meanings are not the creations of language but are antecedent, and the relations of meanings are not determined by our syntactic conventions but are determinative of the significance which our syntactic usages may have. Once we have penetrated the circle of independent meanings and made genuine contact with them by our modes of expression, the appeal to linguistic relationships can enormously facilitate and extend our grasp of analytic truth. But the first such determinations and the final test must lie with meanings in that sense in which there would be meanings even if there were no linguistic expression of them, and in which the progress of successful thinking must conform to actual connections of such meanings even if this process of thought should be unformulated.[45]

Lewis' conception of mind and consciousness is based in the action and survival of the individual organism, not necessarily society. Society -- a system of cooperation -- is a particular way of surviving, a later modification of the thought process; but the human psyche itself is not a social product. Even though matter at the thing-in-itself stage can be interpreted in many different ways, all of them functional, it is still the first thing to condition consciousness via the body that must survive in it. He realizes that "We must express meanings by the use of words; but if meanings altogether should end in words, then words altogether would express nothing."[46]

Lewis is careful enough to differentiate between the way something is expressed and what is expressed. He was also influenced enough by the Logical Positivists to believe that the verifiability principle was not incompatable with a Pragmatic philosophy of action. If action and survival were objective, then so is what can be said about action and possible action.

> The mode of expression of any analytic truths is thus dependent upon linguistic conventions; as is also the manner in which any empirical fact is to be formulated and conveyed. But the meanings which are conveyed by symbols, on account of a stipulated or customary usage of them, and the relation of meanings conveyed by an order of symbols, on account of syntactic stipulations or customary syntactic usage, are matters antecedent to and independent of conventions affecting the linguistic manner in which they are conveyed. ... The manner in which any truth is to be told by means of language, depends on conventional linguistic usage. But the truth or falsity of what is expressed, is independent of any particular linguistic conventions affecting the expression of it. If the conventions were otherwise, the manner of telling it would be different, but what is to be told, and the truth or falsity of it, would remain the same. That is something which no linguistic convention can touch.[47] (emphasis Lewis)

He could be so opposed to Sapir and Whorf because meaning (action) gives rise to objectivity rather than society. Lewis could even use this as a key to look for objective value, whereas Mead says, "There is no science in a statement of value."[48]

In the case of his famous "private language" problem Wittgenstein might have done better to read Lewis rather than Mead -- and perhaps he did, but no one knows. Simply stated, there is no common object or verifiability when one talks about a "private" sensation or the sensation in itself. A favorite passage of Wittgenstein's, often quoted by modern behaviorists is:

> The essential thing about private experience is really not that each person possesses his own exemplar, but that nobody knows whether other people have this or something else. The assumption would then be possible -- though unverifiable -- that one section of mankind had one sensation of red and another section had another.[49] (emphasis Wittgenstein)

Wittgenstein infers that there can be no use in referring to a sensation at the level of sensation itself; for another example he uses the sensation of greenness.[50]

Wittgenstein compares private sensations to a beetle in a box, a box which everyone has, and where no one can see into anyone else's box. Whatever is inside of it, if anything, does not really matter to anyone else. He says that, ". . . one can 'divide through' by the thing in the box, it cancels out whatever it is."[51] It is "irrelevent."[52] He appears to suggest that the sensation itself is not something which one informs others about. No one can give another any information about the qualitative aspects of his mental phenomena, in themselves. Any such description must rest upon what is objective, such as the agreement to call certain kinds of surfaces shades of the color blue; or else rest upon some connection with its natural expression, such as pain-behavior. What Wittgenstein has, here, for the information actually communicated is tendentiousness (similar to H. H. Price) in the case of the emotions. Also here he has linguistic agreement, or similarity of usage, in the case of objective qualities, such as the color red. Wittgenstein stresses that, "You learned the concept 'pain' when you learned the language."[53] (emphasis his) It is "new pain-behavior."[54]

Mead, the social behaviorist, was willing to say, "I see no reason to assume that, if a similar neural access to cerebral tracts were possible, we might not

share with others identical memory-imagery."[55]
Miller's interpretation that Mead would agree with
Wittgenstein on the impossibility of private language
is inaccurate because they were talking about different
things. For Mead there could be no private language
simply because language requires another person to
communicate with and to create language or consciousness. For Wittgenstein the notion of "private language" refers to the object of communication. When Mead
does refer to direct experience he either takes it
mechanistically, as above, or openly states that he
knows them to be different from individual to individual.[56] Thus he lacks the subtility of Lewis and
Wittgenstein.

Lewis says:

> It is one essential feature of
> what the word "mind" means that minds
> are private; that one's own mind is
> something with which one is directly
> acquainted -- nothing more so -- but
> that the mind of another is something
> which one is unable directly to
> inspect.[57]

> We can have no language for dis-
> cussing what no language or behavior
> could discriminate. And a difference
> which no language or behavior could
> convey is, for purposes of communica-
> tion, as good as non-existant.[58]

Lewis explains what he meant by a concept which is
"common to two minds:"

> The concept is a definitive struc-
> ture of meanings, which is what would
> verify completely the coincidence of two
> minds when they understood each other by
> the use of the same language. Such
> ideal community requires coincidence of
> a pattern of interrelated connotations,
> projected by and necessary to coopera-
> tive, purposeful behavior. It does
> not require coincidence of imagery
> or sensory apprehension.[59] (emphasis
> Lewis)

210

Like Wittgenstein, Lewis stresses the concept and the practical significance of the thing or state known. According to Lewis,

> We are concerned with two things in our practical understanding of each other -- with communication and with behavior. My concepts are, from the outside view of me which you have, revealed as modes of my behavior, including my speech.[60]

He continues the paragraph by remembering, "But it is not necessary that when we act alike we should feel alike . . ." (emphasis Lewis) For Lewis what is important to the psychology of purpose is the "relation between anticipation and realization," and it is only known through behavior. He asserts,

> The eventual aim of communication is the coordination of behavior; it is essential that we should have purposes in common. But I can understand the purposes of another without presuming that he feels just as I do when he has them. ...

> I do not need to suppose that either purposes in general or the content of this act in particular are, in terms of immediate experience, identical in his case and in mine, in order to "understand his purposes."[61]

For Lewis, "All meaning is relational,"[62] (emphasis his) and "Meanings are identified by the relational patterns which speech and behavior in general are capable of conveying."[63] Thus, even though the sensory content itself of one mind cannot be conveyed to another, the concept or significance of it is objectified by its relationship to the individual and society. This can be conveyed in speech. Not only were Lewis and Wittgenstein dealing with the same problem, but they reached very nearly the same solution; i.e., that the concept or significance of the phenomena could be objectified and transmitted through language.

That was Lewis' position in 1929, twenty-four years ahead of the publication of Wittgenstein's Investigations. By 1941 he adopted a new outlook; one

211

disavowing the verifiability principle and echoing James's The Will to Believe. He said, "All of us who earlier were inclined to say that unverifiable statements are meaningless -- and I include myself -- have since learned to be more careful."[64] Rather, he found that the belief in other consciousnesses has "empirical sense" even if it is not verifiable, saying: "We significantly believe in minds other than our own, but we cannot know that such exist. This belief is a postulate."[65] He found the belief in other minds to be similar to the belief in electrons and ultra-violet rays.

Lewis puts his final stress on language as the vehicle of education. Because of language humans do not have to learn everything by trial and error or repeat the mistakes of the past. It makes past action a species property.

> Language is . . . essential to that preservation of accumulated learning which is the root factor in the difference between human life and that of other species. It is an indispensable instrument of that continued and progressive human betterment which history reveals. ... Granted real communication, we are warranted in some confidence that there is nothing which is desirable to men at large, and is attainable by any, which will not be eventually shared by all; nor any common trouble which can be obviated by any from which all may not eventually be freed.[66]

He continues to the point of being utopian. Progress is continually accelerating because language has made social learning a cumulative product.

Both Mead and Lewis developed theories of mind as arising out of the action of an organism in its environment. For Mead language is the instrument which creates mind and consciousness, the internal dialogue. In Paul Weiss' words, "The late Professor Mead, though a professed pragmatist, was at heart a metaphysician."[67] Similar to the systems of Freud and Marx, to what could one appeal that possibly might prove Mead's theory wrong? For Lewis language is a tool of cooperation and social memory, but not something essential to the nature or existence of the human mind.

Rather, he showed what were the limits of using language to talk about consciousness, but did not discuss whether he assumes consciousness in itself to exist. As Weiss said of Lewis' Pragmatism in a 1930 issue of The New Republic, it is good work but it lacks an explicit formulation and criticism of the metaphysics which it assumes.[68]

Nevertheless, the formal philosophy of Pragmatism was kept alive, giving men such as John Dewey and Sidney Hook a respectable justification to call for radical change in society. In fact, an offshoot of Pragmatism, called the "behavioral movement," came to dominate the social sciences. Yet, what the Behavioralists and Weiss failed to note was that Pragmatists such as Lewis, Lippman and Hook had transcended the relativism which was essential to its founders. Lewis was more than willing to grant the possibility of real communication. This communication, then, implies the conclusion that Pragmatism may be used to propose and test normative theories within the social sciences. The procedure would be to entertain certain Realist concepts as hypotheses to be subjected to possible falsification.

FOOTNOTES FOR CHAPTER 9

[1] Weiss, Paul. "The Year in Philosophy" The New Republic, CI (December 6, 1939), p. 204.

[2] Mead, George Herbert. The Philosophy of the Act. ed. C. W. Morris et al. Chicago, Illinois: The University of Chicago Press, 1959, p. 404.

[3] Mead, George Herbert. The Philosophy of the Present. La Salle, Illinois: The Open Court Publishing Company, 1959, pp. xxxvi-xxxvii.

[4] Mead, The Philosophy of the Act, op. cit., p. 65.

[5] Ibid., p. 79.

[6] Ibid., p. 403.

[7] Ibid., p. 657.

[8] Ibid., p. 360.

[9]   Ibid., p. 490.

[10]   Mead, George Herbert. Mind, Self and Society; From the Standpoint of a Social Behaviorist. ed. C. W. Morris. Chicago, Illinois: University of Chicago Press, 1934, p. 105.

[11]   Ibid., pp. 76, 78.

[12]   Ibid., p. 38.

[13]   Ibid., P. 8.

[14]   Ibid., p. 11.

[15]   Ibid., p. 6.

[16]   Mead, The Philosophy of the Act, op. cit., p. 480.

[17]   Miller, David L. George Herbert Mead; Self, Language and the World. Austin, Texas: University of Texas Press, 1973, p. 6.

[18]   Mead, Mind, Self and Society; From the Standpoint of a Social Behaviorist, op. cit., p. 79.

[19]   Mead, The Philosophy of the Act, op. cit., p. 372.

[20]   Ibid., p. 517.

[21]   Mead, Mind, Self and Society; From the Standpoint of a Social Behaviorist, op. cit., p. 69.

[22]   Ibid., p. 75.

[23]   Ibid., p. 47.

[24]   Mead, The Philosophy of the Present, op. cit., p. 40.

[25]   Ibid., p. 60.

[26]   Ibid., pp. 64-66.

[27]   Mead, The Philosophy of the Act, op. cit., p. 518.

[28]   Ibid., p. 518.

[29] Whorf, Benjamin. Language, Thought and Reality. Cambridge, Massachusetts: The M.I.T. Press, 1970, pp. 213-214.

[30] Skinner, B. F. Beyond Freedom and Dignity. New York: Bantom Books, 1972, p. 183.

[31] Polany, Michael. Knowing and Being. ed. Marjorie Green. Chicago, Illinois: The University of Chicago Press, 1969, p. 160.

[32] Polanyi, Michael. The Study of Man. Chicago, Illinois: The University of Chicago Press, 1960, p. 60.

[33] Miller, op. cit., p. 67.

[34] Lewis, C. I. Mind and the World Order; Outline of a Theory of Knowledge. New York: Dover Publications, Inc., 1956, p. 85.

[35] Ibid., p. 90.

[36] Lewis, C. I. Our Social Inheritance. Bloomington, Indiana: Indiana University Press, 1957, p. 25.

[37] Lewis, Mind and the World Order; Outline of a Theory of Knowledge, op. cit., p. 211

[38] Ibid., p. 93.

[39] Ibid., p. 115.

[40] Ibid., p. 116.

[41] Lewis, C. I. "Realism or Phenomenalism?" The Philosophical Review, LXIV (April, 1955), p. 234.

[42] Lewis, Mind and the World Order; Outline of a Theory of Knowledge, op. cit., p. 3.

[43] Lewis, C. I. An Analysis of Knowledge and Valuation. LaSalle, Illinois: Open Court Publishing Company, 1962, p. 72.

[44] Ibid., p. 79.

[45] Ibid., p. 131.

[46] Ibid., p. 140.

[47]   Ibid., p. 148.

[48]   Mead, The Philosophy of the Act, op. cit.,
p. 458.

[49]   Wittgenstein, Ludwig. Philosophical Investigations. trans. G. E. M. Anscombe. New York: The
Macmillan Company, 1970, p. 95.

[50]   Ibid., p. 96.

[51]   Ibid., p. 100.

[52]   Ibid., p. 100.

[53]   Ibid., p. 118.

[54]   Ibid., p. 89.

[55]   Mead, The Philosophy of the Act, op. cit.,
p. 377.

[56]   Mead, Mind and the World Order; Outline of
a Theory of Knowledge, op. cit., p. 33.

[57]   Lewis, C. I. "Some Logical Considerations
Concerning the Mental." Journal of Philosophy, 38
(1941), p. 226.

[58]   Lewis, Mind and the World Order; Outline of
a Theory of Knowledge, op. cit., p. 112n.

[59]   Ibid., p. 89.

[60]   Ibid., p. 102.

[61]   Ibid., p. 103.

[62]   Ibid., p. 107.

[63]   Ibid., pp. 109-110.

[64]   Lewis, Journal of Philosophy, op. cit., p.
232.

[65]   Ibid., p. 232.

[66]   Lewis, Our Social Inheritance, op. cit.,
p. 38.

[67] Weiss, Paul. "G. H. Mead: Philosopher of the Here and Now." The <u>New</u> <u>Republic</u>, LXXII (October 26, 1933), p. 302.

[68] Weiss, Paul. "Pragmatists and Pragmatists." The <u>New</u> <u>Republic</u>, LXII (March 26, 1930), p. 162.

CHAPTER 10

THE PRAGMATIC TEST OF PRAGMATISM

Just what would it mean if one were to claim that the American social sciences, especially political science, "worked" in practice?

To answer that question one would be forced to go beyond the empiricism that marks these sciences and into the sciences of ethics and metaphysics. The Marxists have had some measure of advantage here because they are consumate metaphysicians -- perhaps if they could separate the humanistic conception of man as a "species-being" from the mysterious notion of the dialectical interpenetration of opposites (and forget about the latter just as most Christians have the doctrine of predestination), then their humanism might be more appealing. On the other hand, it is possible that the myth of the dialectic reinforces the sense of certitude that is indespensible to the true-believer's eschatology. If this be so, then at least some contemporary "radicals" will be found to be but using Marxist rhetoric for Instrumental purposes.

Robert Heilbroner, for one, believes that the U.S. should promote the Communist myth in the Third World as the most efficient means for progress. "I begin," he says, "with the cardinal point . . . that the process called 'economic development' is not primarily economic at all."[1] The real problem is "backwardness"[2] or the mass of old social habits which are inefficient -- it is a psychological problem. Thus, addressing the problem of the "development" of a social structure, Heilbroner explains,

> It is rather modernization of that structure, a process of ideational, social, economic, and political change that requires the remaking of society in its most intimate as well as its most public attributes. ... The trouble is that the social psychology of these nations remains so depressingly unchanged despite the flurry of economic planning at the top.[3]

"But how to achieve haste? ... I suspect that there is only one way. The condition of backwardness must be attacked with the passion, the ruthlessness,

219

and the messianic fury of a jehad, a Holy War."[4]
Thus, for Heilbroner, ". . . the political force most
likely to succeed in carrying through the gigantic
historical transformation of development is some form
of extreme national collectivism or Communism."[5]

Notice that Heilbroner is a social nationalist in
a style similar to that of Herbert Croly: Heilbroner
can recommend Marxism because he believes that "diver-
gencies of national interest and character" may be
counted on to outweigh any sort of political unity
among states espousing Marxist rhetoric.[6] International Communism is but a myth, especially as countries
compete to modernize,[7] but it is a helpful myth:

> The leadership needed to mount a
> jehad against backwardness -- and it is
> my main premise that only a Holy War
> will bring modernization in our time --
> will be forced to expound a philosophy
> that approves authoritarian and collec-
> tivist measures at home and that uti-
> lizes as the target for its national
> resentment abroad the towering villains
> of the world, of which the United States
> is now Number One.[8]

As if speaking for Sorel, Heilbroner continues:

> Revolutions, especially if their
> whole orientation is toward the future,
> require philosphy equally as much as
> force. It is here, of course, that
> Communism finds its special strength.
> The vocabulary in which it speaks -- a
> vocabulary of class domination, of
> domestic and international exploitation
> -- is rich in meaning to the backward
> nations. The view of history it espou-
> ses provides the support of historical
> inevitability to the fallible efforts of
> struggling leaders. Not least, the very
> dogmatic certitude and ritualistic
> repetition that stick in the craw of the
> Western observer offer the psychological
> assurances on which unquestioning faith
> can be maintained.

> If a non-Communist elite is to
> perservere in tasks that will prove
> Sisyphean in difficulty, it will also

have to offer a philosophical interpretation of its role as convincing and
elevating, and a diagnosis of social and
economic requirements as sharp and
simplistic, as that of Communism.
Further, its will to succeed at whatever
cost must be as firm as that of the
Marxists.[9]

Heilbroner's ultimate ground -- his metaphysical
justification --for employing the Sorelian-Marxist
myth is Utilitarian. As an economist, he believes in
creating the greatest material benefits in the shortest
time for the greatest number of people, regardless of
the means employed. For instance he admits,

Stalin may well have exceeded
Hitler as a mass executioner. ... Yet
one must count the gains as well as the
losses. Hundreds of millions who would
have been confined to the narrow cells
of changeless lives have been liberated
from prisons they did not even know
existed. ... Above all, the prospect
of a new future has been opened.[10]

Success justifies terror: he seems to agree with
Stalin's explanation that "One must break a few eggs in
order to make an omlette." The ultimate rationale is
quantitative.

Even if Heilbroner was trained as a "worldly
philosopher" his foresight is suspect. He makes the
following claim about accepting his view of promoting
development: "It would mean in our daily political
life the admission that the ideological battle of
capitalism and Communism had passed its point of
usefulness or relevance, and that religious diatribe
must give way to the pragmatic dialogue of the age of
science and technology."[11] Although Heilbroner is
not explicit about the nature of a "pragmatic dialogue"
with those whom he would encourage to view the U.S. as
"Number One' among "the towering villains of the
world," one can guess that it might display quite a
bit of friction. Perhaps he thought that the leaders
of the U.S. would be too rational to be alarmed by the
rhetoric of a Communist jihad aimed against them. Also,
there is something rather disturbing in his implied
assumption of the autonomy of means and ends, in assuming that violence (or a violent myth) will not beget
more violence. Even more disturbing is his assertion,

221

"It is clear beyond doubt . . . that historians excuse horror that succeeds."[12] Finally, he betrays his cynicism regarding the relationship between knowing and doing; believing that the masses cannot judge what is good for themselves without the help of a simplistic myth.

Still, what would be the metaphysical fulcrum of a non-Marxist social scientist, or how might one side-step the objections raised to moral objectivity by the "sociology of knowledge" school?

George B. Leonard, author of Education and Ecstasy, let the cat out of the bag when he wrote, "Skinner's scientific and humane impulses meet in his desire to substitute reward for punishment, to rely increasingly on the more subtle and 'beautiful' forms of positive reinforcement."[13] Leonard unknowingly voices what must be among the greatest ironies in the field of the social sciences: in effect, he compliments B. F. Skinner for his good will. All the behavioral techniques of the modern social sciences mean nothing when they are disassociated from the "impulse," the desiring element, or the will to take note of and use them.

William Barrett, in The Illusion of Technique (1978), sheds further light on the problem of "will," or active and conscious desire, as it relates to the social sciences. Recalling that the Pragmatism of James and Dewey was viewed as a form of Idealism, he reminds the reader that "Russell and Moore virtually launch twentieth-century philosophy, at least for the English-speaking peoples, as a refutation of idealism -- to use the title of one of Moore's early essays. And as such it has largely continued to be."[14] "With Nietzsche the history of western metaphysics comes to its close. We have arrived at the end of philsosophy. ... The immense labor of philosophy was to bring science into being; to establish a world of objects over which the subject, mankind, has now to assert its mastery."[15] When science and technology have replaced God and Natural Law all action becomes a matter of the existential will, the wills of men with no guide or direction outside their own whims. Thus scientists gave up on concepts such as "society" and the "nation" in order to measure what individuals do -- i.e., how they actualize their petty wills under their particular socio-economic conditions -- but such observations are a matter of technique, not science. Society might be "healed" or "progressed," but only if

222

one knows what a "healthy" or a "good" society is, only if one holds a normative theory of man and society.

Barrett makes a revealing mistake in thinking that Marxism is not a natural law philosophy:

> The two modern movements of Marxism and Positivism, for example, still exist within the premises of the modern era, though these premises remain hidden to them. Marxism uses the most populist and egalitarian slogans as instruments of its will to <u>come</u> to power. ... As for Positivism, it seeks to drag out the death rattle of philosophy as a series of annotations on science.[16] (emphasis Barrett)

Everything that Barrett says in the quote above is correct, but for the wrong reasons. Marxism promotes a will to come to power precisely because, contrary to its own assertions, it is a natural law philosophy: it proclaims that a human being's <u>natural</u> and good state is realized (or returned to) as a species-being rather than as an alienated class-being. Marxists combine "is" and "ought" through the normative description of what it means to be a species-being. Thus, although Marxist socialism has been discredited if not falsified in practice, it retains its appeal for many outside the Communist world. It claims to justify a moral sentiment on a scientific basis, much as a doctor recognizes health. No wonder, then, that so many find it to be so appealing. Positivism, on the other hand, it will be argued, reinforces the metaphysics of individualism.

Barrett laments the Positivistic culture of contemporary science and offers a Pragmatic way out:

> To try to restore the moral will to a central and primary role in the human personality is bound to appear as an effort against the mainstream of the culture. ... Yet in all this disparagement of the moral will there remains one glaring discrepancy between this culture and our actual life; or, to bring the case closer to home, between ourselves as partisans of this culture and ourselves in the ordinary course of our private lives. We still go about

our everyday business guided by this moral will, and we still discriminate in its terms. We do distinguish the people we know by their virtues and vices, and deal with them accordingly.[17]

Barrett is right in his observations here too, although in this case his reasoning does not go far enough. Still, he offers a start: Pragmatism without the moral will is mere Positivism and, as such, is an insufficient guide for human affairs. We simply must discriminate the "good" from the "bad," the virtuous from the unvirtuous, or the objectively desirable from the undesirable in both our private and our public lives.

David G. Smith reached virtually the same conclusion in an article on group theory in the American Political Science Review:

> In rejecting received notions of public opinion, pragmatist social theory also discarded the metaphysics and epistemology that went with the concept of the "public interest." As people actually used such words, Bentley, Follett and Dewey agreed, interest or interests did not exist, they were generated by activities and the activities were interpreted symbolically, that is recognized. The activities were the "objective" stuff of the interests, in so far as something tangible or objective existed, while views communicated and "known" were the subjective stuff of interests.[18] (emphasis Smith)

> One way of summarizing the argument of this article is to say that the pragmatists discarded too much of the "soul-stuff," "spooks," and formal mechanisms in their discussion of politics and government and that the group theorists have followed their lead too closely. ... Pragmatism and group theories of politics are often misleading intellectual constructs for this interpretation or description of political or governmental situtations since they direct attention in principle to what men are doing rather than to their intentions or dilemmas as well. ...

224

One consequence of such an omission is
that there are a good many activities
of men -- men in government and the
political process -- that group theories
of politics do not explain. They
explain little where the "facts" are
especially important, where "rights"
and due process of law or "forms"
are at stake in a serious way, where
leadership comes into play, or when the
machinery of government is engaged
extensively.[19] (emphasis Smith)

Similar to Barrett's discovery that men in day-to-day
practice depend upon their wills, Smith reminded his
readers how concerned they are over qualities such as
"rights" and "forms." For both scholars the emphasis
was on the practical value of the non-scientific com-
ponent of the contemporary outlook.

According to Bernard Crick, "Pragmatism, when its
gods of affable public opinion deserted it, changed
into positivism, without many noticing the difference.
The political became less interesting to political
scientists than the sociological."[20] Yet there is a
distinct difference between Pragmatism and Positivism.
From World War II until the late 1960s the substitution
of the "sociological" for the political was an afford-
able luxury: the problems America faced as a nation
appeared literally "manageable" as a businessman would
use the word; there appeared to be little or no need
for radical changes, and administration could stand in
for politics. As Crick noted, the prerequisite for the
emphasis on "purely descriptive research" as it is
carried out in the U.S. "is that social and political
conditions remain fairly stable"[21] -- i.e., that the
behavior of people and institutions does not change
rapidly, and that there are no pressing and immediate
problems which must be solved or changed at once. The
queer thing, however, was that when great problems did
arise, such as the seemingly endless and purposeless
war in Vietnam, the most prestigeous journals in
political science continued to carry "sociological"
articles. Something was missing.

One way to distinguish the great Pragmatists is by
noting that they were _romantic_ humanists. The revolt
against reason in America may be looked at as an
attempt to create a better world by abandoning the
forms of its predecessors and substituting the moral
will. The seminal thinkers, such as Beard, Veblen and

225

Dewey, who virtually created contemporary academia had split personalities: they sought to change the world and, for this, they used Pragmatism pragmatically. Here Bertrand Russell compared the similarity of Dewey's objectives with those of Karl Marx. After quoting the essential passage from Marx's Theses on Feuerbach (#11) -- "Philosophers have only interpreted the world in various ways, but the real task is to alter it" (emphasis Marx) -- Russell says, "Allowing for a certain difference in phraseology, this doctrine is essentially undistinguishable from instrumentalism."[22] If the great logician is correct, then Marxism, Instrumentalism, Existentialism, and even contemporary Positivism-Behavioralism all can be viewed as derivations of nineteenth-century Romanticism, or the revolt against reason.

The classical scholar attempted to understand the world and himself so that he could live in harmony with his surroundings. The modern scholar, by comparison, tries to grasp the facts in order that they might better be manipulated. The gnosis, the secret wisdom (and metaphysics), believed in by the old masters of our age is that all true knowledge is simply a means to serve human purposes -- they were good Sophists, technicians who had their hearts in the right place. "Science" was the illusion of certitude that justified their authority. In Crick's estimation, "Croly, for all his elaborate historical analysis, was in fact just making two at first sight simple pleas: that the man of 'exceptional ability' should be honoured, and that such men should themselves develop a craftsman's skill and delight in a particular vocation."[23]

Yet, Crick continues, ". . . it does not seem possible to state -- certainly Croly himself does not -- what in fact are the technical standards of politics. If it is technical, then it can, presumably, be taught."[24] (emphasis Crick) The implication must be that Croly never understood the central problem of Plato's Meno, the fact that virtue or "exceptional ability" seldom is passed on by those who have it to others. If excellence were reducible to (scientific) knowledge, then it would be no more difficult to teach than say mathematics or mechanics. What, in Crick's opinion, Croly actually strives for is to give scientific sanction for the best practices of the time in which he grew up.

In other words, Croly should be criticized for mistaking a dilemma for

226

a solution; his articulation is more interesting than his analysis. He is actually upholding a traditional American moralism, but he tries to re-interpret it to fit the sentiments of his own age, by talk of 'authoritative technical standards.' One moment he points to the shore, at another to the open sea; but he is really just riding with the tide.[25]

The problem is that the Pragmatists were not "scientists" in the best sense of that term. As Crick describes it,

The fact of the matter is that none of the pragmatists really thought systematically about scientific pro-cedures. They thought of science in a cant manner, as the method of observa-tion, experiment and then theory. The prior importance of theory to observa-tion scarcely occured to them. ... Technology, more than scientific method, was the analogy that most obviously impressed them.[26] (emphasis Crick)

The next generation was to mistake technology for science and largely forget the importance of humanistic responsibility. "Perhaps the tragedy of the Progres-sive Era was that the doctrine of intelligent public administration based on technical 'standards' began more and more to supersede the doctrine of personal responsibility: the two halves of Croly fly asunder."[27] The Instrumentalist without the Romantic is sterile, yet, as Crick proceeded to note, "Just as there has been a popular hope to reduce all apparently great problems in American politics to legal terms, so there has been an academic hope to reduce the study of politics to mere technique."[28]

The contemporary fact is that the Instrumentalists won out over the Romantics, even though it was a Pyrrhic victory. They could not help but win because the logic of the Pragmatists, Instrumentalists, Behav-ioralists, and Positivists all had a radically Nominal-istic basis. Following the logic of the masters of these schools ultimately the moral wills of their epigoni became nice but "unprofessional." The masters were entitled to their idyosyncrasies: as David Marcell commented, "Dewey remained a moral idealist

227

while eschewing the traditional basis for such idealism."[29]

> In John Dewey's eyes, humans engendered value upon the world whenever they elected one particular course of action over another. The essence of value was the process of choosing a path that led in a desired direction. Ideas were valuable as parts of a selective process; the valuable idea was "progressive, reformatory, reconstructive, synthetic" in expediting human purpose and extending human will.[30]

Marcell concludes, "Since progress was particularistic and subject to no overarching moral reference, there could be no absolute standard for its assessment."[31] Thus, after the passing of the masters there was bound to be a vacuum. Pluralism in all regards was inevitable: "political pragmatism," in the words of Herbert Schneider, ". . . is primarily a theory of power, or rather of powers, pluralistic and opportunistic."[32] The unbiased human good is but a chimera created out of words for the delight of epistemological Realists and metaphysical Idealists.

Of course the problem was anticipated. For instance in 1928 William Elliott protested, "Pragmatism, Romanticist or Instrumentalist, holds that conceptual logic is vicious because concepts are not 'reality.' But concepts are realities."[33] For the Realist a "forest" has a greater significance than any of the individual plants and trees of which it is composed. Taken to its political extreme, as in Utilitarianism, this view can justify the bloody sacrifice of individuals for the sake of the group -- as in the case of Fascism. The distinguishing feature is that whereas the Pragmatist uses his myth, the Fascist believes in, is wholly committed to, and controlled by his myth. For instance, Heilbroner should be labeled a Pragmatist because his Marxism is intended as but a productive gimmick: it is projected that other people should believe in it, at least until they reach the point where they can think for themselves.

The irony of the Progressive Movement is that the practitioners of the new social sciences continue to believe in a Nominalistic methodology. The supreme irony is that the most consistent advocates of political Nominalism in the U.S. have been John C. Calhoun

228

and Ayn Rand -- radical advocates of States' rights and laissez-faire capitalism, respectively. The critics of American Positivism are correct when they charge that it is inherently conservative and reactionary. After all, it rests upon an onotology which resists transcending the individuals which constitute the whole.

The reason why the early Pragmatists were in fact Progressives was because they were inconsistent. They had in mind improving the health of the Nation while employing a "science" which drew attention to the particulars. They were humanistically Pragmatic in their inconsistency. Their rationality lay in attempting to hold the mean betwen two extreme positions.

One of the last of the great Pragmatists was C. Wright Mills (1917-1962). According to Irving Louis Horowitz, "Mills shared with Walter Lippmann a search for a 'public philosophy,'"[34] a beneficial set of myths, even though he longed for the day that the public could act on reason and knowledge alone. "Mills' feat consisted in combining empiricism and prescriptivism; describing the world of human relations and also presenting solutions (albeit partial ones) to the worst infections of the American social structure."[35] What Mosca, Pareto, Sorel and Mannheim offered Mills was a rational way to explain irrational behavior:

> That the "manipulation" of man was possible Mills did not doubt. But the message of the great sociolologists of the past not only dealt with the mechanisms of persuasion but also, in this very process, provided a system of clarification, provided for Mills that sociology could cure human ills as well as explain them. And any science concerned with human beings had to have this prescriptive value -- just as medicine and psychology.[36] (emphasis original)

In another work Horowitz describes Mills's doctoral dissertation at the University of Wisconsin, Sociology and Pragmatism, as being ". . . not a study of the truth of Pragmatism, but rather a study of its utility. The only comparable work in the sociological literature is Georges Sorel's De l'utilite du pragmatisme."[37] (emphasis Horowitz) Horowitz details Mills's relationship to Pragmatism as follows;

229

In the vacuum created by the modern
pragmatists . . . Mills naturally enough
began to place a new emphasis on the
radical aspects of the "classical
tradition" in sociology from Marx to
Mannheim. ... But if he moved away
from pragmatism as a theory, he moved
nearer to it as a way of life. He
"internalized" the behavior of the
pragmatic man -- at least of Jamesian
man. This is plainly evident in Mills'
one man crusade to present the truth
about the Cuban Revolution to the
American public in much the same fashion
that William James lectured up and down
the Alantic Coast in 1898 in an effort
to alert Americans to the dangers of the
take over of Cuba by American imperialism. ... The force of personalities is
important to the pragmatic mind. This
is diametrically opposed to the imper-
sonal force of history that is important
for the dialectical mind. ... In this
sense, Mills certainly remained a firm
adherent to the pragmatic cannons of
truth as involvement.[38]

If, at the outset, Mills seemed
anxious to use pragmatism systematically, by the close of his career, he had
begun to use pragmatism journalistic-
ally. ... The irony of the situation
is that the "true reformer" (which Mills
certainly was) suffered at the hands of
the true believer turned true scientist,
while at the same time he found himself
celebrated by the journalists and
columnists.[39]

Mills went unidentified as a Pragmatist because his
contemporary Pragmatists were of a degenerate sort:

Increasingly, pragmatism came to
stand for acquiescence in the social
order. ... The new pragmatism linked
arms with logical positivism in the
essential details. It turned its gaze
inward, and attempted to serve as a
philosophical justification of scientism
rather than social reform.[40]

Apparently, even though Mills accepted that men could understand only their own fabrications, he thought that they could choose rational means in order to maximize them. He followed in the spirit of Herbert Croly, and in this Horowitz compliments Mills by faulting his optimism: "Mills was so imbued with the rationalist ideal that he perhaps put too great rather than too little stress upon the curative powers of knowledge. He tended to underestimate the powers of personal and class interest as effective deterrents to change."[41]

Perhaps, as Horowitz suggested, it was the journalists, the descendants of Croly and Lippmann, who retained the Pragmatic vision that is necessary to make sense out of "the facts." In a March, 1984 issue of The Los Angeles Times William Schneider attempted a normative separation of "interest politics" from "issue politics." The former applies to the traditional buying off of coalitions of factions (groups that are out solely for their own benefits), and the latter means problem-solving on the national level. For instance Presidents John Kennedy and James Carter attempted to be problem-solvers. For Schneider, the proper focus is on America as a nation:

> Issue politicians like Carter get into trouble because they have no political base to carry them through the inevitable bad times. "Your base," a politician once said, "are the people who are with you when you're wrong." On the other hand, interest politicians -- Lyndon B. Johnson, for example -- get into trouble because their policies are often neither rational nor efficient. They are exclusively "political." People knew what Johnson did for blacks and for poor people, but he didn't seem committed to finding policies that worked for the nation as a whole.[42]

The same week Michael Kinsley (the current TRB of The New Republic), writing in the same paper, made similar distinctions. In Kinsley's eyes,

> The true leader is one who neither embraces "special interests" nor denounces them like Satan, but tries to make people understand that the special-interest conspiracy against

231

the general interest is one that we've
all joined, and we'll be better off
generally if we relent a bit in our
specific demands on the system."[43]

The "true leader" is his "neoliberal," rather than the
old advocate of interest politics whom Kinsley labels a
"paleo-liberal:"

Put simply, neoliberalism (unlike
paleo-liberalism) shares the widespread
skepticism about many aspects of big
government as it has developed over the
last 50 years, but (unlike neoconserva-
tism) continues to believe that the
government should play a major role in
providing for the poor, creating jobs,
guaranteeing health care, protecting
consumers and the environment and so
on. Neoliberalism wants to rewrite the
liberal agenda, not embalm it (like
the paleos) or discard it (like the
Reaganites). ...

Unlike the Paleos, Neos believe
that economic growth is the best answer
to poverty. Unlike conservatives,
though, they're not complacent about
those whom prosperity passed by and
others who get crushed by the gears of
progress. Furthermore, neoliberals see
some kinds of government spending -- for
education, research, infrastructure --
as valuable capital investment, not
money down the drain. As you can tell,
I find the neoliberal vision pretty
seductive.[44]

What seems needed is an idealistic element in
American social science. Possibly the easiest way to
find that element is to follow the Pragmatic method and
to fabricate it -- call it a working hypothesis. Examples would be the American nation and the rights to
life and liberty. Acknowledging that concepts are both
real and abstractions is not a contradiction; the
reality of abstractions depends upon the purposes for
which they are used, and their advantage is that they
are subject to modification. An honest prescriptive
scientist must include and identify prescriptive concepts among his premises, even if it is only the desir-
ability of sheer survival. Those who wish to transcend

pluralism are forced, if they are honest, to admit much more complex abstractions. The fact that it is possible to do this within the Pragmatic tradition has been demonstrated by the life histories of Walter Lippmann and Sidney Hook: they tested their abstractions in the laboratory of history, and revised them accordingly.

Recapitulating: it should be obvious by now to the reader that the American philosophy of Pragmatism is responsible for the methodological family resemblance of contemporary American social sciences. Further, it has been argued that, given their Nominalistic inheritance, the New Social Sciences may be unscientific or, at least, inadequate. For instance, modern psychology tends to "study" (i.e. record) behavior rather than the psyche, sociology studies mass behavior rather than the society, administration has superseded leadership, and political science finds it difficult to be the architectonic science because it emulates the observational approach of the other sciences. Science, as it is commonly accepted, seems to imply a sterile Positivism where prescriptive utterances are reduced to merely the personal whims of those who make them.

The dilemma -- the forced choice between two equally unsuitable alternatives -- is that under the prevailing system a person might be either a scientist or a politician, but not both at the same time. A "political scientist" becomes a contradiction in terms because of the fact-value distinction.

One solution -- the easiest within the prevailing atmosphere -- is (Pragmatically) to abandon ahistorical Positivism and return to Pragmatism.

Pragmatism is superior to Positivism as a human science because the former admits to being a science of values whereas the latter does not. For instance in any science one can never actually see or measure a law itself, only its effects are known directly and the causal principles are inferred therefrom. In the social sciences this is an historical process. For example, have Germans in the last quarter century discovered themselves to be happier under Communism or Capitalism? Has this "experiment" been repeated under various conditions? One then could argue that Capitalism produces more desirable human conditions than does Communism -- at least under world conditions from Aristotle's time until the present. Similar historical experiments have been performed using the hypothesis of

233

natural rights. Again, the efficacy of natural rights does not <u>prove</u> their ontological existence any more than does the constantly reoccuring phenomena of falling bodies <u>prove</u> the existence of the "law" of gravity as their "cause." Rather, in Anglo-American science since David Hume the "law" of cause-and-effect is simply a recognition that two events are constantly conjoined with one, said to be the "cause," preceding the other. In the human sciences, of course, the exception so "proves" the "rule" exactly because it is an exception to the general rule or law of that aspect of society. (Aristotle taught us that.)

The proper task of the Pragmatic social scientist is to look to both history and the social "sciences," in order to recognize which "fictions" or social hypotheses in fact live up to their promises and "cause" or promote a better world -- at least most of the time. In this sense John Dewey, for all his avowed Pragmatic radicalism, was unscientific in that he allowed his <u>faith</u> in "collectivism" to outweigh the social facts of his time. On the other hand Walter Lippmann and Sidney Hook had the integrity to evaluate their prescriptions time and again in terms of which social constructs produced the most desirable consequences. Of course, in line with their method, their conclusions always are tentative -- but such is the nature of science. The important aspect, however, is that if historical "experiments" are subject to evaluation by their consequences, then a normative science of <u>society</u> is possible within the frame of American academic culture.

FOOTNOTES FOR CHAPTER 10

[1] Heilbroner, Robert. "Counterrevolutionary America." <u>Commentary</u>, Vol. 43, No. 4 (April, 1967), p. 31.

[2] Ibid., pp. 32-33.

[3] Ibid., p. 32.

[4] Ibid., p. 33.

[5] Ibid., p. 31.

[6] Ibid., p. 36.

[7] Ibid., p. 35.

[8] Ibid., p. 35.

[9] Ibid., p. 35.

[10] Ibid., pp. 34-35.

[11] Ibid., p. 38.

[12] Ibid., p. 34.

[13] Leonard, George B. Education and Ecstasy. New York: Dell Publishing Company, Inc., 1968, p. 43.

[14] Barrett, William. The Illusion of Technique: A Search for Meaning in a Technological World. Garden City, New York: Anchor Press, 1978, p. 192.

[15] Ibid., p. 198.

[16] Ibid., p. 199.

[17] Ibid., p. 232.

[18] Smith, David G. "Pragmatism and the Group Theory of Politics." The American Political Science Review, Vol. LVIII, No. 3 (September, 1964), p. 601.

[19] Ibid., p. 610.

[20] Crick, Bernard. The American Science of Politics; Its Origins and Conditions. Berkeley and Los Angeles, California: University of California Press, 1959, p. 175.

[21] Ibid., p. 157.

[22] Russell, Bertrand. "Dewey's New Logic." The Basic Writings of Bertrand Russell. eds. Egner and Denonn. New York: Simon and Schuster, 1961, p. 196.

[23] Crick, op. cit., p. 78.

[24] Ibid., p. 79.

[25] Ibid., p. 80.

[26] Ibid., pp. 92-93.

[27] Ibid., p. 82.

[28]   Ibid., p. 237.

[29]   Marcell, David W. Progress and Pragmatism: James, Dewey, Beard, and the American and the Idea of Progress.   Westport,   Connecticut: Greenwood   Press, 1974, p. 204.

[30]   Ibid., p. 228.

[31]   Ibid., p. 249.

[32]   Schneider, Herbert W. A History of American Philosophy. New York: Columbia University Press, 1947 (third printing), p. 567.

[33]   Elliott, William Y. The Pragmatic Revolt in Politics: Syndicalism, Fascism, and the Constitutional State. New York: The MacMillan Company, 1928, p. 71.

[34] Horowitz,   Irving   Louis.   "Introduction" Power, Politics and People: The Collected Essays of C. Wright Mills. ed. I. L. Horowitz. New York: Oxford University Press, 1963, p. 19.

[35]   Ibid., p. 3.

[36]   Ibid., p. 16.

[37] Horowitz,   Irving   Louis.   "Introduction" Sociology and Pragmatis: The Higher Learning in America by C. Wright Mills. Pain-Whitman Publishers, 1962 (originally written as C. Wright Mills's doctoral dis- sertaion at the University of Wisconsin), p. 30.

[38]   Ibid., pp. 25-26.

[39]   Ibid., pp. 28-29.

[40]   Ibid., p. 29.

[41]   Horowitz, Power, Politics and People: The Collected Essays of C. Wright Mills, op. cit., p. 18.

[42]   Schneider, William. The Los Angeles Times. Sunday, March 25, 1984, Part IV, page 2.

[43] Kinsley, Michael.   "Democrats' Neoliberals and Paleoliberals" The Los Angeles Times. Friday, March 30, 1984, Part II, page 7.

[44]   Ibid, p. 7.

BIBLIOGRAPHY

Allen, Gay Wilson. William James: A Biography. New
York: The Viking Press, 1967.

Ayer, A. J. The Origins of Pragmatism; Studies in the
Philosophy of Charles Sanders Peirce and William
James. San Francisco, California: Freeman,
Cooper and Company, 1968.

Barrett, William. The Illusion of Technique: A
Search for Meaning in a Technological World.
Garden City, New York: Anchor Press, 1978.

Beard, Charles A. "The Idea of Progress," A Century
of Progress. New York: Harper and Brothers
Publishers, 1933.

Bentley, Arthur Fisher. Behavior Knowledge Fact.
Bloomington, Indiana: The Principia Press, 1935.

------. Inquiry into Inquiries: Essays in Social
Theory. ed. Sidney Ratner. Boston, Massachusetts: The Beacon Press, 1954.

------. Makers, Users, and Masters. ed. Sidney
Ratner. New York: Syracuse University Press,
1969 (manuscript began in 1918, completed in
1920).

------. Relativity in Man and Society. New York:
G. P. Putnam's Sons, 1926 (manuscript completed
in 1924, the year he led the Progressive campaign
in Indiana).

------. The Process of Government: A Study of Social
Pressures. Bloomington, Indiana: The Principia
Press, 1949 (original, 1908).

Bernstein, Richard J., ed. Perspectives on Peirce;
Critical Essays on Charles Sanders Peirce.
New Haven, Connecticut: Yale University Press,
1965.

Boler, John F. Charles Peirce and Scholastic Realism;
A Study of Peirce's Relation to John Duns Scotus.
Seattle, Washington: University of Washington
Press, 1963.

237

Boller, Paul F. American Thought in Transition: The Impact of Evolutionary Naturalism, 1865-1900. Rand McNally and Company, 1973.

Brennan, Bernard P. William James. New York: Twayne Publishers, Inc., 1968.

Burns, James MacGregor. Roosevelt: The Lion and the Fox. New York: Harcourt, Brace and World, Inc., 1956.

Clifford, William Kingdom. "The Ethics of Belief" (complete). Religion from Tolstoy to Camus. ed. Walter Kaufmann. New York: Harper Torchbooks, 1964.

Cohen, Morris R. Law and the Social Order: Essays in Legal Philosophy. New York: Harcourt, Brace and Company, 1933.

Commager, Henry Steele. The American Mind; An Interpretation of American Thought and Character Since the 1880's. New Haven, Connecticut: Yale University Press, 1950.

Cork, Jim. "John Dewey and Karl Marx." John Dewey: Philosopher of Science and Freedom. ed. Sidney Hook. New York: The Dial Press, 1950.

Cotton, James G. Royce on the Human Self. Cambridge, Massachusetts: Harvard University Press, 1954.

Crick, Bernard. The American Science of Politics; Its Origins and Conditions. Berkeley and Los Angeles, California: University of California Press, 1959.

Croly, Herbert. Progressive Democracy. New York: The MacMillan Company, 1914.

-------. The Promise of American Life. New York: E. P. Dutton and Company, Inc., 1963 (original, 1909).

Curti, Merle. The Social Ideas of American Educators. New York: Charles Scribner's Sons, 1935.

Dam, Hari N. The Intellectual Odyssey of Walter Lippmann: A Study of His Protean Thought 1910-1960. New York: Gordon Press, 1973.

Dewey, John. A Letter in the New Republic, LXXXVII (October 7, 1936).

------. Characters and Events: Popular Essays in Social and Political Philosophy, Vol. II. ed. John Ratner. New York: Octagon Books, 1970.

------. Context and Thought. Berkeley, California: University of California Press, 1930.

------. "Correspondence: A Third Party Program." New Republic, LXX (February 24, 1932).

------. Essays in Experimental Logic. New York: Dover Publications, Inc.; an unabridged reprint of the 1916 edition by the University of Chicago.

------. Experience and Education. New York: Collier Books, 1972 (original, 1938).

------. "How They Are Voting." New Republic, CIII (September 23, 1940).

------. Human Nature and Its Conduct: An Introduction to Social Psychology. London, England: George Allen and Unwin, Ltd., 1922.

------. Individualism Old and New. New York: Minton, Balch and Company, 1930.

------. Intelligence in the Modern World: John Dewey's Philosphy. ed. J. Ranter. New York: The Modern Library, 1939.

------. "Intelligence and Power." New Republic, LXXVII (April 25, 1934).

------. "Introduction." Challenge to the New Deal. eds. Bringham and Rodman. New York: Falcon Press, 1934.

------. Liberalism and Social Action. New York: G. P. Putnam's Sons, 1935.

------. "Liberty and Social Control" (1935). Problems of Men. New York: Philosophical Library, 1946.

------. Logic the Theory of Inquiry. New York: Henry Holt and Company, 1951 (original, 1938).

------. "Philosophies of Freedom" (1928). The Moral Writings of John Dewey. ed. J. Gouinlock. New York: Hafner Press, 1976.

------. "Policies of a New Party." New Republic, LXVI (April 8, 1931).

------. "Social Science and Social Control." New Republic, LXVII (July 29, 1931).

------. Studies in Logical Theory. Chicago, Illinois: The University of Chicago Press, 1903.

------. "Surpassing America." New Republic, LXVI (April 15, 1931).

------. The Early Works, 1882-1898, Vol. 2 (1887). Carbondale and Edwardsville, Illinois: Southern Illinois University Press, 1967.

------. The Early Works of John Dewey, 1882-1898, Vol. II. ed. G. E. Axtelle, et al. Carbondale and Edwardsville, Illinois: The Southern Illinois University Press, 1976.

------. "The Future of Radical Political Action." The Nation, CXXXCI (January 4, 1933).

------. "The Need for a New Party; The Present Crises." New Republic, LXVI (March 18, 1931).

------. "The Need for a New Party: II." New Republic, LXVI (March 25, 1931).

------. The Public and Its Problems. New York: Henry Holt and Company, 1927 (from lectures given in 1926.)

------. The Quest for Certainty: A Study of the Relation of Knowledge and Valuation. New York: Minton, Balch and Company, 1929.

------. "Who Might Make a New Party?" New Republic, LXVI (April 1, 1931).

Dewey, John and Arthur Fishter Bentley. A Philosophical Correspondence, 1932-1951. ed. Sidney Ratner, et al. New Brunswick, New Jersey: Rutgers University Press, 1964 (from the introduction by Sidney Ratner).

------. _Knowing and the Known_. Boston Massachusetts: The Beacon Press, 1949.

Durant, Will. _The Story of Philosophy: The Lives and Opinions of the Great Philosophers_. New York: Washington Square Press, Inc., 1962.

Dykhuizen, George. _The Life and Mind of John Dewey_. Carbondale and Edwardsville, Illinois: Southern Illinois University Press, 1973.

Elliott, William Y. _The Pragmatic Revolt in Politics: Syndicalism, Facism, and the Constitutional State_. New York: The MacMillan Company, 1928.

Forcey, Charles. _The Crossroads of Liberalism: Croly, Weyl, Lippmann and the Progressive Era, 1900-1925_. New York: Oxford University Press, 1961.

Gallie, W. B. _Peirce and Pragmatism_. New York: Dover Publications, Inc., 1966.

Goudge, T. A. "Pragmatism's Contribution to an Evolutionary View of Mind." _The Monist; An International Quarterly Journal of General Philosophical Inquiry_, Vol. 57, No. 2 (April 1973).

Heilbroner, Robert. "Counterrevolutionary America." _Commentary_, Vol. 43, No. 4 (April 1967).

Hofstader, Richard, ed. _The Progressive Movement; 1900-1915_. Englewood Cliffs, New Jersey: Prentice-Hall, Inc., 1963.

Holmes, Oliver W. "The Path of the Law." _Harvard Law Review_, Vol. X, No. 8 (March 25, 1897).

Hook, Sidney. "A Communication: John Dewey and His Critics." _New Republic_, LXVII, No. 861 (June 3, 1931).

------. "Abraham Lincoln, American Pragmatist." _New Leader_, XL, No. 11 (March 18, 1957).

------. "Contemporary American Philosophy." _New Republic_, LXIII, No. 815 (July 16, 1930).

------. "Correspondence: Marx and Darwinism." _New Republic_, LXVII, No. 869 (July 29, 1931).

------. From Hegel to Marx; Studies in the Intellectual Development of Karl Marx. New York: The Humanities Press, 1958.

------. "Liberalism and the Case of Leon Trotsky." The Southern Review, 3, No. 2 (Autumn, 1937).

------. "Lord Russell and the War Crimes Trial." New Leader, XLIX, No. 21 (October 24, 1966).

------. "Marxism and Values." Marxist Quarterly, I (1937). New York: Greenwood Reprint Corporation, 1968.

------. Pragmatism and the Tragic Sense of Life. New York: Basic Books, Inc., 1974.

------. Reason, Social Myths and Democracy. New York: Harper Torchbooks, 1966 (original, 1940).

------. "Socialism and Democracy." New Leader, XLI, No. 40 (November 3, 1958).

------. "Socialism and Liberation." Partisan Review, XXIV, No. 4 (Fall, 1957).

------. "The Atom and Human Wisdom." New Leader, XL, No. 22 (June 3, 1957).

------. "The Cold War and the West." Partisan Review, XXIX, No. 1 (Winter, 1962).

------. "The Failure of the Left." Partisan Review, X, No. 2 (March-April, 1943).

------. "The Future of Socialism." Partisan Review, SVI, No. 1 (January-February, 1947).

------. The Hero in History; A Study in Limitation and Possibility. New York: The Humanities Press, 1950 (original, 1943).

------. The Metaphysics of Pragmatism; With an Introductory Word by John Dewey. Chicago, Illinois: The Open Court Publishing Company, 1927.

------. "The New Failure of Nerve." Partisan Review, X, No. 1 (January-February, 1943).

------. "The Old Liberalism and the New Conservatism." New Leader, XL, No. 27 (July 8, 1957).

------. "The Philosophy of Dialectical Materialism, I." The Journal of Philosophy, XXV, No. 5 (March 1, 1920).

------. Towards the Understanding of Karl Marx; A Revolutionary Interpretation. New York: The John Day Company, 1933.

------. "What's Left of Karl Marx." Saturday Review, LXII, No. 23 (June 6, 1950).

Hook, Sidney, et al. Social Justice and the Problems of the Twentieth Century. North Carolina State University: The William D. Carmichael Lecture Series, Spring, 1968.

Horowitz, Irving Lewis. "Introduction." Power, Politics and People: The Collected Essays of C. Wright Mills. New York: Oxford University Press, 1963.

------. "Introduction." Sociology and Pragmatism: The Higher Learning in America. By C. Wright Mills. ed. I. L. Horowitz. New York: Paine-Whitman Publishers, 1962 (originally written as C. Wright Mills' doctoral dissertation at the University of Wisconsin).

------. Radicalism and the Revolt Against Reason. London, England: Routledge and Kegan Paul, 1961.

James, Henry. The Letters of William James. Boston, Massachusetts: Little, Brown, and Company, 1926.

James, William. Pragmatism; A New Name for Some Old Ways of Thinking. New York: Longmans, Green and Company, 1943 (original, 1907).

------. The Meaning of Truth; A Sequel to 'Pragmatism'. New York: Longmans, Green and Company, 1909.

------. The Principles of Psychology, Vol. II. New York: Henry Holt and Company, 1890.

------. The Principles of Psychology, Vol. II. New York: Dover Publications, 1950 (a reprint of the 1890 original by Henry Holt and Company).

------. "The Will to Believe" (complete). Religion from Tolstoy to Camus. ed. Walter Kaufmann. New York: Harper Torchbooks, 1964.

------. "What is an Emotion?" Collected Essays and Reviews by William James. ed. R. B. Perry. London, England: Longmans, Green and Company, 1920.

------. "What Pragmatism Means." Pragmatism and American Culture. ed. Gail Kennedy. Boston, Massachusetts: D. C. Heath and Company, 1950.

Kelly, A. H. and Harbison, W. A. The American Constitution; Its Origins and Development. New York: W. W. Norton and Company, 1970.

Kinsley, Michael. "Democrats' Neoliberals and Peleoliberals." The Los Angeles Times. Friday, March 30, 1984, Part II, p. 7.

Laski, Harold J. "The Founders of the Fabians." New Republic, LXXVI (October 25, 1933).

Lenin, V. I. Collected Works, Vol. 38: Philosophical Notebooks. Moscow: Foreign Languages Publishing House, 1963.

Leonard, George B. Education and Ecstasy. New York: Dell Publishing Company, Inc., 1968.

Lewis, C. I. An Analysis of Knowledge and Valuation. LaSalle, Illinois: Open Court Publishing Company, 1962.

------. Mind and the World Order; Outline of a Theory of Knowledge. New York: Dover Publications, Inc., 1956.

------. Our Social Inheritance. Bloomington, Indiana: Indiana University Press, 1957.

------. "Realism or Phenomenalism?" The Philosophical Review, LXIV (April, 1955).

------. "Some Logical Considerations Concerning the Mental." Journal of Philosophy, 38 (1941).

Link, A. S. and Leary, W. M., eds. The Progressive Era and The Great War, 1896-1920. New York: Appleton-Century-Crofts, 1969.

Lippmann, Walter. A Preface to Politics. New York: Mitchell Kennerley, 1913.

------. _Drift and Mastery: An Attempt to Diagnose the Current Unrest_. New York: Mitchell Kennerley, 1914.

------. _Essays in the Public Philosophy_. Boston, Massachusetts: Little, Brown and Company, 1955.

------. _Liberty and the News_. New York: Harcourt and Brace, 1920 (original, 1919).

------. _The Essential Lippmann: A Political Philosophy for Democracy_. eds. Rossiter and Lare. New York: Random House, 1963.

------. _The Good Society_. London, England: George Allen and Unwin Ltd., 1937.

Marcell, David W. _Progress and Pragmatism: James, Dewey, Beard, and the American Idea of Progress_. Westport, Connecticut: Greenwood Press, 1974.

Marx, Karl. _A Contribution to the Critique of Political Economy_. Trans. S. W. Ryazanskaya. New York: International Publishers, 1970.

Marx, Karl and Engels, Friedrich. "Manifesto of the Communist Party." _The Marx-Engels Reader_. ed. R. C. Tucker. New York: W. W. Norton and Company, 1972,

Mead, George Herbert. _Mind, Self and Society; From the Standpoint of a Social Behaviorist_. ed. C. W. Morris. Chicago, Illinois: University of Chicago Press, 1934.

------. _The Philosophy of the Act_. ed. C. W. Morris, et al. Chicago, Illinois: The University of Chicago Press, 1959.

------. _The Philosophy of the Present_. LaSalle, Illinois: The Open Court Publishing Company, 1959.

Miller, David L. _George Herbert Mead; Self, Language and the World_. Austin, Texas: University of Texas Press, 1973.

Mowry, George E. _The Progressive Era, 1900-1920; The Reform Persuasion_. Washington, D.C.: The American Historical Association, 1972.

Noble, David W. Historians Against History: The Frontier Thesis and the National Covenant in American Historical Writing Since 1830. Minneapolis, Minnesota: University of Minnesota Press, 1965.

Novack, George. Pragmatism Versus Marxism; An Appraisal of John Dewey's Philosophy. New York: Pathfinder Press, Inc., 1975.

Patai, Raphael. Myth and Modern Man. Englewood Cliffs, New Jersey: Prentice-Hall, Inc., 1972.

Peirce, Charles Sanders. The Collected Papers of Charles Sanders Peirce. eds. Paul Weiss et al. Cambridge, Massachusetts: The Harvard University Press, 1960.

Persons, Stow. The American Mind; A History of Ideas. New York: Holt, Rinehart and Winston, 1958.

Perry, Ralph Barton. The Thought and Character of William James, 2 Vols. Boston, Massachusetts: Little, Brown and Company, 1936.

Polanyi, Michael. Knowing and Being. ed. Marjorie Green. Chicago, Illinois: The University of Chicago Press, 1969.

------. The Study of Man. Chicago, Illinois: The University of Chicago Press, 1960.

Price, Henry Habberly. "Our Evidence for the Existence of Other Minds." Philosophy, XII, No. 52, 1938.

Robinson, James Harvey. The New History; Essays Illustrating the Modern Historical Outlook. Springfield, Massachusetts: The Walden Press, 1958 (original, 1912).

------. The New Humanizing of Knowledge. New York: George G. Doran Company, 1923.

Roosevelt, Theodore. The Works of Theodore Roosevelt, National Edition, Vol. XIII. ed. H. Hagedorn. New York: Charles Scribner's Sons, 1926.

Rorty, Richard. Consequences of Pragmatism. Minneapolis, Minnesota: University of Minnesota, 1982.

Ross, Dorothy. "The New History and the New Psychology: An Early Attempt at Psychohistory." The Hofstader Aegis; A Memorial. eds. Elkins, S. and McKitrick, B. New York: Alfred A. Knopf, 1974.

Royce, Josiah. Fugitive Essays. Cambridge Massachusetts: Harvard University Press, 1920.

------. Royce's Logical Essays; Collected Logical Essays of Josiah Royce. ed. D. S. Robinson. Dubuque, Iowa: William C. Brown Company, 1951.

------. The Basic Writings of Josiah Royce, Vol. I. ed. I. K. Skruspskelis. Chicago, Illinois: The University of Chicago Press, 1969.

------. The Letters of Josiah Royce. ed. J. Clendenning. Chicago, Illinois: The University of Chicago Press, 1970.

Rucker, Darnell. The Chicago Pragmatists. Minneapolis, Minnesota: The University of Minnesota Press, 1969.

Russell, Bertrand. "Dewey's New Logic." The Basic Writings of Bertrand Russell. eds. Egner and Denonn. New York: Simon and Schuster, 1961.

Santayana, George. "A General Confession." The Golden Age of American Philosophy. ed. Charles Frankel. New York: George Braziller, Inc., 1960.

------. Character and Opinion in the United States; With Reminiscences of William James and Josiah Royce and Academic Life in America. New York: Charles Scribner's Sons, 1921.

------. "Realms of Being." The Works of George Santayana, Vol. XIV. New York: Charles Scribner's Sons, 1937.

------. "Scepticism and Animal Faith." The Works of George Santayana, Vol. XII. New York: Charles Scribner's Sons, 1937.

------. The Birth of Reason and Other Essays. ed. D. Cory. New York: Columbia University Press, 1968.

------. The Life of Reason: Or the Phases of Human Progress. New York: Charles Scribner's Sons, 1953 (original, 1905).

------. The Works of George Santayana, Vol. VII. New York: Charles Scribner's Sons, 1936.

------. "Winds of Doctrine." The Works of George Santayana, Vol. VII. New York: Charles Scribner's Sons, 1937.

Schneider, Herbert. A History of American Philosophy. New York: Columbia University Press, 1947 (third printing).

------. "Radical Empiricism and Religion." Essays in Honor of John Dewey; On the Occasion of His Seventieth Birthday, October 20, 1929. New York: Henry Holt and Company, 1929.

Schneider, William. The Los Angeles Times, Sunday, March 25, 1984, Part IV, p. 2.

Skinner, B. F. Beyond Freedom and Dignity. New York: Bantom Books, 1972.

Smith, David. G. "Pragmatism and the Group Theory of Politics." The American Political Science Review, Vol. LVIII, No. 3 (September, 1964).

Sorel, Georges. From George Sorel: Essays in Socialism and Philosophy. ed. J. L. Stanley. New York: Oxford Univesity Press, 1976.

------. Reflections of Violence. Trans. T. E. Hulme. New York: MacMillan Publishing Company, 1974.

------. The Illusion of Progress. Berkeley, California: University of California Press, 1969.

Steel, Ronald. Walter Lippmann and the American Century. New York: Vintage Books, 1981.

Strout, Cushing. The Pragmatic Revolt in American History: Carl Becker and Charles Beard. New Haven, Connecticut: Yale University Press, 1959.

Taylor, Frederick Winslow. "Scientific Management." Classics of Public Administration. eds. Shafritz and Hyde. Oak Park, Illinois: Moore Publishing Company, Inc., 1978.

------. Shop Management. New York: Harper and Brothers Publishers, 1911 (original, 1903).

------. The Principles of Scientific Management. New York: Harper and Brothers, 1911.

------. "The Principles of Scientific Management." Classics of Organization Theory. eds. Shafritz and Whitbeck. Oak Park, Illinois: Moore Publishing Company, Inc., 1978.

Thayer, H. S. Meaning and Action: A Critical History of Pragmatism. New York: The Bobbs-Merill Company, 1968.

Veblen, Thorstein. Essays in Our Changing Order. ed. L. Ardzrooni. New York: The Viking Press, 1934.

------. The Place of Science in Modern Civilization and Other Essays by Thorstein Veblen. New York: B. W. Huebsch, 1919.

------. The Vested Interests and the Common Man; ("The Modern Point of View and the New Order"). London, England: George Allen and Unwin, 1919 (originally published as separate articles in The Dial, 1918-1919).

------. What Veblen Thought; Selected Writings of Thorstein Veblen. ed. W. C. Mitchell. New York: The Viking Press, 1936.

Weiss, Paul. "G. H. Mead: Philosopher of the Here and Now." New Republic, LXXII (October 26, 1933).

------. "Pragmatists and Pragmatists." New Republic, LXII (March 26, 1930).

------. "The Year in Philosophy." New Republic, CI (December 6, 1939).

Wells, Harry K. Pragmatism: Philosophy of Imperialism. New York: International Publishers, 1954.

Wells, Rulon. "Charles S. Peirce as an American." Perspectives on Peirce. ed. Bernstein. New Haven, Connecticut: Yale University Press, 1965.

Whorf, Banjamin. Language, Thought and Reality. Cambridge, Massachusetts: The M.I.T. Press, 1970.

Wiebe, Robert. The Search for Order 1877-1920. New York: Hill and Wong, 1967.

Wilson, Woodrow. Constitutional Government in the United States. New York: Columbia University Press, 1947 (original, 1908: not his dissertation).

------. The New Freedom: A Call for the Emancipation of the Generous Energies of a People. New York: Doubleday, Page and Company, 1914 (from the campaign speeches of 1912).

------. The State: Elements of Historical and Practical Politics. New York: D. C. Heath and Company, 1918 (original, 1898).

Williams, William Appleman. "A Note on Charles Austin Beard's Search for a General Theory of Causation." The American Historical Review: A Quarterly, Vol. LXII, No. 1 (October, 1956).

Wittgenstein, Ludwig. Philosophical Investigations. Trans. G. E. M. Anscombe. New York: The Mac-Millan Company, 1970.

INDEX

Durant, Will, 1
Dykhuizen, George, 88

Eastman, Max, 105
Elliott, William Y., 228
Engels, Friedrich, 102, 169
England, 45, 51

Fabian, 90, 92, 100, 104
Fanon, Frantz, 42
Forcey, Charles, 51, 52
Freud, Sigmund, 15, 42, 200, 212

Gallie, W. B., 4, 6, 10, 11, 13
Germany, 63, 64, 107, 109, 110, 127, 149, 200
Goudge, T. A., 170
Gulick, Luther, 141

Harbison, W. A., 171
Hegel, 95, 101, 106, 167, 168, 175
Hegelian, 1, 12, 21, 56, 57, 96, 99, 101, 167, 168, 170, 175
Heilbroner, Robert, 219-221
Hitler, 108, 110-112, 115, 221
Ho Chi Minh, 115
Hofstader, Richard, 160
Holmes, Oliver W., 5, 157-160
Hook, Sidney, xii, 76, 78, 87, 93, 102-118, 155, 213, 233, 234
Horowitz, Irving Lewis, 40-43, 229, 231
House, Colonel, 76
Hume, David, xii, 36, 71, 234

Italy, 44

James, Henry, 7, 8
James, William, ix, x, 1-16, 21-39, 42-46, 52, 56, 61, 69, 70, 72-74, 78, 101, 102, 117, 126, 134, 135, 145, 146, 148, 155, 160, 164, 167, 175-177, 185, 186, 189, 197, 206, 211, 222, 230
Jefferson, Thomas, 141
Jones, Robert Edmund, 69
Johnson, Lyndon, 117, 231

Kant, Immanual, 1, 2, 5, 95
Kelly, A. H., 171
Kinsley, Michael, 231, 232

La Follette, Robert, 87, 128, 156, 188
Laski, Harold J., 92
Lenin, V. I., 21, 36-38, 110, 170